ACTA UNIVERSITATIS STOCKHOLMIENSIS
STOCKHOLM STUDIES IN COMPARATIVE RELIGION
28

Kingship, Religion, and Rituals
in a Nigerian Community

A Phenomenological Study of Ondo Yoruba Festivals

by

Jacob K. Olupọna

To Dennis & Barbara Tedlock
friends, teachers & mentors
With best wishes & appreciation
Jacob K. Olupọna
Buffalo, July 20, 1991.

Almqvist & Wiksell International, Stockholm — Sweden

To the memory of
my father Venerable Michael Alatake
Olupọna
and
High chief Adaja Ọlaniyi Awọṣika
in Gratitude

Printed with a grant from Humanistisk-Samhällsvetenskapliga Forskningsrådet (HSFR)

Abstract

Jacob K. Olupọna
KINGSHIP AND RELIGION IN A NIGERIAN COMMUNITY:
A PHENOMENOLOGICAL STUDY OF ONDO YORUBA FESTIVALS

With the growing interest in African and indeed Yoruba religious beliefs and culture, and a corresponding yearning to understand, appreciate and identify its place within the wider context of other religious beliefs and movements in the world, the research into African and Yoruba religions has assumed an important dimension. It has become a more serious and concerned kind of scholarship that benefits from findings in disciplines such as History of Religions and Anthropology. This book focuses on a phenomenological interpretation of the religion of the Ondo Yoruba People of Southwestern Nigeria. Specifically, it deals with the forms, contents, and symbols of Ondo ritual life as it is articulated and shaped by their most significant festivals. The author shows how Ondo civil religion, emanating from the institution and rituals of Sacred Kingship, becomes the focus of the Ondo-Yoruba multi-religious community. The author concludes with reflections on the changes taking place in the concept of sacred kingship as a result of conversion to Islam and Christianity and by social change.

ISSN 0562-1070
ISBN 91-22-01382-2

Printed in Sweden 1991
Textgruppen i Uppsala AB

Editor's note

Funds from the Swedish Council for Research in the Humanities and Social Sciences have enabled us to publish this study of important religious festivals celebrated by the Ondo Yoruba of Nigeria. These festivals have been studied from the point of view of an African researcher, who based his conclusions on extensive field work material. We are grateful to have been given this opportunity.

The editor would like to thank Benjamin Ray, Ph.D., University of Virginia, Charlottevilles, U.S.A., and Joan Marie Lindberg, M.A., Uppsala, Sweden, who have proof-read and commented on the English text.

We hope that Dr. Jacob K. Oluṣọna's presentation of Ondo Yoruba ritual activities will reach many interested readers.

Louise Bäckman
Editor

Acknowledgement

This book is the result of several years of study in Nigeria and the United States. During that time I was helped by many people. It is my pleasure, therefore, to acknowledge those persons, scholars, friends, families and institutions, who have helped me most with my work.

First of all, I am greatly indebted to my advisor and mentor, Professor Merlin Swartz, who saw me through my doctoral program and gave me the privilege and freedom to consult him at all times. My personal thanks go to Profs. Dennis Tedlock and Daniel McCall. Both men, along with Prof. Swartz, supervised the project that forms the basis of this book. I am also deeply grateful to those members of the Department of Religion and the University's Professors Program at Boston University whom I have come to know and work with these years. Most especially I thank Profs. Alan Olson, Daud Rahbar, Herbert Mason, Peter Berger, Lee Rourner, and Howard Kee. Their intellectual stimulation and helpful criticism of several parts of this manuscript and my work in general are deeply appreciated.

I should like to express my gratitude to several other scholars and friends for their assistance and helpful comments on this project: Nancy Schmidt, Robert Emery, Bruce Lincoln, Robert Cohen, Dan Aronso, Evan Zuesse, Margaret Hunt, and Marjorie Senechal.

I also wish to express my indebtedness to the people of Ondo, most especially those with whom I consulted throughout my fieldwork. Since I completed my first period of fieldwork, several of the people I met and who offered valuable help have died: High Chief Adaja Ọlaniyi Awọṣika, Alhaji J.O. Fawẹhinmi, Alhaji S.O. Oyenẹyin, Chief Jerome Ojo, Venerable Ọmọdunbi, and Chief Ṣọra Adegbamigbe, the chief priest of Ọramfẹ, from whom I learned a great deal about the Ondo past. I am particularly grateful to the late High Chief Awọṣika for his encouragement and support. In addition to being my host during my fieldwork, he occasionally accompanied me to those dreadful areas in the field where even the initiated fear to tread. I here place on record my gratitude to all these people, and pray that they may have peaceful rest.

Further I wish to thank my relations and in-laws for their prayerful wishes and moral support during my stay in Boston and after my return. I thank most especially Venerable A.A. Aderẹmi, Mr. S.O. Akinpẹlu, Chief Mrs.

E.A. Fagunwa, Chief and Mrs. J.O. Akintọmide, Chief M.A. Akintọmide, Mr. A. Akanwo and Mr. C.A. Olupọna.

I owe much to my late father Venerable Michael Alatake Olupọna and my mother Mrs. Henriette Olupọna: to both, I cannot sufficiently express my gratitude for their love, understanding and support throughout my years of study at home and abroad. Since I could not secure a grant for my fieldwork, both of them bore a substantial part of my research expenses.

I wish to thank several other people for their contributions to the success of this work, particularly Chief Okunlọla Awọṣika for providing me a place to stay in Ondo, my cousin Dr. Samuel Olupọna for his support too, my friend Ọlafisoye Akintọla who acompanied me to several places on my fieldwork, and finally Nancy Soyring, Martha Seikaly and Rhea Cabin for typing several parts of the manuscript.

Many friends and colleagues at Ọbafẹmi Awolọwọ University (formerly the University of Ifẹ), Ile-Ifẹ, provided me with much-needed suggestions and intellectual criticism of my project. I should like to thank in particular Tunde Lawuyi, Toyin Falọla and Roland Abiọdun.

The final draft of this manuscript was completed during a one-year leave from my University. I wish to thank members of the Centre for New Religious Movements, Selly Oak, Birmingham, U.K., where I utilized a Commonwealth Universities Visiting Fellowship. The Amherst College, Amherst, USA, granted me a Copeland Fellowship, which enabled me to spend the Spring of 1988 at Amherst. At these two institutions I thank Drs. Jack Thompson, Harold Turner, Stan Nussbaum, and John Pemberton 3rd, for their great hospitality.

Of late, I have enjoyed the kindness and assistance of my friends and colleagues at the Department of Religionswissenschaft, University of Bayreüth, West Germany. I hereby express my deep appreciation to Prof. Dr. Ulrich Berner, Mr. Georg Ziegler and Mrs. Menchen. I also thank Prof. Benjamin Ray, who was extremely helpful in preparing the final draft of this manuscript for publication. The publication was supported with a grant from the Swedish Council for Research in the Humanities and Social Sciences. In this regard, I wish to thank Dr. David Westerlund, and Prof. Louise Bäckman, the editor of Stockholm Studies in Comparative Religion, for their comments on the draft of the manuscript.

Most of all, I wish to acknowledge my indebtness to my wife, Modupẹ, and our four children: Abidemi, Busayọ, Bọlanle, and Babajide, for their endurance and patience during this long period of work. To my first daughter Abidemi, whose very name signifies my absence from home when she was born, I owe the greatest appreciation.

Preface

Few, if any, indigenous African religions have been more extensively studied than the religion of the Yoruba-speaking people of Nigeria. A host of Nigerian scholars of religion, Western anthropologists and other authors have continuously added to our knowledge about Yoruba religion. The great interest in this religion is largely due to the fact that it is an exceedingly rich and varied one.

In many works by scholars of religion, however, the great complexity of Yoruba religion has been somewhat obscured due to a Christian theological bias. For a long time, the theological "reductionism" in the study of African religions has remained unchallenged within the discipline of religious studies. With a few exceptions only, it was not until the 1980s that some African scholars of religion began to take issue with some of the generalizations of previous scholars. By applying insights from the phenomenology of religion as well as from anthropology and history, Jacob K. Olupona, who belongs to this younger generation of African scholars, presents in this study an important challenge and alternative to earlier, strongly theologically coloured works on Yoruba religion.

Unlike the emphasis of scholars who belong to what R. Horton refers to as "the devout opposition", Olupona's main emphasis is on ritual activities rather than on doctrines or systems of belief. However, his book differs from previous works in religious studies not only in terms of perspective and emphasis, but also in that it is based on long periods of field research. In contrast, members of the older generation of African scholars of religion have not carried out much organized field work, although they have obviously drawn upon their experience of growing up in African cultures. Since Olupona's study is based on systematic field research, as well as because it focuses interest on the Ondo Yoruba, a group which has been relatively neglected by scholars, it brings a wealth of new information.

The book deals primarily with Ondo religious festivals connected to the traditions of sacred kingship. A key aspect of these festivals, Olupona accentuates, is the articulation of the sacred power of kingship, through which the different social and religious groups "transcend" their differences and conflicts, thus confirming their solidarity and common Ondo identity. In this discussion, Olupona very fruitfully introduces the analytical concept of civil religion. Despite the great significance of civil religions in black African countries, only a few scholars have previously studied this issue. Presumably and hopefully, Olupọna's analysis will be a source of inspiration to other scholars, not only in religious studies, but also in disciplines such as history, sociology and political science.

For studies of civil religion at the national level, Nigeria is a most interesting example; and at the local level the Yoruba area, in particular, seems to provide fertile ground for such studies. Incorporation of new ideas and practices in a most dynamic way is, apparently, a pronounced characteristic of Yoruba history. As a visitor to Ibadan and Ile-Ifẹ in 1989, I was struck by the markedly inclusive religious atmosphere. For instance, in order to better their protection against evil forces, many people freely mix indigenous Yoruba charms with verses from the Quran and Christian crosses.

In the late 1970s, when the proposal to introduce a federal *shari'a* court of appeal and *shari'a* courts at the state level, where such courts did not already exist, was discussed in the Constituent Assembly, Yoruba debaters in general showed a more flexible and compromising spirit than others. True, the recent problem of "fundamentalism", Muslim and Christian, has affected Yorubaland like other parts of Nigeria. Yet the long-standing Yoruba tradition of cooperation and "sharing" across religious borders strongly mitigates the effects of "fundamentalist" inroads in south-western Nigeria.

The author of this book, Jacob K. Olupọna, hails from Ute, Ondo State in Nigeria. He started his academic studies at the University of Nigeria in Nsukka after which he was employed by the University of Ifẹ—now Ọbafẹmi Awolọwọ University. His studies for the M.A. and Ph.D. degrees in religious studies were pursued at Boston University in the United States. After obtaining a Ph.D. in 1983, he returned to Nigeria. Currently, he is a Senior Lecturer at the Department of Religious Studies, Ọbafẹmi Awolọwọ University. He has published extensively in religious studies, including anthropology and sociology of religion, and has edited *African Traditional Religions in Contemporary Society* (New York, 1990) and co-edited, together with Sulayman Nyang, *Religious Plurality in Africa. Essays in Honour of John S. Mbiti* (Berlin, in press); and with Toyin Falọlo, *Religion and Society in Nigeria* (Ibadan, in press).

David Westerlund

Table of Contents

Maps
Yoruba speaking area in Nigeria

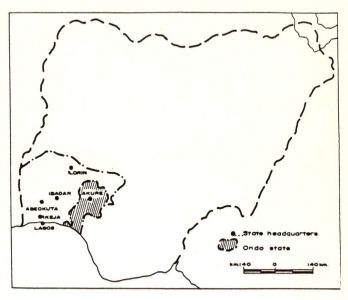

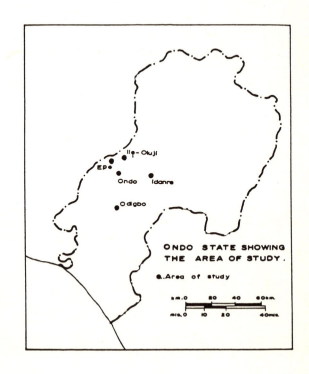

Introduction

This work concerns the festivals and ceremonies of the Ondo people, one of the largest Yoruba subgroups, situated in the Eastern part of the Yoruba-speaking area of southwestern Nigeria. The town of Ondo is about 300 kilometers northeast of Lagos, the capital of Nigeria. It is located in a forest region that is favourable to cocoa, the principal cash crop of Nigeria. The study is based on fieldwork carried out over the period 1979–86. Part of my work focused on the religions of the Ondo-Yoruba and resulted in a dissertation on traditional religion, Islam, and Christianity. Here, I focus on the religious beliefs and rituals related to the kingship. Properly analyzed, I believe that these materials may make a significant contribution to the understanding of both the Yoruba religious world-view and the socio-cultural changes taking place in contemporary Yoruba society.

This study includes a descriptive analysis of a significant aspect of the Yoruba festival cycle, the focus of which is the Ondo kingship ceremonies. The most common Ondo ritual songs indicate that all festivals and rituals are performed for and on behalf of the King (*Ọba mẹ ṣoro yi hun o*). As Peter Lloyd has indicated, the Ondo have a highly concentrated form of kingship.[1] The desire to look into this problem more deeply, especially as it relates to rituals is the concern of this study.

The Yoruba, who number more than 40 million people, inhabit mainly the western part of Nigeria (the Lagos, Ogun, Ọyọ, and Ondo states). They are probably the most researched ethnic group in Africa south of the Sahara. The Yoruba also form part of the population of the Republic of Benin (formerly Dahomey) and Togo in West Africa. Outside Africa, the influence of Yoruba civilization has been strong among people of African descent in the New World,[2] particularly in Brazil and Cuba. In the United States, the Yoruba

---

[1] Peter C. Lloyd, "Agnatic and Cognatic Descent Among the Yoruba," *Man* N.S. (1966) pp. 481–500.

[2] For representative studies on the influence of Yoruba culture in the New World see the following works: Wande Abimbọla, "Yoruba Religion in Brazil," in *Acte du XLVI et Congrès Société des Americanistes*, Vol. 6 (Paris, 1979), pp. 99-108; William Bascom, "The Focus of Cuban Santeria," *Southwestern Journal of Anthropology* 6 (1950), pp. 64-68; Roger Bastide, *The African Religions of Brazil: Towards a Sociology of the Interpretations of Civilizations*, trans. by Helen Sebba (Baltimore: The Johns Hopkins University Press, 1978); William Bascom,

heritage remains a strong unifying cultural symbol for Americans of African descent, especially in the current search for ethnic identity (the "roots phenomenon") in contemporary North American culture.[3]

Yoruba culture in Nigeria, its place of origin, is not in any way monolithic; rather the people can be divided into several cultural subgroups recognized as such by the groups themselves. While such regional differences have been fairly well-documented through literary, linguistic, and ethnohistorical studies, the literature on religion has mainly treated Yoruba culture as homogeneous and monolithic.

Previous scholarship has focused mainly on western and central Yoruba country. The data collected from these areas have become the basis upon which supposedly universally valid categories have been constructed. The report of a research committee established at Ọbafẹmi Awolọwọ University (formerly University of Ifẹ) by the Yoruba civilization conference[4] on the need for future research into Yoruba culture underscores the above remarks. The members of the committee noted the lack of scholarly historical and ethnological data on Yoruba subgroups and they identified the eastern sector, which hitherto has failed to attract the interest of scholars,[5] as specially deserving of attention.

The present study offers an in-depth examination of some aspects of the Ondo religion which remain largely unexplored. With one exception,[6] all the works by Yoruba authors on Yoruba religion are also heavily influenced by models from Christian theology, and the analysis of myth and ritual often lacks the critical approach of scholars in linguistics, anthropology, and phenomenology. This includes virtually every book on Yoruba religion which is currently available. Unlike western religions, Yoruba religions place no emphasis on doctrine or belief, focusing attention instead on participation in rituals and ceremonial activities. Yet, virtually all the available scholarly works focus on doctrine, and specifically on those beliefs which are common

---

Shango in the New World, Occasional Publication of African and Afro-American Research Institute (Austin: University of Texas Press, 1972); George Simpson, *Religious Cults of the Carribean*, Carribean Monograph Series No. 15 (Institute of Carribean Studies, University of Puerto Rico, Rico Pedros, 1980); Judith Gleason, *Oya: In Praise of the Goddess* (Boston: Shambhala Press, 1987).

[3] A few of the studies on Yoruba Culture in the United States are Cult M. Hunt, *Ọyọtunji Village: The Yoruba Movement in America* (Washington: University Press of America, 1979); Joseph M. Murphy, *Santería: An African Religion in America* (Boston: Beacon Press, 1988).

[4] A. Akinjọgbin and G.O. Ekemode, eds., *Reports of the Yoruba Civilization Conference* (Ilẹ-Ifẹ: University of Ifẹ, 1974).

[5] Ibid., p. 676.

[6] Wande Abimbọla, *Ifa: An Exposition of Ifa Literary Corpus* (Ibadan: Oxford University Press, 1976).

to Islam and Christianity. What is needed is a study of Yoruba religion which is in line with and faithful to the ideas and practices of the people themselves in the context of their public religious life.

Fieldwork in Ondo

The primary source of the material presented here was the people of Ode-Ondo (Ondo township) themselves. Information about their religious life was obtained principally through a participant-observation approach, involving interviews with knowledgeable informants. After my initial introduction to the Ondo elders and to my chief informants, I drew up a calendar of the annual festivals. I had the advantage of witnessing several of these festivals and then interviewing the people in charge. In this way, I recorded information on the background, history, and mythology, as well as the process of ritual performance. I also solicited published pamphlets and official documents that my informants might have in their possession. These interviews were followed up by actual observation and participation in the ceremonies.

In addition to using tape recordings to gather information, I photographed the events as they occurred. These materials were used to enrich my written fieldnotes. I also made several visits to the National Archives in Ibadan, where I read relevant personal papers and documents on Ondo. Government papers, particularly the British intelligence reports on Ondo Division, were helpful in reconstructing the Ondo religious life of the past.

Two other important sources significantly aided my work. In 1974, the Yoruba Historical Project was launched at the University of Ifẹ, under the directorship of Professor A. Akinjọgbin. The tape recordings from this research project (largely unpublished) contain detailed ethnographic interviews on the history and cultural life of certain segments of the Yoruba people, including the Ondo. These tapes were made available to me at the time of my fieldwork. Thus, they supplement important aspects of the ceremonies that I was unable to cover because of their timing, such as life cycle rituals and occasional ceremonies such as the *Ọba*'s accession rituals. Through these recordings, I was also able to place some of the rituals in a comparative framework.

The second body of information stems from an unusual source: the reports of the Ondo state chieftancy declaration tribunal. Before I did my fieldwork, the Ondo state government had set up a tribunal to examine the incessant disputes over the chieftancy, with the sole aim of finding a permanent solution to these problems. At the time of my fieldwork, the committee had just completed its findings. One of the results of the tribunal was a monumental collection of oral traditions, folklore, and mythology, gathered through interviews with elders and from papers submitted by community elders as sworn affidavits. The late Dr. A. Anjọrin of the Ọbafẹmi Awolọwọ University was a member of the committee, and he allowed me to read through these Ondo materials. This detailed, sometimes contradictory information was nevertheless a valuable source of information.

A note on the existing literature found in the field, and how it was utilized here, will also be appropriate at this stage. Little exists by way of published material on Ondo religion. The earliest comes from L. A. Leigh,[7] a missionary and pastor of All Saints Church, Ogbonkowo, Ondo. Leigh's monograph, published in 1917, contains the list of Ondo *Ọba* and ample information on the most significant events that occurred during their reigns. In addition, he includes descriptions of several ceremonies, though he makes no attempt to analyze any of the information he collected from the elders of his church. Another book by a local historian, which is not too different from Leigh's study, was published in Yoruba by Chief O. Ojo in 1940.[8]

Two valuable unpublished manuscripts devoted to Ondo are Bishop Charles Phillips'' diary (1877 to 1906) and Canon M. C. Adeyẹmi's work on Ondo customs (1934). The first concerns the pastoral career of the author, who was the pioneer missionary in Ondo and widely acclaimed "Apostle of Ondo People." It covers such diverse topics as Phillips' early missionary encounters with traditional religion and Islam, and events of a political and economic nature in which he was actively involved. These make the manuscript a valuable source of evidence on the religious history of Ondo.

The late Canon Adeyẹmi prepared a manuscript that remained undiscovered until I came across it while doing my fieldwork. I was informed about this manuscript by Chief S. O. Ọladimeji, a retired headmaster who knew the late teacher had been working on a paper before he died. I went to inquire about it from Mrs. Adeyẹmi, who later discovered the manuscript wrapped in cellophane. It has since been deposited at the library of Ọbafẹmi Awolọwọ University . Written as a masters thesis for Edinburgh University and completed around 1934, the manuscript as I found it has no title. For purposes of identification, I have titled it *The History and Customs of the Ondo People*. Adeyẹmi's work contains primary sources on the deeds of Ondo *Ọba*. There is no evidence that he saw Leigh's work; in fact, he produced a list of kings which differs from that of Leigh. There are also references to certain Ondo customs, such as levirate marriage, which Leigh did not mention.

Two other works recently written by Ondo local historians, Patrick Ogun-

---

[7] J. A. Leigh, *The History of Ondo* (Ondo, 1917).

[8] Chief O. Ojo (Bada of Ṣaki), *Iwe Itan Ondo* [Ondo History], n.p., 1940 (Ondo: Fourth Publication, 1962).

ṣakin (1976)[9] and Jerome Ojo (1976),[10] may be mentioned next. Although largely concerned with traditional values and customs, Ogunṣakin's monograph also contains references to the origin and growth of Christianity and Islam and to the personalities involved in the religious history of the area. His accounts were mainly collected from Ondo elders, who were eyewitnesses to these events. The closest thing to a scholarly study of Ondo culture is Jerome Ojo's book. It was first written in the Yoruba language and translated into English by the author's son Valentine Ojo, then a student at Tübingen (Germany). The book is an excellent descriptive monograph, notable particularly for its contribution to Ondo ethnomusicology. The book also contains general references to Ondo cultural history and traditional ceremonies.

Limitations

There are certain limitations to this study which I must point out. Originally, I planned to cover the whole of the religious life of the Ondo Yoruba, including the satellite towns and villages around it, such as Idanre and Ilẹ-Oluji. But this turned out to be overly ambitious. The study ended up being centered on Ode-Ondo, though I have made some reference to research in the satellite towns and villages.

Theoretical Framework

The conceptual framework employed here derives from the nature of the material and the aim of the inquiry. While my primary concern is to try to understand the various beliefs and practices of the Ondo Yoruba, it should be emphasized that it is impossible to separate religion from other aspects of Yoruba culture, since religion expresses itself through all available cultural idioms: music, arts, architecture and even ecology. As a result, Yoruba religion cannot be studied in isolation from its sociocultural context. The nature of the materials and scope of study therefore require that I follow an open-ended analytic and interpretive framework. Since I aim at comprehending the ritual universe of the Ondo-Yoruba, this requires more than a single theoretical frame of reference. The need for a pluralistic and interdisciplinary approach to the study of African religions has long been recognized by scholars. Harold Turner, who has devoted most of his academic career to the study of modern African religious movements, has written:

---

[9] Patrick Ogunṣakin, *Ondo: The People, Their Customs and Traditions*, 1976.
[10] Jerome Ojo, *Yoruba Customs from Ondo* (Acta Ethnologica et Linguistica, No. 37, 1976).

After discussing where the data may be found, the "Is it an animal, vegetable or mineral?" type of question is asked in order to identify the phenomena further and choose the most relevant disciplines. Since the movements are primarily religious, the history and phenomenology of religions are central disciplines; since many movements also claim to be Christian and "Church," Christian theological analysis, which recognizes the divine action, is also essential. The factor of divine action, however, is not only alongside others, but in theological understanding is regarded as operating in and through the secular or "non-theological" factors; these must therefore be studied through the social sciences and other disciplines.[11]

Though Turner was mainly concerned with other aspects of African religions than those I was studying in Ondo, the method of analysis he recommends has informed my work.

Less recently, but in a similar vein, Charles Long has recommended that African religions be looked at through "a unified approach. . . encompassing not only the phenomenology and morphology of religion, but equally the existential, social and practical dimensions of religion."[12] The polymethodic perspective adopted by Benjamin Ray in *African Religion: Symbol, Ritual and Community* (1976) enables him to reveal to his readers "the full semantic, existential, and social meanings of African religious systems."[13]

My study proceeds from the premise that the discipline of the phenomenology of religion provides an especially valuable framework for analyzing the data on the religious life of the Ondo-Yoruba people. Even though phenomenologists today differ on the specifics of this approach, its essential characteristics have been the guiding principles for two important approaches to the study of religion: *epoché* and *eidetic* vision. The former signifies the suspension or bracketing of value judgment while approaching the religious data. *Eidetic* vision, the second principle, is an identification of the essences of the religious phenomena that are being studied.

For the student of religion, the phenomenological task is no simple enterprise. As Olof Petterson has suggested:

The researcher's task does not end with the collection of a greater or lesser number of facts. In his interpretation, he must be aware that a religion is more or less a system of beliefs, ritual behavior and ethical structure. The phenomenology of religion appears as an important factor when it comes to interpreting and understanding the religion.[14]

---

[11] Harold W. Turner, "A Methodology for Modern African Religious Movements," in *Religious Innovation in Africa: Collected Essays on New Religious Movements* (Boston: G. K. Hall, 1979), p. 63.

[12] Charles Long, "Prolegomenon to a Religious Hermeneutic," *History of Religions* 6 (February 1967) p. 256.

[13] Benjamin Ray, *African Religions: Symbol, Ritual and Community* (Englewood Cliffs, N.J.: Prentice Hall, 1976), p. 16.

[14] Olof Petterson and Hans Åkerberg, *Interpreting Religious Phenomena: Studies with Refer-*

The procedure by which such phenomenological investigation is accomplished has also been aptly described by some phenomenologists of religions as a two-tiered process of "morphological phenomenology" and "hermeneutical phenomenology."[15] The first implies the "classification of various types and structures that arise from an examination of the data"; the second, discovering "the essence of meaning residing tacitly within the situation of the phenomenon."[16]

In addition to using categories derived from the phenomenology of religion, I also utilize relevant anthropological models to assist in the search for meaning. In commenting on the contribution of anthropological models to the study of religious phenomena, Douglas Allen remarks:

...such an approach, which can be seen in the investigation of Levi-Strauss and many other anthropologists, plays a large part in the history of religions: the attempt to understand a religious phenomenon *from within*, to penetrate it and communicate with it, especially by deciphering its meaning through its *symbolic structures* ... if the History of Religions really wants to understand what a religious phenomenon means for *homo religiosus* and if it really wants to understand the religious data "from within," the possibility of such interpretation must be reflected in this methodological approach.[17]

The warning becomes even more urgent for the historian of African religions because of the importance of the cultural context in the explanation and interpretation of the religious data collected from these societies.[18] However, the ultimate problem for the scholar of religion, in spite of the assistance which the new methodology offers him, is to avoid falling into the danger of positivism whereby religion is reduced to "a mere epiphenomenon of an empirical cultural and psychological process."[19]

Once again, as Ray remarks (in a statement that most phenomenologically-oriented anthropologists would no doubt agree with), "the process of inter-

---

ence to the Phenomenology of Religion (Stockholm: Almqvist & Wiksell International, 1981), p. 125.

[15] Walter L. Brenneman, Jr., Stanley O. Yarian and Alan M. Olson, *The Seeing Eye: Hermeneutical Phenomenology in the Study of Religion* (University Park and London: The Pennsylvania State University Press, 1982), p. 14.

[16] Ibid.

[17] Douglas Allen, *Structure and Creativity in Religion: Hermeneutics in Mircea Eliade's Phenomenology and New Directions* (The Hague: Mouton Press, 1978), p. 55. In the above text, however, Allen made an ambitious suggestion that "the historian of religion must be cognizant of all the specific anthropological approaches," p. 52.

[18] Wilhelm Dupre, *Religion in Primitive Cultures: A Study of Ethno-philosophy* (The Hague: Mouton Press, 1975), p. 51.

[19] J. G. Platvoet, *Comparing Religions: A Limitative Approach: An Analysis of Akan, Para-Creole, and Ifo-Sananda Rites and Prayers* (The Hague: Mouton Press, 1982), p. 9.

pretation actually begins within the religious materials themselves, it arises from the semantic richness of religious languages and it is expressed in the different interpretations offered by the participants.''[20] Such an entry point may help to guide against the error of reducing Yoruba religion to something other than what it claims to be for its practitioners.

My theoretical scheme can be justified from the very nature of the tradition I am investigating. The sheer exuberance and eclecticism of Yoruba religious expression demands that I approach its study from a multifaceted perspective. In this work, my primary phenomenological task has been to understand and describe the religious rituals, festivals, and attitudes that are obtained through direct investigation. I have endeavored to classify and analyze these data using categories available within the culture, largely without concern for their truth value. The qualitative methods of participant observation and the use of collective and personal interviews with knowledgeable participants in Ondo-Yoruba religious life have greatly enriched the data and analysis.

I have addressed issues in Yoruba studies and religion such as the importance of religious ideology, the socially integrative role of cultural symbolism and ritual performances in contexts of potential social and religious division, the role of rituals in mediating political conflict, and the place of festivals in reflecting and shaping the rhythms of Ondo life.

Significance of the Study

This study has three main aims. The first is to fill in the vacuum created by the neglect of Ondo-Yoruba religious studies. This study will provide new materials on local religious systems and become a source of information on the region. It is hoped too that the study will provide a basis for further regional studies among other Yoruba cultural sub-groups and in Nigeria in general. The study further illustrates that when examined at the micro-level, Yoruba religion possesses a structure and dynamism that contrasts in a number of ways with the general pattern of Yoruba religion as presented in previous scholarship.

---

[20] Benjamin Ray, *African Religion*, p. XII. Also, as pointed out by Donald Stone, the phenomenological overtone in Emile Durkheim's methodology, in spite of his positivistic stance, is evidenced in the following statement: "Let him experience it as the believer experiences it, for it only really exists in virtue of what it is for the latter. Thus, whosoever does not bring to the study of religion a sort of religious sentiment has no right to speak about it. He would be like a blind man talking about colors," quoted from Donald Stone, "On Knowing How We Can Know About Religions," in *Understanding the New Religions*, eds., Jacob Needleman and George Baker (New York: The Seabury Press, 1978), p. 146, cited in Steven Lukes'' *Emile Durkheim: His Life and Work, A Historical and Critical Study* (New York: Harper and Row, 1972), p. 515.

The second aim of the study is to contribute new methodological insights to the study of Yoruba religion. Taking the study of religion outside of normative frameworks and basing it on the life situations of the people themselves made me rethink the narrow methodological and theoretical frameworks within which African religions are often studied. I adopt instead a more all-encompassing approach that would take into account the total context in which the religious experience of a people takes place. It is hoped that this approach will be helpful to others experiencing similar problems.

The third aim is to examine the factors behind the remarkable durability of Ondo ritual. The Ondo people are particularly noted among the Yoruba for their love of traditional festival and culture. For example, they produce an annual almanac of rituals and festivals. In spite of having the largest Christian population among the Yoruba sub-ethnic groups, the Ondo community has retained a substantial part of its old traditions and rituals. There is a need, therefore, to understand why this retention is so strong. The institution of kingship appears to provide the integrating factor that transcends the town's religious, socio-political, and economic cleavages. The kingship rituals become the sacred canopy under which the entire society takes refuge. The way in which these rituals work to sustain a religiously and culturally pluralistic society needs to be explained.

Outline of Work

Chapters I and II provide the historical and ethnographic setting of Ondo society. The purpose of these chapters is to show the cultural and social context in which Ondo religious life functions. Chapter III focuses on the ideology, iconography, and rituals of kingship. It explains how the rituals of the kingship create an invisible sacred canopy that unites Ondo's multi-religious community. Chapter IV examines the myths and rituals of Oramfẹ, the culture-hero and savior god through whose medicinal and ritual acts the Ondo cosmos is "recreated." Chapter V describes the ritual of Ogun, the Yoruba deity of war and iron, the most important deity in the Ondo festival calendar. His role in both ancient and modern Ondo society is shown. In Chapter VI, I focus on two female rituals. First an extinct Ondo ritual was recreated through rigorous interviews with former participants. This is *Obitun*, the girls' puberty ceremony, which is normally integrated into kingship rituals and with which adolescent Ondo are integrated into the cultural life of the community. Second, the *Aje* festival, devoted to Ondo's goddess of wealth and fertility, is examined in this chapter. Chapter VII outlines the coming of Christianity and Islam to Ondo and examines why Christianity became the predominant religion of the town. It also speculates on the future role of such rituals in an increasingly multi-religious and multi-cultural community.

Chapter I
Mythical and Historical Background

The Ondo People: Stories About the Past

In this chapter, I present the mythical and historical traditions of the Ondo people as background for understanding their religious beliefs and practices. This chapter is based on material gathered from Ondo elders during my fieldwork, supplemented by secondary sources.

Origin of the Ondo People: Competing Mythologies

There exist three separate accounts that purport to explain the origin of the Ondo people. Two of them are rejected by the Ondo themselves as being the inventions of the historians. We do not know why these stories are so firmly denied. Outright invention of these accounts also seems unlikely. One of the rejected versions, which deals with the Ọyọ tradition, was first presented by the Yoruba historian Rev. Samuel Johnson. In his classic *History of the Yorubas From the Earliest Times to the Beginning of the British Protectorate* (1912), Johnson claims that the founders of the Ondo kingdom migrated from Ọyọ during the reign of Onigbogi, the third *Alafin* (*Ọba*) or King of Ọyọ. It was in commemoration of this event that Gbogi ward was founded in Ondo and named after the Ọyọ king.[1]

The other rejected version was recorded by the Benin historian Egharevba.[2] This account traces the origin of the Ondo to the Benin kingdom in the present day Bendel state. It says that during the reign of the *Ọba* Esigie of Benin (AD 1504) the king's brother Aruanran, who was the chief of the subordinate town of Udo, threatened the Benin throne. A series of wars against Udo resulted in heavy casualties on both sides. In the last and decisive battle, later referred to as *Okua-Ukpoba* ("the battle of blood"),[3] Aruanran was captured alive. He later committed suicide by drowning after an unsuccessful

---

[1] Samuel Johnson, *History of the Yorubas From the Earliest Times to the Beginning of the British Protectorate* (Lagos: 1912), p. 25.

[2] Jacob Egharevba, *A Short History of Benin*, 3d ed. (Ibadan: Ibadan University Press, 1960), p. 27ff.

[3] Ibid, p. 27.

attempt to escape. From this time onwards, the rest of his people were banned from the city. Shortly after this incident, a man named Osemwugbe (who was the *Iyase*, a chief of Udo,[4] and the subordinate of Aruaran) decided to avenge the death of his master and the humiliation which the Udo had suffered at the hands of the Benin warriors. Osemwugbe renewed the attack on the Benin kingdom, but once more Udo troops were turned back by their opponents. This time a few managed to escape to the western side of Benin kingdom. Among them was their leader Osemwugbe. Benin troops pursued them and for several years kept attacking this remnant guerilla force from two Benin war camps at Akotogbo (Eko-Odobo) and Ikale (Eko-Aile). Osemwugbe and his group surrendered at last, pleaded for mercy, and were pardoned by Esigie. But they stayed in the territory to which they were banished and paid an annual tribute to Benin. From that time the group came to be referred to in Benin as *Emwa n'Udo*[5] ("the Udo renegades"). Egharevba thus claimed that Ondo was a contracted form of the name *Enwa d'Udo*.[6] Similarly, he claimed that *Osemawe*, the title of the king of the Ondo, was a corrupted version of Osemwugbe, the original name of the Udo rebel.[7]

This second account is supported by the fact that there are numerous cultural similarities between the Benin and Ondo people today, not only with regard to their political system, but also with regard to religious and ethical practices. These similarities may, however, be explained by their proximity and frequent contact. This was particularly true during their common trade with foreign merchants along the Benin coast. It is also relevant to point out that a Benin tradition claims that the Ondo ruling dynasty derives from the Ile-Ife area. Whatever the merits of this explanation may be, Ondo sources reject the Benin version in favor of an older account, referred to as the "Ife origin account." Though there are many variants of this myth of origin, there is general agreement on the main events and on the names of the places where these events occurred.

The following version is based on the oral tradition of the Ondo people, as recounted to me by Ondo elders in 1980:

Once upon a time, one of the wives of Oduduwa, the legendary founder of the Yoruba, gave birth to twins in Ile-Ife. This was considered an abomination and a strange phenomenon, *esemare*, as they put it. But because the wife was one of Oduduwa's favorites, her life and those of the twins was spared. They were, however, sent out of the palace with an entourage of slaves and under the guidance of a hunter called Ija.

---

[4] An important chieftaincy title in Benin, perhaps a member of the Benin King's council.
[5] Egharevba, p. 27.
[6] Ibid.
[7] Ibid.

The group wandered around until they came to a place not too far from Ilẹ–Ifẹ, which later came to be known as *Igbo Ijamọ* (the forest discovered by Ija). The group apparently stayed in this place for some time. Eventually they found Igbo Ijamọ unsafe and therefore continued their journey eastward until they finally arrived at a place called Ẹpẹ, not far from the present town of Ondo. There they met a man called Yangede who welcomed them.

The group was in Ẹpẹ for several years, until a hunter was sent out to look for a more permanent abode for these people. As the hunter wandered around in the bush, he spotted some smoke and headed in that direction. There he met a man named Ẹkiri who was one of the original inhabitants of this vast area of land. The hunter returned to Ẹpẹ and reported the result of his mission, saying that he had discovered a suitable location. The Ifa oracle was consulted about the prospects which this new land might hold. The oracle instructed the group to take along with them a yam stake, Edo, as their walking stick. They were to poke this stick into the ground as they went along their way, and wherever the stick didn't stick into the ground, the group was to settle.

The group left Ẹpẹ and proceeded according to the instructions of the oracle. Not far from Ẹpẹ they reached a place near the present-day police headquarters, and there the yam stake wouldn't stick into the ground. The group said in surprise *Edo du do* ("the yam stake would not stick in"). Thus, according to the legend, the word "Ondo" is a contracted version of the sentence "edo du do." When the group arrived in Ondo they encountered three groups of people dispersed widely throughout the territory: the Ifọrẹ, the Idoko, and the Ọka. These indigenous inhabitants recognized the "princely" character of the new arrivals and readily ceded them the authority to rule over the territory. There was no struggle or war between the three indigenous groups and the new group, the former submitting peacefully to the latter. It was one of the twins of Oduduwa, a woman called Pupupu, who became the first paramount ruler in Ondo.[8] In the course of time, the original inhabitants of Ondo were gradually assimilated into the culture of the newcomers. But one of the three groups, the Idoko, still maintains a separate ward, Oke-Idoko, with a separate political structure similar to that of the Ondo. Such political officeholders do not have any authority outside their own quarters.

I shall defer the interpretation of this narrative until the next chapter where I examine the details of Ondo religion. It is difficult to establish to what extent the story represents actual events at the beginning of Ondo history. Here it is sufficient to note that the Ondo accept it as true. It is also reasonable to suppose, as R. G. Willis once observed with regard to a similar story, that "such accounts as this, naming specific places and directions, are not just invented but are based on a series of real events, however much the factual basis may have been distorted in the telling."[9] Ẹpẹ, a relatively small town seven

---

[8] A similar account of this tradition is found in the following works: M.C. Adeyẹmi, *Ondo History and Custom* M.S., 1934; J. Ogunṣakin, *Ondo: The People, Their Customs and Traditions*, 1976.

[9] R. G. Willis, "Traditional History and Social Structure in Ufipa," *Africa* XXIV (4) 1964, p. 345.

miles from Ondo on the Oke-Igbo road, is regarded by the Ondo people as their original town (Orisun), where they lived prior to settling in Ondo township. Until recent times, it was customary to bury the head of the Ondo *Ọba* (king) in this town, while the rest of the body was buried in the Ondo Mausoleum in the palace. Many Ondo festivals and rituals have Ẹpẹ as their starting point. Some are actually celebrated by making a pilgrimage to Ẹpẹ, prior to the time of the festival. But more revealing than all of these is the fact that the Ondo, who are a very proud people, should accept the prime position of a relatively small town such as Ẹpẹ. This is indeed surprising since they rarely accept any claim of superiority over them from any other part of Yorubaland.

Other external sources suggest that during the thirteenth or fourteenth centuries, various Yoruba groups emigrated from Ilẹ-Ifẹ to found new kingdoms. There appears, however, to have been no single motivation for these migrations. Atanda has suggested four main reasons for the emigration from Ilẹ-Ifẹ:

(a) sheer ambition on the part of the more adventurous members of the ruling families anxious to carve areas of power for themselves, (b) population pressures as the land available in Ifẹ and its neighborhood became inadequate, (c) a natural catastrophe like an epidemic or even drought which sent some of the population packing, and (d) a political crisis as a result of which many, if not all members of Oduduwa dynasty had to flee from Ilẹ-Ifẹ to other areas of Yoruba.''[10]

If Ondo oral tradition is correct, the Ondo group left Ilẹ-Ifẹ as a result of the last two factors. The abomination of twin births occurred in the Ifẹ palace. This precipitated a political crisis, and a group was dispatched to find a place of safety for the royal victims.

Early History of the Ondo People Prior to the British Occupation

Reconstructing the history of a people is no easy task, especially in cases where the main source is oral tradition. The Ondo Chroniclers, Adeyẹmi, Leigh, and Ogunṣakin, have managed to compile a kinglist in chronological order. All of them provide rather scanty, though invaluable, records of Ondo beginnings. There is little disagreement on the time and the order in which a certain *Ọba* reigned. It was not until this century that an attempt was made to assign dates to the different reigns with the help of modern historical scholarship. Nevertheless, one can still attempt a general survey of the early history of the Ondo.

---

[10] J. A. Atanda, *An Introduction to Yoruba History* (Ibadan: University Press, 1980), p. 10.

Since the origin of Ondo, forty-two *Ọba* (kings),[11] including the incumbent, have reigned. The chroniclers designate the different periods in Ondo history by the regime of each *Ọba*, no matter how short the *Ọba*'s rule. The reign titles of each *Ọba*, normally honorific titles or *Oriki* (praise names, pertaining to an historic event in his reign), became the official names that designate the historical periods in question. Some examples are: *Niyenoye* ("He who has title and a mother as well") or *Arilekọlasi* ("He who owns a house to store his wealth"). The advantage of such a naming system was that it helped provide the people, as well as the chronicler, with constant reminders of the achievements of each king.

Since it would be pointless to recall the details of each reign, I shall highlight certain noteworthy events from the accounts of the chroniclers and from Ondo oral traditions in general. All of the accounts of early Ondo prior to Ondo contact with the British can be classified under the following four headings, according to subject matter: (1) Heroism and military exploits of Ondo *Ọba* and culture heroes, (2) Ondo's external relations with other Yoruba kingdoms, (3) knowledge of traditional medicine and magic as noble ideals, and (4) accounts of the introduction of certain *oriṣa* (deity) cults and festivals. The following discussion is based on these four classificatory headings.

The first ruler or *oṣemawe* of Ondo was Pupupu, variously believed to have been the twin sister or daughter of one of the twins. We saw in the origin myth that she was accorded the rank of a Yoruba king. She reigned until a very old age, or as one of the Ondo elders put it, *nigbati omi ko teti mọ* ("until her ears were already dried up").[12] The Ondo people asked her to give them a substitute, and she named her first son, who later became known as Airọ, "a replacement", as king. However, the official palace version of this story is different. According to this version, it was usual for this female king not to pay much attention to state matters, since she preferred her domestic responsibilities. One day in the midst of the state assembly, *Uha Nla*, Pupupu suddenly left the meeting to take care of her chickens. The Ondo could no longer tolerate this behavior and the council vowed never again to appoint a female *Ọba*. After her death they appointed her son Airọ to the throne. Regardless of the reason Airọ reigned after Pupupu, he is credited with laying the foundation of the present Ondo kingship structure. He built the *Afin* (palace) and

---

[11] Ondo Kings list is in Appendix 1 of Adeyẹmi's manuscript, *Ondo History and Custom*.

[12] Interview conducted with the *Lọbun*, Ondo, 17 July 1975, by the Yoruba Historical Research team led by Professor Akinjọgbin. Although the above statements are credited to the *Lọbun*, she delegated an informant to speak on her behalf in accordance with Ondo tradition.

the town's ramparts. After his death he was elevated to the status of a deity or at least to that of a supernatural culture-hero in the Ondo pantheon. I heard people swearing in Airọ's name during the Ọramfẹ festival.

The most important culture-hero in Ondo history is *Jọmu* Nla ("*Jọmu* the great"). He rose to prominence during the reign of the third *Ọba*, Oṣemawe Luju. He was revered for his knowledge of medicine and his brilliant performance in battle. He expanded the Ondo kingdom and defended the state against outside attack. When *Jọmu* Nla was on his way home from one of his military expeditions, he mistakenly destroyed Ọka settlement, one of the three original groups of Ondo. He reduced the settlement to three compounds and uttered a curse that the town would never again grow beyond that size. Realizing that their hero might do the same to other Ondo people, *Jọmu* Nla's wives took a big drum to meet him on the way and sang this song:

> *Jọmu* o ma bọ,
> Ogun ma julu alade
> o ma dẹhin
> o.
> *Jọmu*, come back
> War is tearing apart
> a crowned city
> Please return.[13]

Since *Jọmu* Nla's ears were stuffed with cotton, as was the custom in war in those times, he did not hear his wives' songs. Realizing this, his servant and armor-bearer Ọgbọjamukan approached him and took out the cotton. He then heard the cry of the Ondo and vowed never to get involved in war again.[14]

The chronicles also refer to Ondo's dealings with several Yoruba kingdoms, especially the kingdoms of Ifẹ, Ọyọ, Ikalẹ, and Benin. Under the reign of the third Oṣemawe, Luju (1561–1590), Ondo was friendly with the Ọyọ kingdom[15] and the *Ọba* visited this kingdom during Alafin Ajiboyede's reign. He brought back with him the architectural plan of Ọyọ's palace (Afin) as a model for rebuilding Ondo's palace. However, by the time of the seventh *Ọba*, Oṣemawe Lẹyọ, it would appear that relations had deteriorated con-

---

[13] Adeyẹmi, *Ondo History and Custom*, p. 3.
[14] A similar story is found among the neighboring Ilẹ-Oluji people relating to the exploits of Jẹgun Igbo, a past *Ọba* and cultural hero.
[15] Ogunṣakin, *Ondo*, p. 21.

siderably. Lẹyọ's reign witnessed the expansion of the Ọyọ empire into eastern Yorubaland,[16] and this inevitably resulted in a confrontation with the Ondo. The accounts of the clash are very confusing since several versions were recorded. One view has it that Ondo was unsuccessfully attacked by Ọyọ forces in the wake of the eastern expansion. A slightly different version suggests that it was *Ọṣemawe* Lẹyọ who attacked Ọyọ and that on the former's return he was nicknamed Ṣ'ọyọ-Lẹyọ ("making a coward of Ọyọ").[17]

However, other Ondo traditional historians feel that the friendship continued and, indeed, that the reign of *Ọba* Lẹyọ was the watershed of these peaceful relations, so much so that Ondo could rely on the prompt help of Ọyọ forces in case of any outside attack. This was why the Ondo gave *Ọba* Lẹyọ the nickname *Ologun* Lẹyọ[18] ("he who has a ready-made troop in Ọyọ").[19] He received his honorific title Lẹyọ from this relationship with Ọyọ kingdom.

Another sign of cordial relations with Ọyọ supposedly took place during the reign of the sixteenth *Ọṣemawe* Jogude (1759–1777). He is said to have been friendly with *Alafin* (King) Ṣango, who later became deified as the Yoruba thunder god. This is most improbable since Ṣango reigned in Ọyọ centuries earlier than *Ọṣemawe* Jogude. Nevertheless, the story is told about the friendship that existed between the two kings. Jogude was Ṣango's confidant prior to his becoming king, and Ọya, the deified river goddess who later became the wife of Ṣango, was their common friend. Ọya was sent to a Yoruba town called Ṣaki to obtain *awure* (good fortune medicine) from a well-known medicine man who warned her not to open the medicine on her way home. Out of sheer curiosity, she disobeyed the diviner and opened the pot and Ṣango and Jogude appeared to Ọya, and both consumed the medicine.[20] Perhaps it was the habit of emitting flames from his mouth which was the most notable legend about Ṣango, and which made the Ondo associate Jogude with Ṣango. But on the whole, the frequent references to Ọyọ suggest two possibilities: (1) That Ondo was in fact under Ọyọ suzerainty during the latter's eastern expansion, or (2) that they were originally connected with Ọyọ and perhaps shared a common origin with the people, so that the Ifẹ origin myth was a later fabrication in tune with the spirit of the twentieth century Yoruba linkage with Ilẹ-Ifẹ.

---

[16] Robin Law, *The Ọyọ Empire c. 1600–1836* (Oxford: Clarendon Press, 1977), p. 131.

[17] Adeyẹmi, *Ondo History and Custom* M.S., 1934, p. 5.

[18] At this period Ọyọ was referred to as Ẹyọ.

[19] Ogunṣakin, *Ondo*, p. 22.

[20] Adeyẹmi, *Ondo History and Custom*, p. 6.

Benin was also important in Ondo chronicles. I have already referred to the
Benin version of Ondo origin which the Ondo themselves rejected. The
kingdom of Benin has long been associated with powerful medicine and
magical prowess. One tradition suggests that *Jọmu* Nla, the Ondo culture
hero, came from this kingdom purposely to help *Oṣemawe* Airọ wage war
against his enemies and to put the kingdom on a good footing. The people
refer to the early period of Airọ's reign as a time when Ondo was not established per se, *Ondo ko do*. Also, during the reign of Jiṣomọṣun, Ondo was
invaded by the Benin troops at a place called Asokoro[21] and the Benin were
driven out. The *Ọba* of Benin denied any knowledge of such an expedition,
perhaps to safeguard the good relations between the two kingdoms. However,
it was the economic sphere wherein the most important gains in external relations with Benin were made. We shall refer to this when we examine Ondo's
economic system.

Many *oriṣa* (deities) were introduced into Ondoland during this early
period. The first and the most important was Ọramfẹ, introduced during the
reign of Airọ. Suffice it to say here that it was through Ọramfẹ's help that
Ondo finally got started after a series of unsuccessful attempts had been made
to establish the city. Other deities of importance in the past were Babaji
(Ọbatala, the Arch divinity), Agẹmọ, (an Ijẹbu-Yoruba deity) and, Ifa, the
oriṣa of divination. A common pattern in these accounts is that the deities
were each brought from the town of the reigning *Ọba*'s mother. For example,
it was *Ọba* Luyare, the fifth *Oṣemawe*, who introduced Babaji from Ilu-Nla,
his mother's town. The cult gained much popularity in Ondo during the reign
of Jiṣomọṣun, the twenty-seventh *Oṣemawe*. Liyẹn, whose mother came from
Ijẹbu, brought Agẹmọ and a major deity of that group into Ondo. *Oṣemawe*
Agunmade was an ardent patron of the Ifa, and during his reign divination
featured prominently in the palace. The Ẹku festival, noted in Ile-Oluji, was
introduced into Ondo in the reign of *Oṣemawe* Tẹrẹrẹ (1777–1795), whose
mother came from the same town. Today, with the exception of Ifa, a universal deity, these deities are not as important as they are in their places of origin.
Agẹmọ is not worshipped at all except among the Araromi–obu living in an
Ondo town near Ijẹbu-ode, while Babaji and Ẹku are worshipped by very few
people.

Another dimension of Ondo cultural history has to do with the ability to
display magical prowess and medicinal knowledge. These powers are generally
viewed as signs of bravery and acts of valor when they are channelled toward
the benefit of the community. This is a theme that is still very much alive

---

[21] Ibid., p. 8.

among the Yoruba today, and it is in tune with Monica Wilson's observation that " 'medicines' are thought to create dignity, majesty, awfulness. . .and are used by divine kings to buttress their authority in the same way as a modern state or University uses robes of office."[22] The Ondo chronicles credited several Ondo *Ọba* with esoteric knowledge which was used to keep Ondo peaceful during their reigns. The fourth *Ọṣemawe*, Okuta (literally, "stone"), was so named because he lived to a very old age. His longevity is attributed to his medicinal knowledge of *ajidewe* (the medicine of rejuvenation). *Ọba* Liyẹn's knowledge of *egbogi* (traditional medicine) enabled him to sustain a long and peaceful reign over his people, even though he almost destroyed all the houses in Ondo with the fire that gushed from his mouth. He had the same power as his friend Ṣango in Ọyọ kingdom.[23] Many *Ọba* whose reigns were considered disastrous by the chroniclers, were poisoned with the knowledge of the people, aided and abetted by Ondo chiefs. Some of the *Ọṣemawe* who suffered such a fate were: Lowolakun (1822–1826), Jiwọmọ (1826–1833), and *Arilekọlasi* (1861–1866). Such reprisals (referred to euphemistically as "sending the *Ọba* to sleep") were the prescribed punishment for a tyrannical *Ọba*.

Ondo Civil Wars 1870–76

The foundation for the two phases of Ondo civil war was laid during the reign of *Arilekọlasi*, an *Ọba* whose excesses led to his being "sent to sleep." According to oral tradition, when *Arilekọlasi* conceded so much power to the palace slaves that they were molesting the people for no just cause, he was poisoned with the knowledge of the Ondo chiefs. But before he died, he put a curse on the Ondo people, that their habitations would remain desolate,[24] and he asked one of his slaves to avenge his death. Shortly after the death of his master, the slave Kulajolu walked out of the palace and established a rival rule at a place called Igbọdan, from whence he waged several wars with Ondo. A sizeable number of Ondo people fled their homes to take refuge in neighboring villages and hamlets such as Ajuẹ, Igbado, and Erinla, but the bulk of the population fled to Oke-Ọpa (Ọkọpa) where a temporary government was set up. The reigning *Ọba* Osungbede committed suicide at Igbado rather than be taken captive by the invaders. The next king, Ayibikitiwodi (1873–1876), was appointed at Ọkọpa. He sent a delegation led by high chief

---

[22] Monica Wilson, "Divine Kings and the Breath of Men" [The Frazer Lecture, 1959], (Cambridge: The University Press, 1959), p. 7.
[23] Adeyẹmi, *Ondo History and Custom*, p. 8.
[24] Ibid., p. 8.

Lisa Ogedengbe to Kulajolu to make peace. In exchange for conferring an *Ẹharẹ* (high chieftaincy) title on him, Kulajolu accepted and he was made *Ọdunwo*, the third-ranking chief after the *Ọba* in the traditional Ondo political system. Meanwhile, another fairly popular palace slave named Ago, dismayed at the truce worked out with Kulajolu, single-handedly attacked Kulajolu and sent him out of Ondo to Erinle where he died.

Shortly afterwards the second phase of the civil war broke out. It would appear that the throne was very weak due to the previous years of unrest. Under the reign of the next *Oṣemawe* another war occurred. He was Afaidunjoye ("the one who came to the throne at an unpleasant time"), and his throne title indeed reflected the spirit of the times. It happened that Ago, the second palace slave who had rescued the Ondo people from the Kulajolu menace, started another devastating war against the Ondo people. He took advantage of the vulnerability of the Ondo to attack them with the help of Ijeṣa and Ifẹ. He camped his troops at Oke-Igbo and attacked the Ondo from a place called Aise. The core of his army, which came from Ifẹ, formed the first settlers of Oke-Igbo.[25] To this day, Oke-Igbo, a major Ondo state town less than twenty kilometers from Ondo, continues to remain culturally an Ifẹ town, though its geopolitical location falls within Ondo. The battle with the Ondo was a fiasco with heavy casualties on both sides. Ago escaped to Ilẹ-Oluji, a neighboring town nineteen kilometers from Oke-Igbo. There he had a quarrel with one of his soldiers named Osokun. At last, with the help of a group of dissident troops from Ijeṣa and Oke-Igbo and the combined forces of Ondo under the leadership of Ogendengbe, Lisika, and Lekiran, Ago was finally routed out of Ilẹ-Oluji. He escaped to Oke-Igbo and there he was captured and thrown into the Ọni River.[26]

Ondo Under British Rule

The third phase of Ondo history takes place under British rule. The need to gain access to the interior of Yoruba country for trade and administrative purposes prompted the British to enter Ondo. At the request of the prominent Ondo high chief Saṣẹre Peters, Governor Glover of Lagos delegated a certain Abayọmi the task of recalling home all Ondo people who had fled to the surrounding regions as a result of the Ondo civil war. After this initial unsuccessful attempt, the Governor himself arrived to plead with the people to return home.

---

[25] Ọlọgbẹnla Aderin, a prominent ruling house in Oke-Igbo and also in Ilẹ-Ifẹ.
[26] Adeyẹmi, *Ondo History and Custom*, p. 10.

The Ondo Christian mission was founded shortly thereafter when Rev. David Hindrer visited the town in 1875. He appointed two church agents, Mr. Young and Mr. Williams, to minister to the people. In 1876, Rev. Charles Phillips (later Bishop Phillips), who was to become the Apostle of Christianity in Ondoland, arrived to take charge of the Christian mission work.

The British entry into Ondo brought a temporary halt to the incessant wars. The government introduced new administrative machinery, the focus of which was the *Ajẹlẹ* (the British officer), rather than the *Ọba*.[27] As a result of this shift in authority, the focus of Ondo social history in part shifted from the palace events to the *Ajẹlẹ*'s (the British officers) domain. In late 1897 a travelling British officer was sent from Lagos to supervise the Ondo area but was based in Igbo-Benin, a town in the Ikalẹ district. It is not quite clear why the British government preferred Igbo-Benin, a rather small and unimportant town in Ondo province. It is possible that the devastating effect on trade and human life of a civil war fought between Irele and Ondo during the previous year spurred them to take this step. This war was fought during the reign of *Ọṣemawe* Jilo (1894–1896) and had started as a result of a dispute between an Ondo and some Irele traders. The Ondo troops under the leadership of *Lisa* Anjanu and Lijọka invaded an Irele camp and both sides suffered heavy losses. As this was disruptive to peaceful trade, British officers were stationed in Igbo-Benin until 1899 to maintain order. When the British headquarters was moved to Ode-Ondo, a travelling commissioner, J. H. Ewart, was stationed there. The Irele and Ondo wars appear to be the last major war fought by the Ondo people. By that time *Ọṣemawe* Dedenuọla, also known as Fidipọtẹ, was on the throne. A case of indiscipline involving some chiefs was reported, although no detail was given, and the governor's representative came from Lagos to enforce discipline among the Ondo chiefs.

Ọṣemawe Tẹwọgboyes' long reign (1901–1917) allowed for peace and long-term planning in Ondo township. By 1900 the Ondo district office had been established and placed under the newly created western province. A district native court was set up and presided over by the District Officer, thereby superseding the power of the *Ugha* (palace court), which had always been the peoples' court of appeal and the court from which the death penalty could be imposed on the accused. Great progress was recorded in the area of trade, and several British firms opened up offices in Ondo. It was in this period that cocoa and timber products, which were to become the country's main exports, began an impressive growth period.

---

[27] A list of British officers stationed in Ondo is in Appendix 2 of Adeyẹmi's manuscript, *Ondo History and Custom*.

In spite of all these successes, Ondo was not completely trouble-free. Strife broke out once again when a mysterious man named Ẹlẹṣinlọyẹ arrived in Ondo with the apparent intention of settling there. Within a very short time he became a menace to the public, committing several crimes, and the Ondo tried in vain to expel him. Eventually he was approached by a mob and beaten to death. The *Ẹlẹgbẹ* warrior chiefs dragged his body outside the town gate that night and tied it to a tree.[28] The District Officer, who apparently had not been in town when this disturbance occurred, reprimanded the Ondo people severely upon his return and ordered them to pay £250. This fine was levied on the populace.[29] The above incident represents a critical moment of change in the life and culture of the people. One may observe in this incident the warrior group performing a traditionally acceptable function which suddenly becomes unacceptable according to the edicts of the colonizers. The Ondo people were displeased with this new situation, and more especially with the fine. The relationship between the colonizer and the colonized was becoming more intricate. The customary security duty performed by *Ẹlẹgbẹ* had been challenged and henceforth the title became more of status symbol than a true indication of power and authority.

The provincial reorganization of the country in 1914 which accompanied the British amalgamation of the Northern and Southern parts of Nigeria resulted in the creation of the Ijẹbu province. A new Ondo province was created with the headquarters at Akure. Another case of British government intervention in Ondo traditional politics occurred during the reign of Adekolurẹjọ (Gbegbaje) Jiṣomoṣun II (1919–1925). The incident stemmed from the alleged disappearance of a young girl from Ondo, with the *Ọba* falsely accused of being responsible for her disappearance, allegedly for ritual purposes. To add to an already explosive atmosphere, the suspect was found guilty of practicing the long prohibited practice of 'trial by ordeal'. This was brought to the attention of the British government which ordered him exiled to Ilẹ-Ifẹ. Although his body was brought back to Ondo when he died, he was buried in his house rather than in the palace as was the custom in Ondo.[30]

---

[28] Adeyẹmi, *Ondo History and Custom*, p. 12.
[29] Ibid.
[30] Ibid., p. 13.

Chapter II
Social, Political, and Economic Organization

In addition to the mythical and historical background discussed above, it will be necessary to describe briefly Ondo's social and political organization in order to provide a fuller context for the later chapters on kingship and religion.

The Kinship System

The best-documented aspect of Ondo social organization is the kinship system. The available materials were developed as a result of the dialogue between two anthropologists, Peter C. Lloyd and Donald R. Bender.[1] Their discussion centers on the nature of the Ondo kinship system following their field investigations in the same town. More recently, their seemingly divergent findings have been reviewed by J. S. Eades,[2] who has suggested an alternative approach. This dialogue has added considerably to our knowledge of the Ondo kinship system.

Here the positions of the various authors will be summarized and then supplemented with additional data based on my own experience and fieldwork. The Bender-Lloyd dialogue centers on the nature of the Ondo kinship system. Lloyd observes that contrary to the widely-held belief that the Yoruba culture is highly homogenous, there were more than negligible differences among their various sub-ethnic groups. This is clearly demonstrated by the sharp differences in descent systems which are observable among the northern and southern Yoruba kingdoms. Lloyd then argues that whereas in the northern Yoruba kingdoms the basic social unit is the *agnatic* (patrilineal) descent group, the southern Yoruba kingdoms of Ondo and Ijębu in fact manifest *cognatic* elements with descent being traced through the apical ancestor in

---

[1] See the following relevant literature: Peter C. Lloyd, *Yoruba Land Law* (London: Oxford University Press, 1962); Peter C. Lloyd, "Agnatic and Cognatic Descent Among the Yoruba," *Man* (N.S.) 1 (1966), 484–450; Peter C. Lloyd, "Ondo Descent," *Man* (N.S.) 5 (1970), pp. 310, 312; D. R. Bender, "Agnatic or Cognatic? A Re-evaluation of Ondo Descent," *Man* (N.S.) 5 (1970), pp. 71–87; D.R. Bender, "*De facto* families and *de jure* households in Ondo," *American Anthropologist* 73 (1972), pp. 223–241.

[2] J. S. Eades, *The Yoruba Today* (Cambridge: Cambridge University Press, 1980).

both male and female lines.[3] Such a distinction is particularly important for
Lloyd because it seems to be corroborated by marked differences in other
aspects of the social-political structure of these kingdoms. Such differences
have been documented with regard to the patterns of selection and recruit-
ment of chiefs, the rules of inheritance, the population density, and patterns
of town growth of each kingdom. Lloyd implies, therefore, that descent
systems are germane to an understanding of the overall social structure of the
Yoruba kingdoms. In addition to the above, Lloyd argues that membership
in the agnatic northern kingdoms is exclusive to one descent group, whereas
in the cognatic system, multimembership is encouraged and an individual can
identify with more than one descent group if he or she so wishes.

In contrast to Lloyd, Bender expresses the view that the Ondo have both
"observable patrilineal descent groups and a definite patrilineal ideology."[4]
As in other Yoruba kingdoms, an individual in Ondo claims membership only
in his or her father's descent group.[5] Bender goes on to suggest that Lloyd
has over-emphasized the significance of the descent system in the Yoruba kinship system. He cites anthropological literature to demonstrate that descent
may not be easily determined in a given culture and that it may also not
necessarily be the determinant of other social relations, since other factors
may be equally important. He cited Ondo, where people rarely talk about
their descent, as a case in point.[6] It is relevant to point out that Lloyd's
primary research focus has been on land issues in Yorubaland. He observes
that throughout the Ondo kingdom, land is held in trust for the people by the
territorial units (quarter, villages and townslands) and in Ondo township in
particular all land is vested in the *Osemawe* (the king). Therefore, each indigenous member of the community is free to acquire land from any part of
Ondo with the king's permission. Still on the land issue, Bender, in opposition
to Lloyd, argues that there is a clear connection between the Ondo people's
views on kingship and descent and the fact that all lands belong to the king.[7]
Descent groups are also land-holding units in Ondo and not just the territorial
heads, a point Lloyd conceded in the case of the northern kingdoms. The sudden and tragic death of Bender has prevented a continuation of the debate.
Therefore, in the face of these seemingly disparate interpretations of the Ondo
descent system, if not the total kinship structure, Eades has suggested an
"alternative perspective."[8]

---

[3] Lloyd, *Yoruba Land Law*, p. 34.
[4] Bender, "A Re-evaluation of Ondo Descent," p. 73.
[5] Ibid.
[6] Ibid., p. 73.
[7] Ibid., p. 81.
[8] Eades, *Yoruba Today*, p. 50.

After reviewing the theoretical and methodological assumptions of Lloyd and Bender, Eades goes on to demonstrate that the kinship system found among all the various groups of the Yoruba kingdoms is a bilateral system with an emphasis on the patrilineal pattern.[9] He notes that discussions on Yoruba kinship in the past usually recognized the importance of the bilateral element, although different emphasis has been placed on the extent of the bilateral relationship. Eades' most significant contribution to the debate is his recognition that the constantly evolving nature of Yoruba society makes a classification of kinship into an agnatic north and a cognatic south difficult for an understanding of Yoruba social structure.

Furthermore, the imprecise and variable kinship terminology used throughout Yorubaland make such a classification suspect.[10] Eades presents several convincing arguments to illustrate the effect of historical change and political and economic factors in explaining minor variations in the social organization of Yoruba kingdoms.[11]

In my view, it is precisely the lack of a historical perspective in the various analyses of social structure that has clouded our understanding of the true nature of the Ondo descent system. Lloyd himself suggests in his rejoinder to Bender[12] that the confusing information on land issues in Ondo might have arisen out of such changes. There can be no doubt that the increase in scarcity of land as a result of population increase, a sudden rise in cocoa production, and the development of real estate, must have brought on sudden changes in the way people perceive and talk about the system. In conclusion, I would submit that Ondo people normally present their kinship system as bilateral.

Descent, Inheritance and Succession

Ondo kinship ideology today is highly bilateral with an emphasis on patrilineality. Unlike other Yoruba kingdoms, however, the Ondo possess a strong tendency toward matrifocality. This is expressed in the kinship term, *Omiye mi,* which simply means "my maternal kin," but which is a household word and constitutes a fundamental tenet of the ideology of the ancient Ondo society.[13]

---

[9] Ibid., p. 51.

[10] Ibid., p. 50.

[11] Ibid.

[12] Lloyd, "Ondo descent," p. 312.

[13] In explanation of the prominent position that Yoruba women occupy in the traditional socio-political system and religious world view of some Yoruba kingdoms, some authors (H. U. Beier: 1955; Bọlaji Idowu: 1966; B.I. Belasco: 1980) have suggested the possibility that the Yoruba originally practiced matrilineal descent.

The most cited case in Ondo, *Ẹbi Mọdẹ*, from which the Awọṣika lineage branched out, may be traced back to a woman. Bender was right in pointing out that a female progenitor was quite common for many lineages among the Ondo.[14] However, he did not see it as a result of a cognatic descent structure, a matrilineal past.

What then is the importance of this for Ondo myths and rituals? The palace coup d'etat in which the woman *Ọba* was replaced by a male line in the Ondo myth of origin must have had an impact on the way Ondo populace view their descent system and perhaps also on other aspects of the social structure. Airọ, the name of the male king that succeeded Pupupu, the female king, means "a substitute." The *Lọbun*, who is considered a king in her own right, emphasized this fact by saying: *a fi parọ ni* ("We make him replace someone").[15] Thus the Ondo myth of origin may indicate that at some point in the distant past Ondo women played a powerful political role, the remnants of which are still preserved in the *Lọbun* institution, one of the most revered titles in Ondo today. It is a daughter of the *Lọbun* or a woman within the lineage that succeeds her. That an institution of such crucial ritual importance to the state has survived (for without the *Lọbun* no king can be enthroned) suggests the importance of women in the past and may represent a sort of compensation for women's lost power.

Even today the Ondo live with the paradox of suppressed female political power.[16] *Lọbun* is still referred to as *Ọba Obinrin* ("the woman's king"). This paradox is further demonstrated in the all-night "*Opepee* festival", "a ritual of reversal" in which the society's suppressed urges are brought into the open. Such rituals, as analyzed by Max Gluckman, always end up by reinforcing the stability of the status quo. The young men and women take to the street and sing *Ọba wa N* (referring to the personal name of the incumbent king) *Ṣe duo ku di Lọbun jẹ* ("Our king N, die and let us elect a *Lọbun*"). The ritual implications of this will be discussed in a later chapter.

---

[14] Bender, "A Re-evaluation of Ondo Descent," p. 76.

[15] Ibid.

[16] All the most recent studies of female political or ritual power in the past suggest that though *some* women may enjoy political power at some times this is not reflected in "female dominance" in the rest of the society. In fact, it usually goes along with increased *male* dominance everywhere except at the top. Moreover, whenever a woman ruler begins to suggest verbally or symbolically that male dominance should be challenged, she is immediately removed by the men. This is what may have happened to Pupupu.

Ẹdili (Lineage) Uli (Family) Pattern

The most significant social unit among the Ondo is the lineage group, or *ẹdili*. This is a corporate descent group consisting of members who trace their origin to a common male founder (Baba Nla) through a line of male descendants. Reference to the primacy of lineage abounds in the vocabulary of Ondo people, especially in the naming system. For example, the daughter of one of my informants was named *Ẹdiliọla*, literally "a wealthy lineage." She is an example of the ideal to which many Ondo families aspire. The lineage can be broken down into family units or *uli*. An *uli* is a compound family unit consisting of a father, his wives, children, and immediate relations. Membership in the family is by birth and a child born into an *uli* automatically becomes a member of the larger lineage, thereby obtaining access to its rights and privileges. The oldest living member of the lineage (*Baba Agba*) in principle becomes the lineage head (*Olori Ẹdili*). He is the sole guardian of the lineage, the one who holds intact the tie of kinship (*Okun ẹbi*). The genealogical bond (*ajọbi*) existing between members of the lineage represents the central link of trust within the lineage and quite often people will swear or pray in the name of their *ajọbi* in order to give validity to a statement or a point. The decline in the traditional lineage structure today and the emergence of new social ties outside the lineage structure is vividly portrayed by the Yoruba proverb, *Ko si alajọbi mọ, alajọgbe lo ku* ("there is no longer a kinship bond, what is left is a co-residence bond").[17] This is in reference to the new pattern of relationships and neolocal residency that is common in most Yoruba urban areas today.

Residence

Residence is patrilocal in traditional Ondo society. A male child born into an *uli* remains there until death. A female sibling, however, leaves the residence upon marriage and joins the *uli* of her husband. Children born of the marriage are born to the husband's lineage or *ẹdili*. Today, however, residence in Ondo society is patterned differently. Each male child aims at establishing his own household upon marriage and will move out of the family residence once his house is completed. It is noteworthy, however, that firstborn male children sometimes remain in the family house even when they have built their own personal houses somewhere else in the town.

There are three reasons for this type of residence pattern: (1) The notions

---

[17] Personal communication with Professor Akin Akiwọwọ, University of Ifẹ, Ile-Ifẹ, August, 1980.

of residence and home have a mythical character; so the idea is to keep the spirit of the lineage alive by maintaining continuity with the departed ancestor. (2) All ceremonies and activities pertaining to any member of the lineage, such as the rites of passage (marriages, naming ceremonies, etc.) are by convention performed in the ancestral home. Such houses have a niche (*Ojubọ*), usually marked with three cowries stuck into the floor, as I observed in Ṣọra's (the priest of *Ọramfẹ*) house in Ondo. (3) The Yoruba generally cannot conceive of a home without a male head member. A house without a male head is thought of as virtually empty, as suggested in the saying *Baale* Ile *ku* Ile *di ahoro* ("the death of the head of a home turns it into an empty one"). Therefore, the firstborn male child is referred to as *Opo mule ro* (the pillar of the house), and it is more appropriate for him to stay in the home permanently.

Marriage Arrangement

The Ondo marriage pattern is exogamous. A man may not marry within his *ẹdili* (lineage) but can marry within the town. There is a general distaste for marriages contracted outside the town, though there was never a rule against it. Polygyny was the custom in former days and there was no limit to the number of wives a man could take. Generally, a marriage is contracted once the traditional puberty rites (*Obitun* for girls, *Apọn* for boys) are completed. (However, one of my informants told me that *Obitun* is the equivalent of Christian baptism and that there was no need for it today, since Christianity has taken root.) Apart from this standard type of marriage, another form of marriage quite common among traditional Ondo is the levirate, vestiges of which are still to be found. The two kinds of levirate practices are anticipatory levirate and posthumous junior levirate. The practices are described as follows:

When a man dies the children of the deceased, if of tender years, remain with their respective mothers under the guardianship of the deceased's next younger brother. If, however, the deceased is a man of position with many wives (such as a traditional chief), his brothers and sons, if grown up, will have already in all probability paired with one or other of the wives of the deceased while he was still alive. (The Ondo-Yoruba terms used to express this relationship translate literally as "playing with".) In this case each relative will take one wife together with her children. The remaining wives and children will come under the guardianship of the younger brother of the deceased, who will marry them or not, as the case may be. On the other hand, if any of the wives wish to marry again outside the family they are at liberty to do so. Their new husband will pay a dowry to the younger brother of the deceased. The children of wives that do so will remain with the family of the deceased.[18]

---

[18] Adeyẹmi, *Ondo History and Custom*, p. 27.

An elderly woman, who was one of my informants, confirmed the above statement and added that her late father never allowed his older sons and junior brothers, whom he suspected of 'playing with' his wives, to eat with him from the same plate, for he believed that this would shorten his life span.[19] She recollected her father's statement *awọn e ti baya mi ṣere yi* ("Those who have already been playing with my wives") in reference to these older sons and junior brothers. The junior brother of a deceased man by rule becomes the surrogate father and provider for the children and widow of his deceased brother. The marriage system, as we can observe from Adeyẹmi's statement, is not primarily for the purpose of having a relationship, but rather a means of ensuring the support of the deceased's offspring. That is part of the reason why older women with grown children are excluded from it. It has been asked how the levirate institution could be sustained in a society where age seniority plays an important part in social relations. To put it in a different way, when a levirate wife is older than the surrogate husband, is that not a conflict in itself, especially when it is assumed that the wife had to obey her husband? This problem is easily resolved in the pattern of the Ondo kinship terminology. When a woman gets married she refers to her brothers-in-law (i.e., husband's male siblings) as 'my husbands', *Ọkọ mi*, or 'my senior brother', *ẹgi mi*. Whenever levirate occurs, she assumes such positions in the real sense without much friction. Concubinage (*ale*) is not an unusual practice among the Ondo, but concubines are not included among legitimately-acquired wives,[20] since the husband neither pays a dowry nor performs the formal wedding ceremony, both of which are considered essential in Ondo.

The organization of the day-to-day activities in the Ondo home is quite simple. The wives prepare the husband's food in rotation, usually on a weekly basis. The sleeping pattern is on the same weekly basis. The husband sleeps in rotation with the wives. The senior wife takes a prime place in the home. She is highly respected by her co-wives, who refer to her as *lyale* (mother at home). As the husband marries more wives she practically withdraws from household duties, including sleeping with and preparing food for the husband, until she becomes a kind of 'wife emerita'.[21]

---

[19] Interview conducted with an Ondo elder in Ibadan, August 30, 1980.

[20] Edward Ward, *Yoruba Husband-Wife Code*, Washington D.C., Catholic University of America, 1938, p. 16.

[21] Alfred E. Hudson, *Kazak Social Structure*, Human Relations Area Files Press, 1964 (Yale University Publication in Anthropology No. 20), p. 49.

Inheritance

The property of a deceased man is inherited by both his siblings and his children. Upon the death of an individual, the next of kin (usually the maternal cousin) becomes the overseer of his properties. Adeyẹmi suggests that three people are appointed by the *ẹdili*.[22] The executor gathers together all the movable goods of the deceased and takes an inventory of all his immovable property. A sizeable portion of the goods is distributed among the deceased's junior siblings. Senior brothers and the widow(s) of the deceased are forbidden to inherit his property. The rest is divided into the number of wives he had, with each wife and her children representing a stock (*idi*). The senior wife's children have the rights to a higher proportion of the property. Certain private immovable properties such as farmlands and the deceased's domicile are never distributed but corporately owned by all the children. These are kept under the care of the firstborn male child. If the deceased happens to be the head of his lineage, properties held in trust for the *ẹdili* are automatically taken over by his successor, usually the next oldest man in the lineage. While the above is generally applied to all of the Ondo-Yoruba, there may be minor variations from one town to another. When a woman dies, her properties are divided among her children and relations.

Kinship Terminology

It is relevant here to mention just a few kinship terms commonly used by the Ondo people. The Ondo make a distinction between two sets of consanguinal relations: (1) *Omiba*, the paternal relations and (2) *Omiye*, the maternal relations,[23] though the former word is rarely used. In spite of the fact that Ondo is ideologically patrilineal today, maternal kin occupy an equally important position in the life of the Ondo individual as do paternal kin.

A child calls his or her father and any adult male around his father's age and above *bai* ("my father"). This is purely a sign of respect and an indication of the place age plays in the social system. An Ondo boy refers to his grandfather as *Bamiagba* ("my older father"). A similar greeting pattern of *kee o* is expressed towards both. His senior siblings are designated *ẹgi*. This title is, however, often joined to the name of the referent; for example *ẹgi Ọmọlolu*, would mean, "my senior brother Ọmọlolu". *Ẹgi* could equally apply to cousins and other unrelated senior males. It appears that *ẹgi* is in use in Ondo

---

[22] Adeyẹmi, *Ondo History and Custom*, p. 7.

[23] A. A. Adegbamigbe is of the opinion that *omiba* is used in Ilẹ-Oluji. This should be the case in Ondo but it appears that this is rarely used.

township alone. It is interesting that in far distant places like Ibadan and Lagos, Ondo people are generally jokingly referred to as *ẹgi*, distinguishing them from other Yoruba groups.

An individual refers to his or her mother as *yei* ("my mother"), and as is the case of a boy's father, *yei* could equally be used to designate any female adult of the ego's mother's age group or older. As a result of the polygynous nature of the Ondo marriage system, a separate terminology is reserved for the senior wife as a sign of respect. The house of High Chief Adaja Awọṣika, where I stayed most of the time during my fieldwork, is a case in point. The senior wife is referred to as *yei* or *mama*, and one of the wives is referred to even by her own children as *anti*, the English kin term for aunt. However, it is in daily greetings that the degree of affinity between two individuals is better shown. When an Ondo child meets and greets an elderly relation (either a paternal or maternal relation), the individual greeted responds with the child's or his family's praise names, or he may simply say *wa lani o* ("may today be good for you"), assuming the individual who has greeted the elderly person is only slightly known by the latter. He may improvise a very detailed response. For example, I was greeted by a few of the older Ondo people I met who had known my father, a clergyman, as *ọmo alago ajilu* ("the son of the early morning bell-ringer"), an idiomatic reference to the church bell which called people to the daily morning prayer. Ondo chiefs are greeted in the praise names associated with their position.[24] The individual stands in front of the chief, stretches forth his fists three times while simultaneously calling out the chief's title praise names.

Ondo Political Organization

In his seminal essay on the state of research into the traditional processes of the preliterate society, Ronald Cohen laments the lack of a framework (ethnographic, analytic or theoretical) that could serve as a heuristic tool for anthropological investigators for research into political life as it is encountered.[25] In the absence of such a working model, Cohen suggests we look for the authority structure of a given political system, and establish how it is related

---

[24] For a complete list of the *Oriki* (praise names) of Ondo chiefs see chief Dudu Logboṣẹrẹ, *Orukọ Awọn Ọba ati adugbo ni Ondo* (Ondo Kinglist and Names of Streets) (Ondo: Regina Press, 1976).

[25] Ronald Cohen, "The Political Analysis" in *A Handbook of Method in Cultural Anthropology*, eds. Raoul Naroll and Ronald Cohen (New York: Columbia University Press, 1973), p. 484.

to decision-making processes in the body politic.[26] Since religion is our central concern we shall examine Ondo political structure in light of the religious dimensions to political authority.

The Ọba (King)

The Ondo-Yoruba have a complex political structure, the central focus of which is an elected divine kingship. The position of the *Ọba* (king) is hereditary and in Ode-Ondo this rotates among five lineages (i.e., Arilekọlasi, Jiṣomọṣun, Aroworayi, Jilo and Fidipọtẹ). The *Ọba* derives his authority partly through his mythic descent from the primogenitrix of the town, *Ọba* Pupupu, the first woman-king and the daughter of Oduduwa, the legendary founder of the Yoruba ethnic group. The reference to Pupupu as Ondo's primogenitor warrants further elaboration in light of the existence of three indigenous ethnic groups, the Ifọrẹ, Idoko, and Ọka people, prior to the arrival of the Oduduwa group. In the Ondo myth of origin, it is alleged that these three original groups surrendered to the newcomers without much of a fight, and that all rights and privileges pertaining to the territory were readily ceded to the newcomers. This story is acted out during the ritual of succession of an *Oṣemawe* (the title of Ondo *Ọba*). The *Ọlọja* of Ifọrẹ ritually reenacts the original pledge of surrender of the territory while *Oṣemawe* concedes certain medicinal powers and the control of a sizeable portion of the land, the Idoko ward, to the *Ọlọja* of Idoka.

The symbol of *Oṣemawe*'s authority is the sacred beaded crown which, as for any Yoruba *Ọba*, is his most prized possession, since it represents his link with the autochthonous Yoruba founder, Oduduwa. It is said in Yoruba myths of origin that Oduduwa gave out beaded crowns to his children as they departed from Ile-Ifẹ to found new kingdoms. Therefore, the claim to the possession of the original Oduduwa crown has become a claim to authority and seniority among the numerous Yoruba *Ọba* that exist today. A supposedly ancient symbol of *Oṣemawe*'s authority, the sacred staff of authority, *Ọpa Oye*, is actually an innovation introduced by the colonial government. This is presented to the enthroned *Ọba* as a symbol of government sanction for his rule.

The most visible signs indicating the *Ọba*'s presence are the large umbrella (*abuada Ọba*) carried by his emissaries and the blowing of the ivory tusk bugle, *Ọhẹnhẹn*. The presence of these two signs set off the responsive shouting of *abaye O* ("may his reign be long") by the public. Although

---

[26] Ibid., p. 497.

regarded as a symbol of *Ọṣemawe*'s authority in Ondo today, the big umbrella does not seem to have been part of the *Ọba*'s costume in earlier times. This fact is borne out by a letter written by a certain Major J. H. Ewart, the travelling commissioner stationed in Ondo, to the colonial secretary in Lagos, in which he urged the latter to obtain a 'big umbrella' for the *Ọṣemawe* similar to those used by the chief of the Gold Coast (the *Ashantehene*).[27] Thus, we may assume that it was introduced as a royal symbol in the beginning of this century, perhaps at the request of *Ọṣemawe* himself.

Chiefs, Royals and Priests

The *Ọba* rules through an institution of chieftaincy which is constructed hierarchically. First in this hierarchy is the council of senior grade chiefs, who together with the *Ọba* are referred to as *Ẹharẹ* (the *Ọba*'s council). These high chiefs are titled *Lisa, Jọmu, Ọdunwo* Saṣẹrẹ, and *Adaja*. Each one has both ritual and social functions to perform on behalf of the *Ọba*. They are grouped into pairs for these purposes: *Lisa* and *Jọmu* are one pair, *Saṣẹrẹ* and *Adaja* another.[28] One symbol of authority of the *Ẹharẹ* chief is the big umbrella (actually slightly smaller than that of the *Ọṣemawe*), which he always carries with him during public functions. *Ẹharẹ* chiefs also wear coral beads on their wrists and ankles. But the most distinctive symbol of *Ẹharẹ* is the sacred *Ugbaji* drum.[29] A ritual regularly performed in the house of an *Ẹharẹ* chief consists of the marking of his *Ugbaji* drum with white and red chalk, after which prayers are offered for long life and god's protection for the King and the Chief in question. During any celebration, an *Ẹharẹ* chief dances to the tune of his *Ugbaji* drum, the rhythm of which signifies the authority and power that he possesses. This rhythm has been interpreted by Ojo[30] as follows:

> wei ṣe le, wei ṣe le, wei ṣe le
> Ọkan yi wa jẹ gbẹyin
> Ọkan yi wa jẹ gbẹyin
> Ọkan yi wa jẹ gbẹyin

---

[27] Quoted in Jerome Ojo, *Memorandum Submitted to the Ondo State Chieftaincy Review Commission*, Akure, 1979. Ref. S 26/1, memo 3.

[28] It is not clear who pairs with the *Ọdunwo* since the position was vacant during my fieldwork and so he did not feature in any of the rites I witnessed.

[29] The *Ugbaji* set of drums consist of three drums: a large drum which is *Ugbaji* proper, a second smaller drum referred to as *Akọ Ugbaji*, and a third, *gangan* drum. Several gongs are used along with these drums. Jerome Ojo, *Yoruba Custom from Ondo*, Acta Ethnologica et Linguistica Nr. 37, 1976, p. 33.

[30] Ibid., p. 80.

You will never try this again,
This is the last that you will become
This is the last that you will become
This is the last that you will become

The first line of the above song is a reference to the 'burden' inherent in the *Ęharę* title, a title that an incumbent, were he given another chance, might not take on again. However, the symbolic dimension of the position is expressed in the second through fourth lines. *Ęharę* is the highest and the ultimate title an Ondo citizen can possibly attain, and a man may not be made an *Ęharę* unless he has previously taken a lesser title, preferably an *Ekulę* title. The drum rhythm also has a symbolic overtone. Except for a very few of the *Ekulę* chiefs, non-*Ęharę* may not own the sacred *Ugbaji* drum. The few *Ekulę* chiefs who do possess the drum are forbidden from dancing to the above rhythm except, of course, if they do not aspire to becoming an *Ęharę* in their lifetime. Out of the five senior chiefs, *Lisa* is second in line of authority to the *Ǫba*. He is referred to as *Ǫba Ode*, literally *the outside King*, since the *Ǫba* is more heard than seen. It is the *Lisa* who represents him in his functions outside the palace.

Jǫmu, the third-ranking *Ęharę*, is a hereditary title. The title probably dates back to the time of the second *Ǫba*, Airǫ. Some Ondǫ historians have suggested that the first holder of the title, *Jǫmu Nla* (Jǫmu the Great), used his influence to make it hereditary. However, this does not explain why such a title is similarly hereditary in the neighboring Ilę-Oluji town. In general, the power of the *Ǫba* is less concentrated on a single person than one might expect in such a monolithic structure.

The *Ekulę* are the lower grade chiefs, next in rank to the *Ęharę*. They are seven in number arranged in the following order: *Ǫdǫfin, Arogbo, Logbosęrę, Ǫdǫfindi, Sagwę, Sara,* and *Lotuǫmǫba*. The first four of the above chiefs are deputies to four of the higher chiefs. *Jǫmu* does not have a deputy. Each *Ekulę* in turn has a set of junior grade chiefs under his supervision. Apart from the assistance which the *Ekulę* in general offer to the *Ęharę* chiefs, a certain number of them perform other functions for the state. The *Sagwę* is the state treasurer and recorder. *Logbosęrę* is the head of the lower court that takes care of minor judicial cases. In addition, he takes charge of the *otu* chiefs, a group of palace staff residing in the vicinity of the palace (Oreretu, Ęnuǫwa, and Odojǫmu Streets). *Sara* is in charge of the palace stewards, and the last *Ekulę* chief, *Olotu-ǫmǫba*, is the head of the association of royals, whose well-being and continuity are of primary importance to the state.

We must not lose sight of the fact that the *Ǫba* himself is a member of this group. To avoid disrespect for the *Ọba* and the conflict that may result from the *Ọba*'s dual position as a head of state and his membership in the "royal company of equals',[31] the *Olotu-ọmọba is temporarily referred to as Ọdọle*[32] whenever he is in the presence of the *Ọba*.

In Ondo an *Ọmọba* may not take an *Ẹharẹ* title. This rule is designed to prevent them from exercising very much authority either in support of the *Ọba* or in opposition to him, as the case may be. However, they are eligible for the second and third grade titles. Closely related to the *Ọmọba* is a larger royal kinship group called *Ọtunba* (royals). This name refers to both male and female members who claim descent from the ruling lineages. As a mark of his or her royalty, every *Ọtunba* has three vertical strokes marked on the right breast at birth. Even though the practice of giving Ondo ethnic markings to every child has virtually disappeared, many royal lineages still apply the *Ọtunba* royal markings to newly-born children.

Ẹlẹgbẹ is the third and lowest grade chieftaincy title. As their name suggests, they are the warrior group chiefs, fifteen in number, corresponding to the original fifteen quarters that made up Ondo town. This is an indication that the quarters in Ondo were political as well as military units.

The fifteen *Ẹlẹgbẹ* chiefs include *Ayadi, Ọrunbatọ, Ṣokoti, Gbogi, Luogho, Losare, Lijọka, Lijofi, Loyinmi, Ọdọle*, and *Saogho* and others. I was told that a certain *Ẹgbẹdi* was formerly the head of the *Ẹlẹgbẹ* chiefs. His function was similar to the *Arẹ-Ọna KaKanfo*, or generalissimo, of the Ọyọ-Yoruba army. *Ẹgbẹdi*, however, was deposed by the second Ondo ruler, Airọ, and his position was taken over by Ayadi. The *Ẹgbẹdi* title is gradually being restored to a prominent place among the *Ẹlẹgbẹ* and I saw him favorably featured in the annual Ogun festival during my fieldwork. The Ondo people's idiom succinctly describes Ayadi's position. Thus *Ayadi baba Ẹlẹgbẹ, Okọmọ lẹhin yọ yọ yọ* ("Ayadi, father of the *Ẹlẹgbẹ*, 'He' who moves around with children followers"). This is in reference to his role as the head of the Ondo army. The installation rites of the Ayadi are made up of dances to warlike music. Ayadi himself is the custodian of the *Idau* sacred war drum, the music of which signals the approach of war and a warning of danger to the people. He plays a very prominent role in the festival of Ogun, god of iron and war. The fifteen members of *Ẹlẹgbẹ* constitute the Ayadi company (*ẹgbẹ Ayadi*), which is responsible for the security of the town. They form the regiment leaders in the fifteen Ondo wards. The presence of the *Ẹlẹgbẹ* grade in Ondo social structure is said to be responsible for the absence of an Ogboni

---

[31] L. A. Fallers, *Bantu Bureaucracy* (Chicago: University of Chicago Press, 1965), p. 231.
[32] Ojo, *Yoruba Customs from Ondo*, p. 33.

Society,[33] common among the rest of the Yoruba for providing security and carrying out executions. Ayadi is supported in his police functions by the *Ọrunbatọ* and *Legiri*. He is also the town's chief executioner. Each *Ẹlẹgbẹ* chief carries a baton as a symbol of authority.

Another group of leaders in Ondo is the *Alaworo*, priest-chiefs. They are largely the heads of indigenous, pre-Oduduwa groups now in a position of 'ritual superiority' over the newcomers. The *Alaworo* are *Ọlọja Oke-Idoko, Ẹkiri* of *Iforẹ*, *Ṣora*, and *Akunnara*, the last two being *Ọramfẹ* priests. All the priest-chief titels are hereditary and candidates are elected from the lineages concerned.

The female chiefs are referred to as *Opoji*. They have a set of hierarchies (like their male counterparts). The paramount female chief is *Lọbun*, the most revered title in Ondo. The office of *Lọbun* is surrounded with mysteries and taboos. Since the change in chieftancy from female to male, women nevertheless have the right to have a woman leader, *Lọbun*, also referred to as *Ọba Obinrin* (woman king).

The fact that the word *Lọbun* refers to a village market (*ọbun*) is an indication of the important place of the market and of trade among Ondo women. Apart from *Lọbun*'s major duty of installing a new king,[34] she is in charge of Ondo markets and is the priestess of *Aje* (god of wealth and prosperity). She opens new markets and performs any ceremonial rites that pertain to this. Many taboos surround the *Lọbun* title and getting a replacement when the position falls vacant is very difficult. An important norm concerning the position is that, whenever a *Lọbun* dies, a new one cannot be appointed until the reigning *Ọba* dies. The new *Lọbun* is thus elected for the main purpose of installing the new *Ọba*. Once a *Lọbun* is appointed it is forbidden for her to engage in any domestic duties. She may not step on an unswept floor early in the morning, and she may not eat any food prepared the previous day. The price for keeping her "holy" is that the town must cater to her throughout her reign. The women's chief council is made up of the following titles: *Lisa-Lọbun, Jọmu-Lọbun, Ọrangun-Lọbun, Saṣẹrẹ-Lọbun*, and *Adafin*. Other female chiefs of lesser grades include *Ọdọfin-Lọbun, Ogede-Lọbun, Sama-Lọbun*, and *Awoye-Lọbun* among others. While the *Lọbun* is selected by the *Ẹharẹ*, other women's titles are elected by the high women chiefs, though their

---

[33] Adeyẹmi, *Ondo History and Custom*, p. 24.

[34] Contrary to the view expressed by Atanda 1980; Robert Smith 1976, that *Lisa-Lọbun* is the highest woman chief whose function it is to carry out the *Ọba*'s installation, the installation is performed by the *Lọbun*, the head of the women chiefs. Normally this misinformation may be due to the usual absence of *Lọbun* Once the *Lọbun* dies, the title is left vacant until the *Ọba* himself dies, when a new one is appointed to install the *Ọba*.

appointments are still subject to confirmation by the Saṣẹrẹ, who does so on behalf of the *Ọba*.

Succession to the Kingship

In this section I shall discuss the very complex rules of succession to the throne in Ondo. The Ondo dynastic institution is based on the 'royal descent group'.[35] Here kingship rotates among the five descent groups that constitute the ruling class. The gap between the death and the succession of an Ondo *Ọba* is of critical importance to the state. Whenever an *Oṣemawe* dies,[36] it is the duty of the palace chiefs *Bajulaiye* and *Tutugbuwa* to confirm it and inform the regent, the *Lisa*. The announcement of the *Ọba*'s death is concealed from the public until all the necessary burial arrangements have been made, apparently in order to guarantee a peaceful transition. But the general state of confusion that follows the death of an *Ọba* is symbolized by the chaotic dismantling of the town's marketplace. Once the death is officially announced by the *Ọba*'s crier, the *Lisa* takes over the affairs of the state in the interim period, and in his absence the next senior chief in line assumes his duties. It is important to note that the *Ẹharẹ* chiefs are forbidden from becoming *Ọba*. This constraint theoretically guarantees their neutrality in their role as kingmaker.

The process of installing a new *Oṣemawe* involves both selection and appointment. The *Ẹharẹ* kingmakers notify the next royal lineage in line to present a candidate for the throne. The law recognizes five lineages. The head of this royal lineage in turn calls the meeting of the *Ọtunba*, the royal kin group, to select from the list of candidates who have made their intentions known. There is sharp disagreement in Ondo with regard to the rules which define eligibility. It is this disagreement that was partly responsible for the very long lapse between the death of the last *Ọba*, *Oṣemawe Tẹwọgboye*, and the selection of the present one, *Oṣemawe* Adekolurẹjọ. Most people agree that the candidate, in addition to being a male descendant from a ruling house, must be physically and mentally fit and devoid of any past criminal record. However, they disagree on the following two issues: (1) Should the candidate

---

[35] Jack Goody, *Succession to High Office* (Cambridge: University Press, 1966), p. 26. Three other types of dynastic institution suggested by Goody are (a) Stem dynasty; (b) familial dynasty; (c) dynastic descent group; pp. 26–27.

[36] It is never said among the Yoruba that an *Ọba* dies, rather the *Ọba* is said to have "ascended into the ceiling," *Ọba waja*. This metaphor suggests the motif of 'ascent' and 'descent' which characterizes the mode by which divinity and superhuman beings manifest and disappear into the world of humans.

necessarily be a son of a past *Ǫba* or is a grandson equally eligible? (2) Should the candidate necessarily be born while the father is already *Ǫba* (i.e., what in Idanre would be called *ǫmǫ-ori-opo*)? At the time when I did my fieldwork these issues had yet to be resolved and were under consideration by a chieftaincy review commission.[37] However, an anthropologist named Ward, who visited the *Afin* of the *Ǫba* in 1934, made some observations that may shed light on the issues.

Ward spent four years in Ondo district. He had visited the *Oṣemawe* and urged the *Ǫba* to show him around his courtyard. Ward believed that his mission was to obtain an understanding of the general layout of things and to see how the wives reacted to the presence or conduct of the husband, since he had "heard so much about the sanctuary where so few men are privileged to tread."[38] The *Ǫba* agreed and both of them visited the courtyard one morning. Ward described his experience as follows:

The king was friendly with all of them [his wives] and all of them except one or two greeted him with delight. He asked all of them how they were and how their children were. He beckoned a smiling female of about thirty towards him. He pointed to the little child on her back and said proudly, 'This is my son'. I wondered why he had picked him out from the rest and I asked Anthony [Mr. Ward's escort] about it. He told me that that was the first male child of which the king was father since he came to the throne and that he might reign some day. The other male children, and there were dozens who were born before that event, were not in line for succession. I had to pat the little chubby child on the head and asked his overjoyed mother all about him.[39]

The popularity of a candidate among the people very often influences the choice of the royal lineage. At the lineage meeting a vote is cast among male children and the candidate with the highest number of votes is forwarded to the kingmakers, i.e., the *Ẹharẹ* chiefs. The kingmakers then ask the Ifa diviner, Bapaiye, to divine the choice of the lineage "since the human choice often requires the confirmation of divine authority."[40]

An unfavorable prediction constitutes sufficient grounds for the rejection of a candidate by the *Ẹharẹ*. In the absence of any major reason for his rejection, the candidate is appointed by the *Ẹharẹ* as the new *Ǫba*. However, the

---

[37] In 1979, a chieftaincy review commission of enquiry was set up by the Ondo State Government to probe into the incessant succession disputes that normally follow the death of traditional rulers in the State and to review the customary law regulating the selection and appointment of Ondo State *Ǫba*. It is hoped that an updated chieftaincy declaration for Ondo would result from the work of the Committee.

[38] Ward, *The Yoruba Husband-Wife Code*, pp. 52–53.

[39] Ibid., p. 53.

[40] Jack Goody, *Succession to High Office*, p. 12.

Oṣemawe is not crowned (*igbade* ọba) until three years after his installation, *ifọbajẹ*. No explicit reason is given for such a long delay, although it may be assumed to represent a period of probation for the new *Qba*. During this interval the administration of the state is carried out by the *Lisa* in consultation with the new *Oṣemawe*.

Age-Set

Another aspect of Ondo social structure is the age-set. Because of the ease with which the age-set disappeared in Ondo it is very difficult to reconstruct how it operated in the past. In Ondo, the age group is referred to as *Otu*, and on performing the puberty rite an individual enters the first age grade. Promotion to the next set takes place every five years. The main purpose of the age-set is to form a corporate group as a source of labor for community projects and to provide a ready-made force in the event of emergencies such as war, epidemics, and drought. With the rapid change of traditional values in Ondo, a new form of association has emerged whose allegiance is towards individual members of the community, rather than the community oriented collective force described here.

The Network of Government

Having examined the hierarchies of citizenship and authority in the Ondo political system, it is now important to consider the ways in which the daily decision-making processes are carried out by this body.

In the past, Ondo was surrounded by a large rampart with five gates which had been built during the reign of *Oṣemawe* Luju.[41] The city gates were assigned to the *Ẹharẹ* chiefs for their supervision. The location and the distribution of the gates were as follows: *Lisa* took charge of the Oke Lisa, the western gate, leading to Oke-Igbo and Ẹpẹ. *Jọmu* was in charge of the Kee, the eastern road; *Saṣẹre* controlled Odoṣida, the southwestern gate; and *Ọdunwo* was assigned to Agbabu, the south road; while *Adaja* took charge of Ododibo, the north gate, that leads to Akurẹ.[42] Each of these gates was manned by a gatekeeper (*Onibode*) referred to as the *Lagbogbo*. These gatekeepers were always tough criminals or ex-convicts on parole, so they could be relied upon to prevent unwanted outsiders from entering the city. They were also in charge of toll collection (*owo bode*), a major source of

---

[41] M. C. Adeyẹmi, *Ondo History and Custom*, p. 3.
[42] J. O. Ojo, *Yoruba Customs from Ondo*, p. 32.

revenue for the kingdom. The unity of Yoruba culture is expressed very vividly in the gatekeepers' tradition. Throughout the kingdoms they were generally regarded as notorious criminals and many tales are told concerning their deeds. In Ondo I did not hear the kinds of tales that are attributed to the notorious *Onibode Lalupọn* in Ibadan legends, but the fact that the street on the Akure road in Ondo is named *Lagbogbo Oke* would suggest that that particular gatekeeper must have been a legendary figure. The traditions surrounding *Onibode* in general are still an unexplored area of research in Yoruba history and culture.

The primary political unit in Ondo is the quarter or ward. Although the *ẹdili* (lineage) possesses its own internal structure, it does not have any political influence outside the lineage. The same observation was made by Lloyd when he wrote that "in none of the Yoruba city states did the government consist of a committee of lineage heads; always the government consisted of a separate set of institutions standing apart from lineage."[43] As the Ondo town population increased, new quarters were added by subsequent *Ọba* and by 1934 forty major quarters were counted.[44] Each of the quarters was under the supervision of an *Ẹharẹ* chief and a set of *Ekulẹ* chiefs. The only exceptions were *Logbosẹrẹ, Ọdọfin,* and *Ọdọfindi,* who took charge of other state matters. The *Ẹlẹgbẹ* chiefs were also assigned to different quarters. In peacetime they were subordinate to the *Ekulẹ* and *Ẹharẹ* within their quarters, but in wartime they became the quartermasters, so to speak, under the leadership of Ayadi, the war chief who was directly responsible to the council of chiefs.

Adeyẹmi describes the ways in which these intricate legislative and judicial processes were carried out: "Normally every title holder, however small, had certain judicial powers. A minor chief might decide petty cases between members of two compounds under his control, while the head of the quarter was a court of appeal in such cases. Suits between members of two compounds not under the control of the same minor chief are brought to the head of the quarter for arbitration."[45] From the above it would appear that in the past power was highly concentrated among the hierarchies of chiefs. The head of the quarter in a sense was the high chief who took care of both judicial and legislative offices. However, a separate court of appeal recognized by the state also existed in the *Logbosẹrẹ*'s court, which handled cases from any quarter of the town. Cases that left the *Logbosẹrẹ*'s court unresolved were sent to the *Ọba*'s (State) council meetings or *Ugha.*

---

[43] P. Lloyd, "Political System of the Yoruba," *Southwestern Journal of Anthropology,* 10 (4), p. 382.

[44] *Ondo District Intelligence Report,* Ondo Prof. 1/1 30172.

[45] M. C. Adeyẹmi, *Ondo History and Custom,* p. 12.

Ugha Council Meeting

The State council meeting, referred to as the *Ugha*, is presided over by the *Oṣemawe*. Two forms of such meetings are conducted: (1) *Ugha Kekere*, a smaller assembly meeting that takes place on a daily basis, where the *Oṣemawe* deliberates with his *Ẹharẹ* on the affairs of the state; and (2) The *Ugha Nla*, the supreme state assembly, which meets weekly to discuss matters of interest to the kingdom and is attended by all grades of chiefs. Decisions arrived at in the *Ugha Nla* are passed into law and formally announced to the public. The Ondo people have great reverence and respect for *Ugha* council. One of the ritual songs I recorded during a festival refers to the Ugha State Council.

> 'Me faya Ọba
> Me ma fẹ tujoye
> Ohun a gbe mi kunle N'uha
> O ṣoro O!
> I have not seduced the wife of the king,
> Nor have I seduced the wife of a chief.
> What else could make me be summoned (kneel)
> before the councils meeting is unthinkable.'

Besides adultery, which is a crime commonly referred to the *ugha* (especially if it involves abduction of a chief's wife), other crimes such as murder, theft, and witchcraft are brought to the *ugha*'s jurisdiction. It is not unusual to ask litigants involved in a dispute to swear to a deity such as Ogun or Airọ (Ondo's deified culture-hero and King). However, in the past it was often necessary to resort to trial by ordeal to prove innocence, since such practices produce quicker results. For example, someone accused of witchcraft may have been asked to drink from a ritual mixture prepared with the sasswood powder. If that person died from it, it was assumed that he or she had committed the offense.[46]

---

[46] Ibid., p. 24.

Economic Life

Occupation

Traditionally, Ondo people have always been engaged in two major professions: farming (*agbẹ*) and trading (*owo*), which correspond almost completely to the division of labor between male farmers and women traders. Agriculture is the mainstay of the Ondo economy. The annual cycle contains two seasons: The dry (*Igba ẹrun*) and rainy (*Igba ojo*) seasons, which correspond with the annual agricultural cycle of planting and harvesting. Two types of farmland are cultivated: (1) small parcels of land located within walking distance of the town, *Oko etile* or *Igo*, where foodstuffs such as *agbado*, maize (*Zea mays*), *gbaguda*, cassava (*Manhot esculenta*), *eree*, beans (*Virgna unguiculate*) and *iṣu*, yam (*Discorea*) are mainly grown; and (2) the farmland referred to as *oko ayunsun*, large farms located far from the town, where cash crops such as cocoa and kola nut are planted. Unlike the small nearby farms which are cultivated on a daily basis, farmers stay at the large distant farms throughout the week and only come back to town for weekends or the fortnightly *ẹgbẹ* (society) meeting, and in modern times for the Muslim (Jumat) prayer or Christian Sunday Services.

As the hamlets and villages developed to accommodate more people, the farmers stayed longer on their farms. Those who had enough money would build houses with corrugated iron roofs. The *Ọba* would deputize a town chief to supervise the area for him and the chief invariably would become the *Ọlọja* (head chief) of the area, thus establishing a micro-sociopolitical setup for community rule. Such hamlets were sometimes named after the first founder. When the distant farmlands developed to this stage, the inhabitants only returned home for major traditional festivals, or if they were Christians or Muslims, for the major 'church' ceremonies as *Keresimesi* (Christmas), *Ikore* (harvest thanksgiving), and *Ileya* (*id al-kabir* festivals). Today cash crops such as kola nut and cocoa are mainly grown on the distant farmlands. On both types of farms an individual may engage the assistance of his close friends or age group on the farm at the time of planting. He too must offer the same assistance to those who have assisted him. Such cooperative effort expressed in the form of labor exchange between friendly individuals is referred to as *ọwẹ*. The spirit and the ethics behind this cooperative enterprise are best expressed in the Yoruba proverbs, *oni loni njẹ, ẹni a bẹ lọwẹ* ("Today is the day for the one who has accepted help on farm work"). Ondo farmers believe that they get much more done through participating in *ọwẹ*.

Once the farmland is cultivated, a portion of it is divided among the farmer's wives who are not engaged in trading activities. This land is used to cultivate less labor-intensive crops like *ata* (pepper), *gbaguda* (cassava), and vegetables. Each wife takes care of her piece of land and she is solely responsible for the planting and weeding. It is not unusual for Ondo women to cultivate cash crops, especially on farmlands inherited from their parents.

The sole responsibility for marketing the excess food crops from the husband's farmland lies with the wives, although most of the crops are reserved for home consumption. The cash crops, however, are mainly sold by the head of the family himself.

As mentioned above, the second mainstay of the Ondo economy is trade and it is conducted solely by women. Among their articles of trade are *aṣọ oke* (woven cloth), *iyun* (coral beads), and *ẹni* (mats). The center of the trading activities is the market, *ọja*, or *ugele*. This institution has both religious and social functions as well as economic importance.

Ondo Women in Trade

The importance of women's role in the market economy in this town is indicated in the title of the paramount female chief as *Lọbun* (the women chiefs bear *Lọbun* suffixes in their titles, e.g., *Lisa-Lọbun, Ọrangun-Lọbun*).[47] The word *Ọbun* refers to a rural or village market in Ondo dialect so the female chiefs are "owners of the village markets." Most villages and hamlets under Ondo administration started as farming and market centers. The point is also made by Samuel Johnson that, "the principal market of the town is always in the center of the town and in front of the house of the chief ruler. This rule is without an exception and hence the term *ọlọja* (one having a market) is used as a generic term or title of all chief rulers of towns be he a king or a Bale. . .".[48] The Ondo appear to be an exception, since the market is far from the palace center. However, this does not diminish the importance of the market as an institution in Ondo kingship structure, since intimate connection between the two is observable elsewhere. The point must be made once again that what appears to be a crucial institution in Ondo is brought under the domain of the woman head by making her (literally) the "one having a market," *Lọbun*. This marks an important distinction between Ondo and the rest of Yorubaland. Women clearly have a primary position in Ondo social and economic structure.

---

[47] Niara Sudarkasa has aptly remarked, "Available evidence suggests that women have been involved in the distribution of goods for as long as the Yoruba have lived in urban areas, and that the historical precedent for present-day trade by women can be found in their participation in the markets within the towns in which they resided." See, *Where Women Work: A Study of Yoruba Women in the Marketplace and in the Home* (Ann Arbor: The University of Michigan Press, 1973).

[48] Samuel Johnson, *History of the Yorubas*, quoted from Niara Sudarkasa, Ibid., p. 27.

The head of the Ondo market, *Lọbun* (and in her absence the *Lisa-Lọbun*), is supported by the cabinet of chiefs. They are responsible for maintaining order in the town's marketplace and they carry out the ritual purification of the market whenever the need arises. There are four types of markets in Ondo: The daily market, *ugele*, held from morning until dusk; the evening section, designated *ugele alẹ* (evening market); and two periodic markets held at four and eight day intervals. Both are referred to as *ọrun* (five-day), and *isan* (nine-day) markets; *Odojọmu* market belongs to the latter. (In the Yoruba method of counting, the day of the last market and the day of the following market are both counted.) A few Ondo markets are held every other day, *ọja ijọ mẹtamẹta*. The most elaborate markets are the *isan*, also referred to as *ọja nla* (the big market) in the neighboring Ilẹ-Oluji. In addition to food commodities, an important article of trade in major Ondo markets is the locally-woven cloth referred to as *aṣọ oke*. This is commonly worn by the people, especially on ceremonial occasions. In a recent study, Lamb and Holmes observed that, "until recently, Ijẹbu Ode and Ondo were important weaving towns; today the craft survives on a much more reduced scale in Ijẹbu-Ode but has virtually disappeared in Ondo."[49] Before the advent of colonial rule and the introduction of European currency, the medium of exchange was the cowry shell, *owo ẹyọ*. Cowry shells continued to be used as currency several decades after British currency became the official coinage. Cowries are still being used in several parts of the kingdom not as a means of exchange, but for ritual purposes. As there were no banks, people saved their cowries by putting them in pots and burying them in secret spots, especially on farms and banana plantations. There have been cases in which such stores of wealth were discovered long after the death of the owner. It would appear that Ondo people were also engaged in trade with the Portuguese as early as the sixteenth century. An account of the early Portuguese trading activities on the West African coast mentions that their "pilot (sailor) bought from the captain of Rio dos Forcados (the Forcados River) and the *Lysa* (*Lisa*) jointly four hundred manillas of yam for the cargo."[50] It is most likely, as Ryder has suggested, that the latter referred to the Lisa of Ondo.

---

[49] Venice Lamb and Judy Holmes, *Nigerian Weaving* (Lagos: Shell Petroleum Development Company, 1980), p. 170.

[50] A. F. C. Ryder, "An Early Portuguese Voyage to the Forcados River," *Journal of the Historical Society of Nigeria*, 1 (4) 1959, p. 319. As suggested earlier, the *Lisa* (*Lysa*) is next in rank to the *Ọba* of Ondo and not fourth as suggested by Ryder (1959:318n). In Ondo, he is called *Ọba* Ode, "The Outside King," which suggests his function as the official representative of the kingdom in its external relations.

Special Occupations

Apart from trade, there are many occupations in Ondo which are restricted to men only and in most cases limited to certain lineages. The three most common professions are drumming, blacksmithing, and hunting. All are guild professions and all have religious characteristics. Hunting is a well-established guild profession with a head hunter, *Olori-Odẹ*, named by the *Ọba*. The hunters can be called upon by the *Ọba* to solve any riddle or problem, since they are believed to have a rapport with mysterious human or animal beings in the bush. Apart from a few domesticated animals such as goats, fowl, and pigs, animals killed in the bush, *ẹran igbẹ*, are a major source of food, especially on festive occasions. The animals most commonly hunted are *ẹtu*, antelope, and *ẹdun*, monkey. The last is mainly used for ritual purposes and in Ondo it symbolizes upward mobility, since the monkey lives in trees, unlike other animals that live below.

The workshop of the blacksmith is held sacred by all because it signifies the Ogun's sacred spot. Blacksmiths are also producers of iron implements connected with the cult of this divinity.

One other professional group that requires a much more detailed study than I can provide here is brassworkers. As I mentioned earlier in the chapter, the Ifọrẹ, one of the Ondo aborigenes, were specialists in brass production. I was told by several of my informants that they had the best guild system in Ondo. In fact, the Ondo praise name (*oriki*) refers to the prominence of brass in their beginning, *ẹkimogun ọmọ alade igbo, a fi agogo idẹ momi* ("Ẹkimogun, the son of the forest chief, who drinks with a brass cup"). The Ifọrẹ people I spoke to could be accused of boasting of their glorious past achievements in brasswork, but no excavations that support this have been carried out. However, a few references to this ancient craft are still found in their ritual context. For example, it is taboo in Ondo for anyone to wear a brass necklace or bangle during the Ọramfẹ festival. The traditional guild groups by and large have been replaced by modern professionals such as carpenters, tailors, drivers, and barbers. They are devoted to Ogun, the most popular deity in the Ondo pantheon. Lastly, one should also mention the drummers who play a most signficant part in Ondo social and religious life. The drumming profession is hereditary, in Ondo as in other Yoruba towns. It is they who keep that Ondo tradition alive.

Revenue Collection

The Ondo kingdom had a well-organized revenue system prior to the arrival of the British. There were two main sources of income for the state: 1) Tolls and tributes collected on booty and goods entering the town's gate. The gatekeeper, *Lagbogbo*, was also the toll collector and he could be relied upon to enforce the law strictly. 2) The quarter levy, which is the amount of money needed to run the affairs of state, supplies expenses for state rituals and ceremonies that are initiated by the king's council as the need arises. These are levied among the quarters (wards). Each quarter collects its own share and keeps proper records of defaulters. The money is paid to Sagwẹ, the treasurer. There are also impromptu levies mainly for ritual purposes, especially in time of great calamities and epidemics, when an urgent sacrifice is prescribed by Ifa divination. Apart from these two main sources, fines imposed by the king's council on erring individuals and tributes from villages and hamlets under Ondo, *iṣakọlẹ*, mainly go to the purse of the *Ọba* and the *Ẹharẹ* chiefs who supervise these villages.

Ondo Special Festive Diet

Ondo people have a special diet for rituals and other festive celebrations. The two most important items are the hot spicy soup, *ọbẹ ase*, which is eaten along with pounded yam, *iyan*, and barbecued goat meat, *asun*. *Asun* is the distinguishing item of the Ondo diet, for there is no other place in Yorubaland outside the Ondo district where this food is eaten. *Asun* can be given in both a ritual and a non-ritual context. No ceremony in Ondo is deemed complete without *asun*, whether it be a housewarming, a naming ceremony, a wedding, a funeral or the general purpose *saara* (propitiatory sacrifice) which is quite common in Ondo. All are occasions for *asun*. The guests, who are usually the celebrants, gather together all neighbors and kin groups in the celebrant's house. They all sit either in an open place in the courtyard or on the front veranda, or even in the celebrant's sitting room. If the *asun* is organized outside the lineage circle, for example by the *ẹgbẹ* society, it is held in the house of the *Olori-ẹgbẹ* (the chairman) of the society. Whatever the nature of the gathering, once the guests are seated the goat is brought forth with a cord tied around its neck and prayers are offered for the purpose for which the *asun* is held. The prayer is optional, however, since the *asun* may not necessarily be for a ritual purpose. The goat is slaughtered and the skin is burned on a wood fire. It is then cut into pieces and put on a long iron rod, *ọpa asun*, especially made for the purpose of *asun* (virtually every house in Ondo owns one). The goat meat is then roasted on the same wood fire prepared in the open courtyard. Once roasted, the meat is cut into small pieces on a flat board and is mixed with slightly ground hot pepper. This is served to the guests along with *ẹmu* (palmwine) or other beverages. The goat's intestines and hind legs are reserved for the celebrants, and some elders who are either indisposed or too old to attend are sent portions of the unroasted meat.

Chapter III
Ọdun Ọba:
The Ideology and Rituals of Sacred Kingship

The most important aspect of Ondo religion today is the system of royal rituals and ideology under which all other aspects of cultural life are sub sumed. In the Ondo political system, the king's role is critical in terms of its executive, judicial, and ritual functions. In this chapter I will discuss in detail the central place of royal ritual and ideology in Ondo religion and society. The chapter is divided into two sections. The first provides a brief analysis of the kingship ideology, which is relevant to an understanding of the rituals of kingship. The second section focuses on the myths and rituals of kingship as portrayed in two major ceremonies: *Ifọbajẹ*, the King's installation ceremony, and *Ọdun Ọba*, the annual festival of the King.

The Kingship Ideology and the Ritual Life of Ondo

The Ondo kingship ideology is expressed in various forms: oral traditions, proverbs, and songs. The most widely-used epithet describes the *Ọba* as *Ugba gbọmọla* ("the great saviour of his subjects," referred to as his "children"). This refers to the role of the king as the protector of the weak, the widows, the orphans, and the poor.[1] The *Ọba*'s palace in the pre-Colonial days acted as the sanctuary for those who were being persecuted and a place of succor for the suffering. Every prayer formula and ritual invocation spoken on any chiefly occasion in Ondo is answered by the shouts of *abaye o* ("may you live long"), a reference to the subjects' wishes for the king's immortality. In the exercise of his power, he is accorded the epithet *o ya joko iro* ("swifter than the early morning cultivation of farmland"). The *Ọba*'s divinity is expressed in other attributes already mentioned in this introduction; he is *alaṣe* ("the one who welds power and has authority"), which signifies his absolute sovereignty over every living thing in his kingdom. In practice, however, this

---

[1] Paul Radin, "The sacral chief among American Indians" in *The Sacral Kingship/La Regalita Sacra* (Studies in the History of Religions), (Leiden: E. J. Brill, 1959) p. 88.

power is curtailed through power-sharing with his chiefs and by means of a series of checks and balances. For the Ondo people and the Yoruba in general, the *Ọba* shares in the divine attributes; he descends from Oduduwa, whom the Yoruba origin myth regards as a deity. The Ondo king is hailed as *ekeji Orịṣa* ("the one whose power is like that of the *orịṣa* or gods")[2] and also as co-equal with death, *Uku*.

The above epithets and praise names indicate the two apparently separate modalities of kingship described by Frankfort[3]: the king as god or the king as representative of god on earth. These two modalities of kingship are hardly kept separate in Ondo kingship. For the Ondo people, the *Ọba* is identical with the *Orịṣa* and possesses the ambivalent characteristics of being the source of both life and death, yet he is also the *Orịṣa*'s representative (vice-regent) on earth.

The death of an *Oṣemawe* signals a period of mourning and a temporary return to chaos. Harmony with nature and the cosmos is brought to an abrupt end, symbolized by the cutting down of leaves and branches of sacred trees around the town.[4] The interregnum, during which the *Lisa*[5] acts as regent, is no less chaotic, for it is the period when the eligible princes contest each other for the throne. Only through the accession of a new king is stability and normality of life restored.[6]

The accession ceremony is a socio-religious performance; it is an occasion for the "greatest display of the myths, symbols, arts and skills"[7] of the Ondo people.

Ifọbajẹ: The Making of a New *Oba*

The process of selecting a new king is a lengthy one. It is perhaps the most crucial step in the transfer of power from one regime to another. I shall very briefly discuss the selection process.

---

[2] The following outline of the ceremonies and ritual proceedings may be useful to keep the festival in mind. *Dida ọjọ ọdun ọba*—The announcement ceremony or fixing the day for the king's festival.

[3] H. Frankfort, *Kingship and the Gods*. Also, Robert Ellwood's *The Feast of Kingship* contains an interesting review of substantial works on kingship studies in the history of religions.

[4] The ascension or installation ceremony (*Ifọbajẹ*) as it is often called is quite distinct from the coronation (*Igbade Ọba*). The latter takes place in Ondo two years after the former and it is held with less fanfare. In the interim between *Ifọbajẹ* and *Igbade-Ọba*, the king is held under probation and there are limited functions that he may perform. In theory the town is ruled by the *Lisa* during this period.

[5] *Lisa* is the highest-ranking chief in Ondo political structure.

[6] Wilson, *The Divine King of the Shilluk*, p. 17.

[7] Ellwood, *The Feasts of Kingship*, p. 3.

As observed in Chapter II, there are four patrilineal kingship houses from which kings are chosen. All trace their descent to the first female king and by implication to *Oduduwa* in Ile-Ifẹ. Whenever there is a vacancy on the throne, the kingmakers, consisting of the five *Ẹharẹ* high chiefs, meet to decide on the next patrilineage and inform them accordingly. Succession takes a long period as there are always struggles among the princes. After the prolonged succession period, the patrilineage meeting is called to decide on a new king. Their choice is made known to the kingmakers who then instruct the chief-diviner to determine, through Ifa divination, the appropriateness of this choice.

Once the candidate is confirmed by Ifa, the arrangements for the accession ceremonies begin. These include the appointment and installation of a new *Lọbun*[8] (if the post is vacant) and a series of preparatory rites such as the propitiation of the Ondo deities and the deceased ancestral *Ọba* to inform them of the mandate of the people.

The *Ọba*-elect leaves the town for a nearby village and resides there until the ceremonies begin. The *Ẹharẹ* dispatches a group of *Odibo* chiefs led by *Sagwẹ* and *Sama*, to 'call home' the *Ọba*-elect for installation. Upon reaching the village, these emissaries take hold of the *Ọba*-elect as an offender accused of eloping with the *Lisa*'s wife. The *Ọba*-elect pleads innocent to these charges, after which he is informed that he is to be made the new *Oṣemawe* of Ondo. An *akoko* tree (new *bordia laevis*) is planted on the spot where this official pronouncement is made and the village is hereafter referred to as *Egure Ọba* ("the king's village") to commemorate the event.

We see in the first stage of this ceremony a ritual of confrontation with the authority of the powerful *Ẹgharẹ*. In other words, to gain access to the throne the king-elect must have a foretaste of "the power of the elders and of tradition"[9] with which he will have to deal throughout his reign. Secondly, by adopting an attitude of humility, the king-elect undergoes a change in his ontological status, a change that will become a permanent part of his new status. The king-elect is led to the town to meet the *Ẹgharẹ* in the house of Saṣẹrẹ (or Adaja), where he passes the night and receives a woven cloth (*aṣọ oke*) from his host. The first day of the official installation ceremony is filled with joy, merriment, and entertainment in the town.

The following day, the king-elect is escorted to *ile-iboju* (the circumcision house) in Chief Babẹha's residence and there he remains in seclusion for three months. The first week in the circumcision house is a critical time. During this period, he is totally secluded and forbidden to see any outsider, at which time

---

[8] See Chapter I on the importance of *Lọbun* in the Ondo social structure.
[9] Monika Vizedom, *Rites and Relationships*, p. 46.

the distinctive Ondo facial mark of one vertical stroke is cut on both cheeks by a priest. The etymology of the title of the *Ọba*'s host, *Ọba-bu-sẹwa* ("the king-adds-to his beauty") suggests the importance of the rite. The adornment of the *Ọba*-elect is a necessary part of the initiation ceremony. *Ẹwa* ("beauty") is seen as part of the new identity which the *Ọba* is in the process of acquiring. More significant are the Ondo facial marks which constitute beauty in this context; they mark the identity of one truly born in Ondo town and of Ondo parentage. Through this rite, the *Ọba* undergoes a symbolic death and rebirth represented by his seclusion and reappearance, as in the eight-day circumcision ceremony after child-birth. The king emerges with a new physical and cultural identity and thereby becomes the embodiment of Ondo tradition. The new *Ọba* is now in a liminal state, which is certainly the most salient and dangerous time of the entire ritual. As Mary Douglas aptly describes a similar situation in southern Africa:

Danger lies in transitional states simply because transition is neither one state nor the next; it is undefinable. The person who must pass from one to another is himself in danger and emanates danger to others. The danger is controlled by ritual which precisely separates his old status, segregates him for a time and then publicly declares his entry to his new status.[10]

A Return to the Center

At the end of the three month long seclusion, the *Ọba*-elect is accompanied by the Ifa chief priest to the neighboring village of Ẹpẹ. Here the priest performs several prophylactic rites aimed at keeping the king-elect in good health (an essential quality of kingship) and of preventing evil forces from hampering him. (It was explained in the first chapter that Ẹpẹ was where the Ondo first migrated, having left Ile-Ifẹ before finally arriving at the present site, and that until recent times the heads of dead kings were buried in this town.) By going to Ẹpẹ to perform this essential rite, the *Ọba*-elect undertakes a pilgrimage towards the center, the place of origin where communion with an ancestral past is renewed.[11]

On his way back in the evening from Ẹpẹ, the king, robed in white clothes tied around his neck in the form of a tunic, heads straight for Ọlọja Idoko's residence where the latter and his chiefs await his arrival. The *Ọṣemawe*-elect meets the *Ọlọja Idoko* sitting and both of them mutter certain words to each other and they exchange pacts. A traditional chief from Idoko quarter explains that this pact consists of the following:

---

[10] *Purity and Danger: An Analysis of the Concepts of Pollution and Taboo* (New York: Prager Publishers, 1966), p. 96.

[11] Older accounts of kingship installation also suggest that the king-elect spends some time in Ilẹ-Oluji. This has been denied, however, by the present day Ondo historians.

The Idoko people promised that we would continue to perform the rites necessary for the well-being of the Ondo people; that we would solely be responsible for the ritual removal of the body of those who commit suicide by hanging in Ondo; that we would perform the burial and purification rites of women who die during pregnancy and childbirth; and that whenever a house is destroyed by natural fire (arson is not considered part of this) we would perform the rites necessary to appease the gods.[12]

When the *Saṣẹrẹ* Idoko, a chief of Idoko quarter in Ondo, was asked to explain what this rite means, he remarked that at the age of six, every male born in Ondo was brought to Idoko for initiation (he calls this baptism) as a prophylactic against evil forces such as *ọrọ* ("whirlwind"), which could cause paralysis.

In return for Idoko's obligation, the *Oṣemawe* of Ondo promised the Idoko people an unlimited right to acquire land anywhere in Ondo. In addition, the Ondo were to celebrate, along with the Idoko people, the *ọdunmoko*, Idoko's major annual festival.

In an atempt to fully understand the significance of this ritual covenant, it is necessary to reconstruct the position of the *oṣemawe* and Idoko in the Ondo sociocultural context. The Idoko people were the most powerful of the three pre-*Oduduwa* aboriginal groups which later surrendered to the Oduduwa group (now represented in the *Oṣemawe*). They still exercise important ritual rights (if not ritual superiority) over the more recently arrived Ondo, while the Ondo themselves exercise a predominantly secular authority over the land. The ceremony between the Idoko chief and the *Oṣemawe*-elect signifies a territorial surrender of the land to the *Ọba*-elect in exchange for ritual rights over the citizens. The covenant is a reaffirmation of the primordial exchange whereby the Idoko surrenders his right over the land to the newcomers and claims special ritual privileges in return. Such new rights include payment for the piece of land on which any Ondo who dies during the annual *Ọdunmoko* is buried.

As the *Ọba* is a living representative of his subjects, "he is the symbol and totality of his people and country,"[13] and as such he is responsible for their destiny. It is therefore to the King's advantage to make this covenant with the Idoko, who claim to be the guarantors of his subjects' welfare. By this ritual the king is then able to "further the good of his people and able to keep within bounds the pernicious power of illness, plagues, war, generosity, beneficence."[14] The *Saṣẹrẹ*-Idoko boasts of the magico-religious superiority of

---

[12] This source is from the interview with Chief Akingbohungbe Saṣẹre of Idoko by the University of Ifẹ, *Yoruba History Research Group*, in 1965.

[13] *The Sacral Kingship*, p. 57.

[14] Ibid.

the Idoko people and their ritual potency, especially their control over an illness called *ategun* (another form of paralysis). This ailment is believed to be caused by the whirlwind spirit, the tutelary deity of the Idoko people. He cites two instances when such esoteric power was put to use in the service of the Ondo people. According to him, the Idoko people once saved the Ondo people from subjugation to the Oyo kingdom to which they were paying very heavy annual tribute.[15] Long after the establishment of British rule, it was still customary for the government to call on the Idoko people to perform the ritual cleansing of any polluted space in Ondo.[16]

The Broken Covenant

As a seal of this covenant, the *Oba*-elect and the *Oloja Idoko* avoid each other for life; once the ceremony ends, the king-elect is forbidden to pass through the area again. Such an avoidance taboo between the *Osemawe* and the *Oloja Idoko* was removed during the installation of the last *Osemawe* Adenle II. According to the *Sasere Idoko*, the chief informant on this aspect of Ondo kingship, "we decided to follow the Christian way, and we put the Bible between the two of them, so they could continue to see each other; if it were to be the olden days, once they departed that night, that was the last they would see of each other."[17] The explanation for this change may be found in Ondo's conversion experience. The Ondo Christians saw this occasion as a significant religious landmark. Hence, the first time the *Oloja Idoko* worshipped in St. Stephens Anglican Cathedral at Oke-Aluko, a special anthem was composed for the event.[18] But according to the Idoko people, the Ondo have not kept the promises made to them, especially Ondo's refusal to participate in Idokos' rituals. This broken covenant has been interpreted by the *Sasere* as the cause of a variety of disorders in the Ondo community, such as women's infertility and impotence among young men.

---

[15] Among the tributes Ondo used to pay the Oyo kingdom according to Sasere Idoko were 200 *eru* (slaves), 200 *awo* (dishes), 200 *aso-oke* (pieces of woven native cloth) and 200 *akun* (coral beads). All the above items were the most prized possessions of the Ondo people in the olden days.

[16] Sasere Idoko further elaborated on how this process was carried out: "Whenever there was a case of suicide, the government would inform the Osemawe who would call the Idoko for the purification rite. It is after this that the health superintendent would visit such homes to make sure that proper sanitation is maintained." *Yoruba Historical Research Group*, tape recorded interview, 1965.

[17] Chief Akingbohungbe, the Sasere Idoko, interview.

[18] Ogunsakin recorded the first stanza of the song: *A'ayin Oluwa, A'ayin Oluwa, 'Loja oke'doko wo sosi* ("Praise the Lord, Praise the Lord, Olojo Idoko worshipped in the church"), Ogunsakin, *Ondo*, p. 46.

Once the covenant is reenacted and the *Ọba* in theory takes possession of the territory, he then performs two short ceremonies: the first signifies the extension of his authority over the warrior class. I observed earlier that Ondo originally was divided into fifteen quarters, each quarter representing both a political and military unit; the military functions were performed by the *Ẹlẹgbẹ* chiefs directly under the leadership of *Ayadi*, the army chief and the chief-priests of Ogun (the deity of war). In this ceremony, the *Ọba*-elect is led from the oke-doko to the house where he meets his army chief, and the latter pledges support of the *Ẹlẹgbẹ* warrior groups. He also offers sacrifices on behalf of the king to Ogun, the quintessential deity of war "capable of assuring him of victory"[19] in his military exploits.

The remark made by M. W. Young that "kingship exists by virtue of the consent of the various groups and offices involved in the ceremonies"[20] is true of the next stage of the king's installation rituals, which confirms his authority over the nobles. Such consent is also coerced by tradition and by implicit or potential force. As the king leaves the *Saṣẹrẹ*'s house, he is led to Oke-Ọtunba where he meets the *Olotu-Ọmọba* (the head of the nobles), who represents the royalty from whose membership he has been chosen to be king. There *Olotu-Ọmọba* confronts the king-elect and asks him the question: "What do you want here?" The *Ọba*-elect replies, "I have come to take up my father's title."[21]

Hereafter, *Olotu-Ọmọba* warns him not to pass through the site again.[22] Once again, the king is forbidden access to a ritual space. As we saw in the case of *Ọlọja-Idoko*, such prohibitions and ritual affront in principle limit the degree of his participation in political affairs to the barest minimum.[23]

Other smaller rites follow these two ceremonies. They include making sacrifices at *Ogun Aiṣẹrọ* (a quarter shrine to the Ogun deity) and receiving the blessing of Akunnara, another important chief of the *Ọramfẹ* cult, at Oke-dibo, where the king is also forbidden to pass after this ceremony.

The next stage is the most delicate part of all the ceremonies. The *Ọba*-elect

---

[19] Brown, *Ritual Aspects of Mamprusi Kingship*, p. 92.

[20] "The Divine Kingship of the Shilluk," *Africa* 36 (1966), p. 107.

[21] Ogunṣakin, *Ondo*, p. 34.

[22] Ibid.

[23] Robert Ellwood, *The Feast of Kingship*, p. 29. Ellwood pointed out a similar custom among the Polynesians, where the sacred chief is so prohibited by ritual taboo that he may not conduct ordinary political affairs. These affairs are handled by a sort of Prime Minister called the "talking chief." I pointed out in a previous chapter that the *Lisa*, also called *ọba ode* (the outside king) handles such functions on behalf of the king in Ondo.

is led to *igbo-oṣi* (the mausoleum)[24] where he is blindfolded and asked to pick out two of seven sacred swords,[25] symbolizing wealth, war, famine, poverty, long reign, short reign, and abundant life. By performing this ceremony at the royal mausoleum, the rite establishes continuity with the ancestral spirits and the past *Oba* who are the givers of the sacred swords.

Investiture of the Oba

The last and main series of rituals of the Ondo accession consist of the actual investiture of the new *Oba* by the *Lobun*. Here the new *Oba* receives the final authority to exercise his rule over his subjects. It is essential that we quote the *Lobun*, the chief ritual specialist on this aspect of the installation rites, as she relates the mythic beginning of the rites and her role in the kingship system. The following passage was recorded during the installation of the present *Oṣemawe* in an interview conducted with the *Lobun*. In response to the question, "What is your role in the installation?," the *Lobun* replied:

I.

Didun inu wa ni wipe
Bi imọ ti ṣe njade yi
O gba ọna otitọ
Bi ti ọjọ owurọ
Ni igba atijọ ri
Nigbati a bẹrẹ oye nilẹ yi
Ẹniti o kọ jọba oun lo ni ile yi
O lo ojidinirinwo ọdun ni ori itẹ
Omi ti kuro leti
Afi bi enia ba kọja lẹgbẹ ẹ
Igbayẹn la ṣe ri
We ri pe arugbo ti de?
Ibẹ ati fi mama
Wa ba wọn fẹ ẹniti o ma

---

[24] Ogunṣakin translates *igbo osi* literally as "the bush of woe." According to him it is located in Igelemoroko and an akoko tree marks the spot today, as the place has virtually ceased to exist in importance. Afọlabi Ojo, who has studied Yoruba palaces and their traditions extensively, translates *ile oṣi* or *oju oṣi* as the mausoleum, a house or sacred bush within the palace yard where past *Oba* are buried (see his *Yoruba Palaces*). Traditions in Ondo seem to suggest, at least in recent times, that no such public burial place is available, though one is not quite sure whether this is just a recent occurrence or something that goes very far back into history.

[25] There is also disagreement on what the seven swords symbolize. Other possibilities apart from the above are epidemics, scarcity, and calamity.

dipo Ọba fun wa
Ẹ ẹ hi wo ti dagba
Pupọ ọrọ wa wei gbọ l'agbọ fin
Ibẹ o ti kele si - - -
Arẹmọ ẹ ọkunrin, Airọ,
Oun la npe ni *Amuparọ*
O fi pạro ara ẹ
Ibẹ oti mulọ si oju ọna
Ibiti o gba lọ si ori oye
Ohi mu kunlẹ
O gbe ade e dehio
O ṣi n'ohiho ara ẹ
O fi d'e họnhiho
Nigba mẹta
O fi daka mu a wọ ibe hi
Dan ka mu a lọ
Fi ohun na kẹ, dẹn wa
Bo dẹn ti fi ibi yi
O ma ti gun ori opo
Ibẹ o ti ṣuba ko nibẹ ẹyẹn
O hi ṣuba ẹ hun.
Bi tan eleyi ti ri niyẹn

II.

Ọmọ mi ni
Bayi nisinsinyi
Ki ade pẹ lori
Ki bata pẹ lẹsẹ
Bi ẹnikan ba lọ fun ẹnikeji
Bi o ba ṣe oun (Lọbun) lo kọ ku
   Ṣàju lọ bayi
O dọ jọ yi ohun kẹ kuro lori tẹ
Dẹn tun gbọdọ
   Mu ọnumuhẹn dipo ẹ
Nitori a tun ni rẹni
   —ṣuba fun
Bi o ti jẹ niyẹn.

* * * * *

It is a great joy for us
That as knowledge spreads out today,
It follows the path of truth
  as in the beginning of time.
In the olden days,
In the beginning of kingship in this town.
This building we are in (*Lobun*'s titled residence)
  was owned by the first person to be king
  in this town.
She reigned for 220 years.
Her ears were already dried up.
It is only when someone passed by her
That she could notice his presence.
Don't you see how old she was?
So we approached her one day
  and called her: "Great Mother,
Find someone who will be king for us
Since you are too old.
Most of what we have to say to you
  you could hardly hear."
So, she agreed and called
  her first son *Airo*
That is the one we call, *afiparo* (a substitute).
She took him from her place;
She led him to a road path where
  he would pass through
  to be made king.
She made him kneel down,
Her crown on her head,
She removed the crown and placed it
  on his head,
Three times.
And asked the people present to make him
  pass through this place
  (pointing to a street outside)
  and take him home.
And she said that she would soon join them.
When she arrived at where
  he would ascend the throne,
She made a few rites for him.
That is how the story goes.

When *Lọbun* was asked about the relationship of her title to the kingship, she explained further:

II.

The king is my son.
Now, may his reign be long.
If one dies before the other, If I die before the king,
Not until the king himself leaves the throne (dies),
Can the town elect another person to replace me.
Otherwise there will be no one to install the new king.
That is the way it is.[26]

The above narrative provides considerable insight into the nature of Ondo kingship rituals. First, it clearly demonstrates all the qualities of a political charter-myth, by narrating the beginning of sacral kingship in Ondo and expressing "an ideology that legitimizes both political institutions and the king's royal dynasty in terms of events believed to be of great antiquity."[27] Second, the myth provides a basis for male rule as a substitute for a former female rule, perhaps even a suppressed matriarchal kinship system. It provides, as Levi-Strauss has said in a different context, "a logical (but mythic) solution to an irreconcilable problem."[28] Third, the myth confirms the narrator's role as the most important ritual specialist connected with the accession ceremony, for without her (*Lọbun*) there can be no king in Ondo. Unlike the previous ritualists who had maintained avoidance taboos with the king, *Lọbun* and the king maintain no taboos between them. When asked whether such avoidance exists, the woman herself explained this point: "*Ọmọ mi ni, mo le ri*" ("He is my son, and I can see him"). This suggests that a special ritual kinship relationship exists between the *Lọbun* and the *Ọba*. Acting as his ritual sponsor, the *Lọbun* mediates between the ancient past and the present.

The myth also contains the ritual models for the ceremony, thus demonstrating a central thesis of Mircea Eliade. According to Eliade, every ritual has a divine model, an archetype, and these rituals acquire meanings, reality, solely to the extent to which they repeat a primordial act[29] and par-

---

[26] Conversation with *Lọbun*, *Yoruba Historical Research Group*, on tape, 1965.

[27] Thomas A. Reefe, *The Rainbow and the King* (Berkeley: University of California Press, 1981), p. 41.

[28] Mara E. Danabar, "Kingship Theory in the Patriarchal Narrative (Genesis 11:27, 35:29)," *American Academy of Religion, Abstract of Proceedings* (Missonda: Scholars Press, 1976), p. 165.

[29] *The Myth of the Eternal Return or Cosmos and History* (Princeton: Princeton University Press, 1974), p. 5.

ticipate in a transcendental reality. The central motif of the last part of the
accession ceremony is the ritual enactment of the primordial prototype and
the actualization of the mythic event just narrated by the *Lọbun*. It is no
wonder, then, that the *Lọbun* rejoiced at the fact that as knowledge expands,
it takes the path of truth as posited *ab origine*[30] by the ancestors.

The final ceremony begins when the *Lọbun* takes the right hand of the *Ọba*
(an act that signifies the transfer of the sacred power), lifts up his hand, and
circumambulates the sacred *akoko* tree, the *axis mundi*. Amidst the acclaim
and shouts of *abaye o* (a shout of homage and acceptance) the *Lọbun* pro-
claims him king three times. Then the new king is taken to another sacred spot
called *oridẹn*, the *omphalos*. Here he kneels, and one of the high chiefs places
an *akoko* leaf on his head and pronounces the following admonition:

> Today, you become the *Oṣemawe*.
> May your reign be long,
> Take heed,
>   you must not plot against your people
>   nor do them any evil deed.
> Take care of them all, if anyone
>   offends you, ask for repentance
>   or report him to the elders.[31]

The final rite is performed when the *Lọbun* again takes the king's hand and
leads him up the primeval mound[32] called *masikin*. The ascent to this sacred
spot marks the final public declaration of the new king. Several weeks of
feasting follow the accession ceremony, while the new *Ọba* spends the following three months in the *Bapaiye*'s or the *Logbosẹrẹ*'s house for other minor
rites. Then he departs for the palace at the end of his three-month seclusion.
It must be emphasized that while the accession ceremony marks the beginning
of his reign, the *Ọba* is allowed to participate only in limited political decision-
making. Not until his coronation ceremony, a less-important ceremony two
years later, is he fully a king. In the interim, most state functions are performed by his deputy, the *Lisa*.

---

[30] Ibid., p. 6.

[31] Ogunṣakin, *Ondo*, p. 34. This is not a verbatim quotation of the high chief's words.

[32] C. J. Bleeker reports a similar rite in Egyptian coronation ceremonies, "The prince who
ascended to the throne actualized the mythic deed of the sun god, his ideal father, who in mythic
times climbed a primeval hill, thus causing the day to break." *Egyptian Festivals* (Leiden: E. J.
Brill, 1967), p. 95.

The *Ọdun Ọba*: Festival of Kingship

This section presents a phenomenological description and hermeneutical explanation of the *Ọdun Ọba*. The rites and ceremonies of this annual royal festival, viewed from a phenomenological perspective, embrace a significant central religious meaning and function: the renewal of the Ondo kingship, cosmos, and society. An exploration of the structure and meaning of the entire festival will be conducted along this line. There are nine significant aspects of *Ọdun Ọba*. Each is examined in turn. In presenting these materials, the description of the ritual processes and their interpretations are dealt with separately, thus differentiating descriptive from hermeneutical phenomenology.

The Announcement of the Ọdun Ọba Ceremony

The annual *Ọdun Ọba* festival takes place in July. The auspicious and sacred time of the festival is ritually fixed by the king's diviner. The time is very suggestive of a renewal motif. First, it corresponds to the climax of the yearly agricultural cycle, the end of the sowing and planting season, and the beginning of the harvest season; it is the first festival in the Ondo ritual calendar. Second, the period marks the end of the rainy season, when the last of the year's rain falls with full force at the approach of the dry season (harmattan). To all intents and purposes the ceremony exhibits the characteristics of a new year celebration "when the life forces are at their lowest ebb,"[33] thus making the rejuvenation of the cosmos absolutely necessary. The intent of the festival is to energize the cosmos, to transform its profane nature into a life-supporting sacred power through a recreation of the "primordial age," the pure time of origin.

Nine days before the actual day, the preparatory ceremonies begin with the official announcement ceremony referred to as *dida ọjọ ọdun ọba* (literally, "announcing the date of the king's festival"). In the afternoon of the announcement day, people gather in the front yard of the palace where the ceremony will take place. The chiefs of the *Ekulę* and *Ęlęgbę* (the second and third grade chiefs) sit according to rank on the left and right sides in the open yard (fig. 1). Then *Sagwę*, the chief in charge of the procedure of the day's ceremony, ushers in two of the highest-ranking chiefs, *Adaja* and *Saşęrę*, and leads them to their seats on the left side of the *Ọba*'s elevated throne where the *Ọba*'s big umbrella also stands. The other chief priests, *Ọdunwo* and

---

[33] Bodde, *Festival in Classical China*, p. 54.

Aogbo, enter the courtyard, dancing to the tune of *Ugbaji* (a sacred drum). The special manner of seating the high chiefs and the chief priests is referred to as *rire wole* (i.e., "they are persuaded to come in").

Meanwhile, the *Ekule* and *Elegbe* come out of their seats in pairs to pay homage to the high chiefs. Standing a few feet from a high chief, each *Ekule* and *Elegbe* chief in turn raises his closed fists towards the high chief three times, while simultaneously murmuring the chief's praise names. Finally, he prostrates himself on the floor. Shortly afterwards, the *Oba* emerges from the inner room and is ushered into the elevated throne amidst the sounds of trumpets and the voices of his subjects praising him and saying *abaiye o*. The rites and ceremonies of the day follow immediately. The *Sagwe*, the *Oba*'s messenger, ushers in the two highest-ranking chiefs, *Lisa* and *Jomu*. Dressed in gorgeous traditional dresses covered with white sheets, they perform the ritual dance by which they demonstrate their loyalty and submission to the king's authority. The ritual homage which starts as the sacred pair dances towards the king is accompanied by the solemn rhythm of *Idau* music and is performed in the following form (fig. 1). Each of the two chiefs takes three steps forward in a clockwise and counter-clockwise direction respectively, stopping to pay homage to the king in a manner comparable to the Muslim ablution rite. Together they kneel down, touch the ground with their hands, put dust on their arms, chest, back, and head, and finally touch the ground with their foreheads. They then rise up and dance three more steps forward and repeat the same act of homage. The display of obeisance is carried out three times before they finally arrive in front of the king. The dance completed, the two chiefs remove their ceremonial white cover sheets and take their seats on the right side of the *Oba*.

Next, the royal drummer kneels in front of the *Oba* and, accompanied by his drum, recounts the names of virtually all the past *Oba*. Then he places the drum in the hands of the *Oba* and prays for a long reign and good health in the coming year. He also prays for himself, that he may be alive to perform the ceremony for the *Oba* the coming year. When I asked an informant whether it is possible for the drummer to remember all the names of the thirty-six past *Oba* that have reigned in Ondo, he answered:

Normally the drummer may skip through certain names, but what he *must* not do is to forget to recount the name of the first female *Oba*, Pupupu. It is a common belief among the people that if the drummer fails to follow this procedure, he may not live to perform the festival the following year.

At the conclusion of his performance the drummer is presented with a token gift referred to as *adiitu* (literally, "what is closed up that must not be opened"), a gift that he may not open while he is still in the presence of the

A Representation of the Sitting Arrangement and the Rites of the Announcement Ceremony

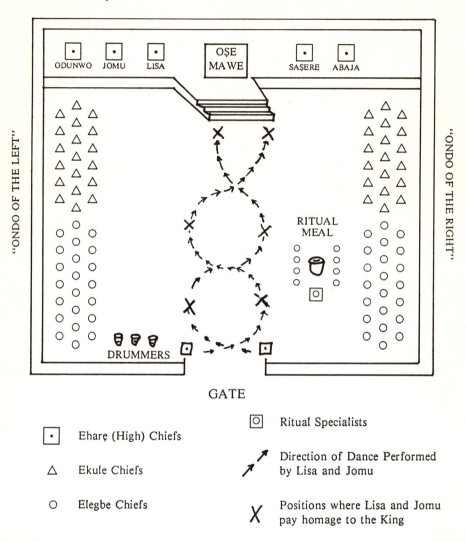

Figure 1.

king.[34] Next, a food offering is made to the ancestors and the invisible spirits. This consists of the typical Ondo festival meal, pounded yam with a stew made of monkey legs and palm wine, all set out on a flat stone (fig. 1). Fifteen minor chiefs from each quarter, holding their brass batons and staffs of office, form two rows on both sides of the "meal table'. The priest-chief in charge of the rite, the *Aogbo*, stoops down in front of the 'meal table' and pretends to be eating the food in communion with the past heroes. He pours a wine libation and then points his sword seven times towards the king as he prays for prosperity in the coming year. It is through this ritual that he demonstrates his willingness to continue to communicate with the ancestor world on behalf of the king and the people present.

Invitation to the Ọba's Festival

The main purpose of the first-day ceremony, as stated earlier, is to announce the date of the *Ọba*'s festival. Once the meal is completed, the *Sagwẹ* calls for silence (*okere o*) and loudly recalls the names of most of the second-grade chiefs in order of their rank. He then calls on the general public, *ọtun Ondo, osi Ondo* ("Ondo on the right and on the left") and greets them on behalf of the *Ọba—Ọba ma kin wọn o* ("the king greets you all"). The people then respond with the shout of *abaiye o*. The five *Ẹharẹ* high chiefs stand up from their seats and kneel in front of the king in two rows. They decide jointly on the auspicious date for the *Ọba*'s festival, but in actual fact the day has already been decided and everyone knows it will be held the ninth day following the announcement. After this deliberation, the *Jọmu* then recites the invitation formula to the people:

> Okere, okere, okere
> Ọba ma ki wọn o
> Hi, nigi lugbagbọ ṣe ọdun tiẹ
> họn bọ ṣe
> Nigi lumọle ṣe ti ẹ
> họn bọ ṣe
> Bi loiṣa ṣe ti wọn
> họn ba wọn ṣe
> Ajailaye hi, "ọdun hun disanni ni o"
> Di, ọni ho ko, do bọ
> Di, gbogbo aiye bahun ṣọdun hun o.

* * * * *

---

[34] The gift wrap contains *ẹgbaata* (sixpence).

> Silence, silence, silence
> The king greets you all.
> He says, when the Christians had their festival he
>   celebrated with them.
> When the Muslims had theirs, he joined them in
>   celebrating it.
> When the *Orişa* believers (traditional religion)
>   had theirs he celebrated with them.
> Ajailaye ("My Lord, or owner of the universe")
>   says that his festival is in nine days time.
> Let the person on the farm come back home.
> Let every person celebrate with him.

In response to this announcement the people shout, *abaiye o*, and the King stands up and walks to the entrance of the assembly and back to his seat two times, thus making his appearance to the people. On the third occasion he walks to his inner palace, to the tune of special music.

The king's festival is an all-encompassing rite; "in one and the same ceremony" the Ondo people "bring about their entrance into a new period of time, the renewal of their kingdom and the 'reconstruction' of the world."[35]

The announcement ceremony, the first ritual performance, ushers the community into active participation in the reality of sacred time. The role of the royal master drummer is precisely to help recreate this primordial sacred time with his talking drum. Since his memory can be relied on to accomplish the task successfully, he recites the king list, the chain of authority that links the present with the mythic past. For the present to be validated, the past must be ritually reaffirmed. This point reminds us of the analogous role played by the *isnad*, the chain of authority that validates an authentic *ḥadith* corpus in Islamic tradition.

Through the invocation of the names of the past *Ọba* and ancestor kings, their acts and deeds, which have become the paradigmatic model for the living, are also recounted. As we observed earlier, Ondo traditional chroniclers group different epochs of history around the personalities of their kings. Past kings are known officially by their honorific titles, which depict major events of cosmic quality during their reign. Therefore, "there is a very close relation between the particular being of the king himself and the life of the people."[36] By reciting these 'sacred names', the master drummer releases

---

[35] Dominique Zahan, *The Religion, Spirituality and Thought of Traditional Africa*, trans. Katezva Martin and Lawrence M. Martin (Chicago: University of Chicago Press, 1979), p. 78.
[36] K. A. H. Hidding, "The High God and the King," in *The Sacral Kingship*, p. 57.

into the immediate world of the Ondo this 'transcendent power', the *sine qua non* of the genuine ritual.[37] And, through that which is "considered most sacred, real, holy and powerful"[38] to the people, a meaningful and ordered cosmos is created and the Ondo world is once again renewed. With this completed, the sacred drum is handed over to the king, and through it he reaffirms his kingship in communion with the previous users of the same drum. I remarked earlier that in return for orchestrating the rite successfully, the master drummer[39] is offered a token gift by the king. What is most important to him is not the gift received, but that through this rite he renews his own life, as evidenced in the exchange of blessings *Wa ṣe amọdun* ("you will do this next year") between him and the king. Here, the spoken words (ọrọ) are used to renew life and kingship. It is significant that it is a taboo for the drummer to forget to name *Pupupu*, the first woman-king and founder of the kingdom in his drum recollection. This implies "a connection through the person of the culture-hero and founder of the kingdom." As Ugo Bianchi has suggested, there is a connection "between the story of the first beginnings of the world and the renewal of the year's life."[40]

Roger Callois, in a similar way, comments that one of the various methods employed by archaic cultures to "recreate the fecund time of the powerful ancestors (is) the recitation of the myth of origin."[41] Thus, through recreating the life-giving force of the sacred in ritual, the royal drummer makes the profane community life sacred once again.[42]

Omi Abẹ: The Boundary Rites

Between the announcement ceremony and the actual festival day, the boundary rite takes place at the border between Ondo and Ileṣa. This rite is called *omi abẹ*. No one knows its origin or how it became associated with this festival. One thing remembered by everyone is the circumstances by which the priest in charge of the ceremony became involved with it.

It was once the prerogative of a small group of Ondo people to perform the

---

[37] "Ritual," in *Introduction to the Study of Religion*, ed. T. William Hall (New York: Harper & Row, 1978), p. 72.

[38] Ibid.

[39] For the role and status of Yoruba drummers see Ayọ Bankọle, Judith Bush, Sadek H. Samagn, "The Yoruba Master Drummer," *African Arts* VIII (Winter 1975), p. 48–55.

[40] Ugo Bianchi, *The History of Religions* (Leiden: E. J. Brill, 1977), p. 113. He further indicates that the recital of the *Enuma Elish* in the celebration of Akitu, the Babylonian New Year, suggests a close connection between the creation of the World and new beginnings.

[41] Roger Callois, *Man and the Sacred*, p. 109.

[42] Bianchi, *History of Religions*, p. 39.

boundary rite for the *Ọba*. While doing so they were often molested and sometimes killed by a group of people referred to simply as 'strangers' living on the other side of the boundary. This caused great disturbances during the king's festival, so much so that it became almost impossible for the king to perform this part of his festival.[43] A powerful medicine man named Akingbade approached the king and promised to carry out this rite for him and put a stop to the incessant disturbances caused by the 'enemies'. This promise was made on the condition that the medicine man would be made the official priest in charge of the rite. The king consented, and the man was installed as *Lotualẹwa* (literally, "the autochthonous controller or owner of the land from the time of the beginning"). As promised, he carried out the rites during his lifetime without further disturbances. The warlike song[44] heralding Akingbade's return from the *omi abẹ* site has become a ritual song for this aspect of the *Ọba*'s festival and a signal to the people that the boundary ritual has been successfully completed.

The boundary ceremony, *omi abẹ*, expresses several motifs. It reestablishes the Ondo space and territory over which the king exercises his power and dominance. In this regard, Evan Zuesse makes an interesting comment: "It is a common feature of African royal ceremonies that all ceremonies for the renewal of the year as well as those consecrated to the renewal of the kingdom among African royalty once included and to this day still include rites concerning the restoration of the cosmos."[45] Although we possess no actual historical details about the origin of this ceremony or how it came to be associated with the king's festival, certain details accompanying the performance are suggestive. The rite itself is performed on behalf of the king by a medicine man whose title, *Olotualẹwa*, suggests a renewal motif. He is the 'autochthonous owner' of the land; i.e., the land *ab origine*, the mythical time of Ondo beginning. The medicine man makes his pilgrimage to the site in order to regenerate the creative period and thereby renews the Ondo cosmos. It is pertinent to ask why, if the Ondo share boundaries with four other 'alien people', did *omi abẹ* and not any of the other four places become the ritual

---

[43] Oral interview with Chief Ojo, August 6, 1980.

[44] In the interview conducted with Chief Ojo, August 17, 1980, the song is rendered as follows:

> Akingbade nbọ, Akingbade nbọ
> Ojẹgun nbọ
> Akingbade is coming
> Akingbade is coming
> The brave one is coming.

[45] Evan M. Zuesse, *Ritual Cosmos: The Sanctification of Life in African Religions* (Athens, Ohio: Ohio University Press, 1979), p. 78.

site? It would appear that the place where the ceremony is performed constitutes, according to Thornton, "the boundary along which competitive interaction among various groups is likely to occur."[46] The aim of such a ceremony, Thornton suggests, is therefore to "ritually demarcate the boundary that creates the frontiers."[47] The available evidence underscores the above idea. The story recognizes an outside threat from a group of alien people referred to simply as *Igbira*. The outsiders' motive appeared to be one of destabilizing the successful execution of the boundary rite and, by implication, the existence of the kingdom itself.[48] While the above may be true, the central intention of the *omi abẹ* ceremony is undoubtedly to remake and resanctify Ondos' boundaries and to purify the land that they enclose.

Ughasu: The Assembly of the Palace Chiefs

On the evening of the king's festival, the ceremony of *Ughasu* in commemoration of *Oṣemawe Esu* takes place. Though not mentioned in any of the lists of Ondo kings, *Esu* is said to have been a woman who once reigned in Ondo. The scarf worn as part of the regalia for this occasion suggests a probable connection between the origin of the king's festival and the *Oṣemawe Esu*. The ceremony is mainly performed by the *Otu* (the palace chiefs). They gather in the house of their organizer, called Salaja, for a feast of lamb. At this time a sheep is sacrificed on an altar referred to as *oẹnẹn*. These chiefs are then dressed in their ceremonial costumes (scarves around their necks and swords of office in their hands). They move to the main street *Oreretu* (literally, "the Otu's quarter") located in front of the *Ọba*'s palace. The *Ọba*, also dressed in his ceremonial white clothes, sits alongside the high chiefs on one side of the street, while the *Otu* chiefs gather on the opposite side.

The *Otu* chiefs stand up in pairs and dance on their side to pay the *Ọba* homage, pointing their swords at him three times. This completed, they dance back to the other side to perform the same rite for the *Salaja* and the other senior *Otu* chiefs. The rite is a ritual display of their desire and willingness to perform their duty as protectors of the king. Like a modern day royal brigade of guards, displaying their combat readiness in a national day parade, the *Otu* chiefs oscillate between the king and their leaders, in an apparent display of

---

[46] Robert J. Thornton, *Space, Time and Culture among the Iragw of Tanzania* (Studies in Anthropology), (New York: Academic Press, 1980), p. 26.

[47] Ibid.

[48] See Lucretia Ojo's essay: *Ọdun ọba ni Ilu Ondo*. (The King's Festival in Ondo), N. C. E. Long Essay, College of Education, Ikẹrẹ, June, 1980, p. 18.

force. The *Salaja*, the head of these palace warrior-chiefs, is the last to perform the dance in homage to the *Ọba*. With this, the circle moves down the
street where the same ceremony is performed. At the end of the third homage
dance, the king and his entourage return to the palace.

Asingba: The Ceremony of Bringing Tributes to the King

Another important aspect of the festival is the presentation of ceremonial
tributes, referred to as *asingba* to the king. In the morning of the day of the
king's festival, the second and third grade chiefs present ceremonial gifts to
the *Ọba* as a show of his lordship of 'the harvest of the land'. This ritual consists of the joint presentation of four goats by several groups of about six
chiefs per group. To reinforce the ties of royalty and benevolence between the
king and his subjects,[49] the king returns two of the goats to the chiefs for
sacrifice and feasting. In the evening of the same day, the king dances around
the town, stopping at the ritual spot on his way to make offerings of kola nut.
In the late evening, he receives the ceremonial gifts of ram from the *Ẹgharẹ*
chiefs. We see here the place of gift exchange and royal distribution of wealth
and favor in Ondo kingdom. In reality, Ondo society frowns upon acquisition
of wealth and property which is not put to the use of those who have none
at all.

Beyond its religious and symbolic meanings, the king's festival is related to
the secular domain of Ondo social organization. In Chapter II, I have described the nature of socio-political dealings between the chiefs and the *Ọba*,
observing that the Ondo possess a highly-stratified political structure. There
are three hierarchies of chieftancy titles, each of which perform separate
duties and functions for the community. Here I must emphasize the role of
the king and his ceremonies in integrating the Ondo society and resolving religious cleavages. The royal ceremonies provide the occasions during which
the community acts together to renew and reaffirm the basic structures that
undergird its existence.[50] The festival helps to display and to reaffirm this
hierarchical structure. Of particular importance is the position of the *Ẹgharẹ*,
the five high-ranking chiefs. While they all sit on the elevated platform
alongside the king, the preeminent position of the first two and highest-ranking chiefs, the *Lisa* and the *Jọmu*, is emphasized by their seating on the king's

---

[49] Derk Bodde, *Festivals in Classical China* (Princeton, N.J.: Princeton University Press,
1975), p. 139.

[50] Bardwel L. Smith, *Religion and Legitimation in South Asia* (International Studies in Sociology and Social Anthropology), (Leiden: E. J. Brill, 1978), p. 167.

right side. This reinforces their display of loyalty and submission on the part of the people to the king's authority in their highly stylized and dramatic ritual dance (Fig. 1). While the presentation of *asingba*, the ceremonial gift, illustrates the role of gift exchanges and royal distribution of wealth and favor, it is also another occasion on which the Ondo hierarchical structure is displayed. Whereas the second- and third-grade chiefs present four goats to the king, each *Egharę* presents a ram, a domestic animal of higher monetary value and status than the goat.

At various points in the festival, we see a display of moiety grouping that suggests Ondo symbolic classification. In Ondo the universe of persons and objects is divided into two halves. This is reflected in the invitation formula. Here a call is made by the *Jọmu* to the *Qtun Ondo* ("Ondo to the right") and *Osi Ondo* ("Ondo to the left") to celebrate wholeheartedly the king's festival. Pairing-up is also conspicuously displayed in the various ritual dances and the division of the rank and file of chiefs into two halves in the seating arrangement, as I have indicated above (Fig. 1). Both are reflections of the dualistic structure implicit in the ways of thought and social organization of the people, but more important is the fact that the moieties are unified in the celebration of the kingship.

Perhaps the most vivid and meaningful action that reflects this same dual structure is the marking of *Ugbaji* drums (the symbol of authority and continuity in office of the higher-ranking chiefs) with white and red paints at the home of individual high chiefs on the morning of the announcement ceremony. The ceremony, accompanied by the ritual song *Qba mę șoro yi hun o* ("It is for the king that this rite is made"), is meant for the chiefs, and is a rite of renewal of their own chieftancy as well as the renewal of the kingship and the community at large. It is apparent that these two halves are thought to promote the life-giving rhythm of the universe and nature by means of their ritual activity. The red and white chalk markings symbolize the two elements of procreation: blood and semen.

Kikun Awọn Ọmọ Ọba: The King's Household Ceremony

Kikun awọn ọmọ Ọba (literally, "adding to the king's children") is observed in the evening of the third day of the king's festival. This ritual is meant for the members of the king's household, particularly the royal children and their mothers. Childless wives may not take part in this ritual. At about 3.00 p.m. on the appointment day, the king and his chiefs (many female chiefs feature prominently in this ceremony) sit in a small building located in a corner of the front yard of the palace. While the people wait in anticipation for the members of the king's household to arrive, the children's masqueraders, referred to as *odokoo*, appear before the audience carrying whips. These masqueraders, about twenty in number, are dressed in red flowing cloths and masks and act as policemen to clear the path for the procession of the royal children. In so doing, the masqueraders also act as a source of humor, entertainment and amusement for the waiting audience, thus sparing them from the boredom caused by the apparent delay of the king's household.

The king's wives are dressed in white and their children in fine *aṣọ-oke* (a locally-woven ceremonial dress). The wives' bodies are also dotted with red and white chalk marks, the symbols of sacredness, and their hair is unplaited, transforming them into the sacred state of being. The elaborate arrangement of the royals is organized by the wives of the deceased former *Ọba*, thus showing a sign of continuity between the royal patrilineages. As the members of the royalty line up in the inner palace for the procession to the site of the ceremony, a dramatic and highly symbolic event occurs when the king's emissary *baba mesi* is sent out twice to 'hurry' them up, since the people are becoming impatient. On both occasions he returns with the message that they are still busy preparing and that the king should give them more time. When this drama has reached a climax and the waiting audience is very anxious to see the nobles, *baba mesi* emerges from the inner courtyard with the royal members in procession. The first to emerge are the king's children in order of their birth, starting with the firstborn; they are followed by the king's wives led by the most senior. It is significant to note that those wives who are nursing babies carry their babies on their backs, while those whose children are grown carry dolls instead and pretend to be carrying babies. As the procession moves past the waiting crowd, women and children shout *abaye o* and pray thus: *ma ri wọn mọdun o* ("may we see you next year"). Many also pray for good health, vitality, fertility, and prosperity in their trade and business. As the king's household reaches the inner yard, a rope tied around the neck of the sacrificial ram is placed on the hands and heads of an individual child and wife. This animal, along with kola nut and palm wine, is then offered as a sacrifice on their behalf. The blood of the animal is sprinkled on their heads, after which they return to the inner courtyard where more rejoicing takes place.

Besides its dramatic and entertaining aspects, the king's household ceremony has important cultural signficance that makes it the most impressive and emotionally intense part of the actual festival. I have in mind, in particular, the conduct of members of the king's household throughout this rite. How should we understand the apparently delayed arrival of the king's household for a rite planned in advance and purposely meant for them? No doubt this delay represents the common day-to-day burden of the family institution as well as the stereotypical image of women and children as synonymous with delay. However, and most importantly, it was an attempt to put to test "the quiet dignity and the patience"[51] of the king at the most appropriate time and place, i.e., in the presence of all his subjects and at the most critical ritual time. As the king's household represents a microcosm of the larger society, the king's endurance, shown by his patience in waiting for the household to arrive in spite of all these delays, serves as an example for his subjects to emulate in the conduct of their daily lives.

The ceremony also discloses an implicit motif in the Yoruba world view, referred to in Ondo beliefs as *Iye l'ọmọ*, "the nursing-mother" or child-bearing motif.[52] The procession of the king's household is in tune with this ideal. Reference has already been made to the custom of forbidding the king's childless wives from participating in the rites and letting mothers whose children are grown carry substitute dolls on their backs. Both customs indicate that what is celebrated in this festival is motherhood and the procreative power of these women. This is no doubt a ritual display of an axiomatic principle of Ondo society: "they value children as a way of clinging to eternity through perpetuation of the family."[53] It is no wonder then that many prayers offered on this occasion, and in other similar ceremonies, are directed to infertile women in the hope that they may bear children by the following year. By offering prayers as the royal procession moves past them, the people demonstrate their belief that the maternal, nurturing, and procreating power generated by the royal wives can act as a source of self-renewal for them.

The invitation formula recited by the *Jọmu* on behalf of the king has the most far-reaching significance in the king's festival. Beyond the open call to worship with the king, it illustrates the civil religious nature of the king's festival. According to the sociological theory of Rousseau, Durkheim, and more recently Robert Bellah,[54] any functioning society must possess a set of ultimate symbols that integrate it and tie it to a higher order. The traditional Yoruba festivals have often proved to be a source of common religion that has supplied an "overwhelming sense of unity in a society riddled with realistic conflict."[55] Accordingly, I suggest that we should regard the king's festival as a

---

[51] Sam Gill, "Seeing with the Natives Eyes" in *Contribution to the Study of Native American Religion*, ed Walter H. Capp (New York: Harper and Row, 1976), p. 46.

[52] A similar motif in the history of Greek religions is the *Kourotrophos*. See Theodural Hadzistelon Price, *Kourotrophos: Cults and Representation of the Greek Nursing Deities* (Leiden: E. J. Brill, 1970), p. 1. For a detailed discussion of this motif in World Religions, see pp. 2—9 of the same book.

[53] Ibid., p. 1.

[54] See Robert Bellah, *Beyond Belief: Essays on Religion in a Post-Traditional World* (New York: Harper & Row, 1970).

[55] Robin M. Williams, *American Society* (New York: 1951) quoted by John F. Wilson, *Public Religion in American Culture* (Philadelphia: Temple University Press, 1979), p. 158.

form of civil religion. The rites, ceremonies, and beliefs in kingship are derived from and pertain to the collective experience and destiny of the people. In the face of the pluralistic nature of Ondo society, especially in matters of religious beliefs and practices, the king's festival acts as a common faith and bridge, binding together the diverse elements of Ondo society.[56] At the same time, it also recognizes the legitimacy of individual religions, in which, incidentally, the king also takes part. Note that the formula makes a distinction between the king's festival and regular *orisa* worship. Thus one must emphasize the role of the king and his ceremonies in integrating all Ondo society and in resolving these religious cleavages. Furthermore, the ritual formula presents the picture of a traditional society in the process of change and shows how these traditional forms of beliefs and rites reflect and respond to these new changes. While the ritual formula could not have originated earlier than 1889, when Islam and Christianity were finally established in Ondo, it still possesses the authority of tradition, an authority which overshadows potential social and religious cleavages within Ondo society.

A rẹbọ kadi: Offerings to the Palace Deities

The next day, the king makes offerings to the many deities and the royal ancestors enshrined in and around the palace. As these powers are held to be his protective deities, whose blessings should be invoked before any major activity takes place within their domain, they are honored and remembered as part of the renewal ritual. It is not clear how many such deities inhabit the palace nor which ones are actively propitiated. However, each offering is made according to the taste and specification of the god concerned. While renewal ceremonies are more visibly connected with the powers of the ancestors and culture-heroes in several African kingdoms, they do not constitute the absolute source of regenerative force of the cosmos; the participation of the tutelary gods and spirit deities located in and around the palace are needed to complete the regeneration process. Consequently, the second-day ceremony is devoted essentially to feeding such divinities with the king's thanksgiving offerings. On the next two days, the third and fourth days after the main ceremony, the ceremony of *aṣeyi ṣamọdun*, offering felicitations to the king, takes place in the palace. The three grades of chiefs, the *Ẹharẹ*, *Ẹlẹgbẹ* and *Ekulẹ*, visit the palace to congratulate the king and to offer wishes for the coming year.

---

[56] Robin Horton's thesis on "Conversion," *Africa* (1971), pp. 85–108, is relevant to this analysis. Here the King's festival developed into an autonomous overarching system in response to the enlargement of scale of the Ondo microcosm produced by the effect of modernism and conversion to Christianity and Islam.

Upẹnko: Cessation Ceremony

The last ceremony of the king's festival, referred to as *Upẹnko* ("the sharing of the farm proceeds"), connotes the cessation of farming activities and other civil obligations for a time of leisure and merriment. The central meaning of *Upẹnko* in the context of the king's festival, however, is that it is a holiday for the *Ekulẹ* and *Ẹlẹgbẹ* ranks of chiefs, the two work-groups in the Ondo political system. All civil duties and the rule of law are temporarily suspended. Any criminal caught during this period is locked up until the end of the festival when the chief's court will once again be opened and offenders put on trial. This temporary interruption in the daily working routine is aptly expressed in the proverb: *oloriburuku so ni jọ upẹnko* ("It is the unlucky one that offends during the *upẹnko* ceremony"),[57] since the chiefs who would preside over this trial and thereby bring him to speedy judgement are on vacation. On the early morning of the *upẹnko* day, the chiefs gather in the house of their leaders. Events of the previous year are formally reviewed and given closure, and plans are made and approved for the new year. Within the rank and file of the chiefs, problems such as quarrels among members are discussed and settled and, if need be, heavy penalties may be imposed on offending chiefs. Gifts received by the chiefs are shared here. The spirit of the day in general is that of joyous celebration and merrymaking. This officially ends the king's festival, and signals the beginning of a new ritual cycle in Ondo.

Conclusion

The religious aspects of Ondo kingship remain the most challenging part of my research on Ondo religion. From the perspective of my fieldwork experience, it is the most significant aspect of the entire festival. It has been demonstrated that the ideology and rituals of Ondo kingship play not only a central role in Ondo traditional religion, but are also the source of an "invisible" civil religious system. The primary ritual and symbolic representation of Ondo civil religion is seen in the king's festival ceremony, performed annually in July. All those born in Ondo, irrespective of their sectarian preferences, participate in this festival, and all other traditional rituals and ceremonies are performed for and on behalf of the king. The significance of this lies in the fact that the king's status in Ondo gives the *Orịṣa* worship a major civil religious function in maintaining Ondo identity. This is because the king's "sacred" status has an immediacy in civil affairs, rather than a strictly "cultic" focus, which

---

[57] Conversation with Chief Ojo, August 19, 1980.

could be attacked or eroded by Christianity and Islam. The institution of kingship preserves the "cosmic unity" of the Ondo "nomos" in the face of an otherwise corrosive effect of disintegration in the society. As David Laitin points out, the Yoruba proverb, "The king is the patron of all religions" (*Ọba oni gbogbo ẹsin*), indicates that the king is the source of the religious unity of the city-kingdom.[58] My point is that the king's role as the patron of all the town's gods and religions forges the cults of these separate religious groups into a unified civil religion.

The central article of the Ondo civil religion, read on behalf of the king at the king's festival, is a major finding in my research. This ritual formula constitutes an important and fascinating cultural document whose significance reaches beyond the study of Ondo. Just as the myths, symbols, and rituals of the American civil religion came from Judeo-Christian tradition, the Ondo civil religion draws upon and embraces the traditional religion to give an overarching sense of unity to the religiously pluralistic society. The king joins his subjects in celebrating their objects of worship, be it the *Orişa* worship, Islam, or Christianity, thus unifying all Ondo citizens in celebrating the king's festival. This analysis has also demonstrated the responses of traditional beliefs to secularization and religious pluralism. The increasingly secular atmosphere no doubt creates situations of anomie and normlessness, and here we see the kingship system taking hold on the society, counteracting the disintegrative values of the new secularism.

I should also add that this finding has methodological and practical significance. The methodological significance of this proposal is that future study of Yoruba religion from local perspectives should identify the central (civil) religious ideology, the rituals, and the general sociocultural context. In reality, all maintain very loose boundaries. For the research student, therefore, it is necessary to differentiate between the substantive and the functional understanding of religion, i.e., between what religion is and what religion does in a local community. The practical significance of this approach also justifies such efforts; at present, several of the Yoruba towns and cities face the dilemma created by failing to distinguish between religious attitudes involving civil and traditional beliefs. In recent times, some *Ọba* have been faced with a conflict between their personal religious preference and civil rituals demanded by communal tradition. This is more profound in the case of Muslim *Ọba*, who have accepted Islam's radical monotheism; to the displeasure of their people, some *Ọba*, preferring their personal religion, have

---

[58] David D. Laitin, *Hegemony and Culture: Politics and Religious Change Among the Yoruba* (Chicago: University of Chicago Press, 1986).

rejected the civil ceremonies. One such *Ọba* was quoted as saying that, "on his coronation, he received the crown of the prophet (God) (*o gba ade anabi*), and not the crown of Agẹmọ,"[59] the central *Orişa* of his people through whose blessings he maintains a peaceful reign.

[59] This is in reference to Allah (God) in the Muslim tradition.

Chapter IV
Ọramfẹ: Myths and Rituals of Cosmization

I shall now discuss a festival connected with the deity referred to as Ọramfẹ. The festival is variously called Ọramfẹ (Ọra) or *Ọdun Odua* (*oduduwa*)[1] in reference to its origins in Ile-Ifẹ. When I witnessed the festival in October, 1980, I noticed that it differed in nature and context from the festival as I had previously observed it in Ondo. First, I shall set forth the historical context.

Historical Background

The Ọramfẹ festival is one of the very few traditional ceremonies whose historical development can be reconstructed with the help of oral and written sources. Although the origin of the ritual is told in the mythology of the Ondo people, the changes that have occurred within its practices in the recent past, especially as regards ritual sacrifice, may have far-reaching implications for the study of Yoruba religious festivals, and even for Christianity and Islam in Ondo. According to the Ondo people, a human sacrifice was the major offering made to this god until the arrival of the British in the town. A significant point in the history of the cult arises with the coming of the missionaries. There are ample references to sacrificial practices and the attempts made to stamp them out in the diary of Bishop Charles Phillips, the first missionary sent from Sierra Leone in 1870. After his arrival, the church converts were forbidden to participate in the ceremony. In July of the same year, Phillips met with two Ondo high chiefs to solicit their support for the abolition of human sacrifice (no mention is made that he wanted to prohibit the entire festival). As the bishop recorded in his diary on March 30, 1877, "there was a human sacrifice at *Sọra*'s funeral." He therefore opened up negotiation with the Lisa on July 23, 1877, to discuss putting an end to this aspect of the ritual.

Having failed to persuade the *Lisa*, the bishop sought the help of the British government. When a British officer named Johnson arrived in Ondo, Bishop

---

[1] Ọdun Odua (*oduduwa*) refers to its origin in Ile-Ifẹ. It is connected with the founder and culture-hero, Oduduwa. Very often, the ceremony is simply called *ọra* rather than the full *ọramfẹ* as is obtained in Ile-Ifẹ. These terms will be used interchangeably in this work.

Phillips met him (on July 16, 1886) to work out a plan through which the practice would be eradicated. Perhaps it was through this effort that he reported on July 28 of the same year that "the *Ṣọra*'s (the chief priest of this cult) mother was buried without a human victim; rather, a goat was sacrificed in place of the normal human victim."[2] Shortly after this, there was a public clamor for a renewal of human sacrifice. This outcry apparently occurred on July 15, 1887, and as a result of widespread public support for the protest, human sacrifice was reinstated. The bishop once again reported, on September 12, 1887, that "Ondo has offered another victim to *Ọramfẹ*" at the festival. The only option left to him was to take his case to the governor's office in Lagos. On November 12, 1887, Governor Molony came to the bishop's aid and wrote a sharply-worded letter to the Ondo community, dated November 20, 1887, asking for an immediate prohibition on human sacrifice to *Ọramfẹ*. Although there is no further documented evidence of human sacrifice in *Ọra*'s history, during the reign of *Oṣemawe* Jiṣọmọsun II it was alleged that a girl was kidnapped, and since the abduction coincided with the ritual period, the king was held suspect. This was most probably a convenient excuse for the Colonial destruction of a center of indigenous religio-political power. All the high-ranking chiefs were arrested and taken to the British residence, and the king himself was exiled. This put a stop, at least temporarily, to the festival. According to the cult members whom I interviewed, it was Moses Akinṣọwọn, a member of the *Ṣọra*'s lineage, who was credited with reviving the festival, with the help of Adaja Akintewe. The story goes thus: As the festival was about to be obliterated due to the long years of neglect, a meeting was summoned in the palace of the previous *Ọba*, Oṣemawe Tẹwọgboye, and an agreement was reached with the *Ṣọra*'s family that they could continue the festival. Shortly after this incident, Adegbamigbe, my chief consultant, was installed. At the time of my visit, much enthusiasm was shown by the people for the festival. In fact, one could still see the public advertisements in the form of wall posters announcing the celebration. A sheep had been officially substituted for the normal human victim as a sacrifice.

The brief history recounted above sets the stage for a discussion of the intricate nature of the festival and the problems that I experienced in my efforts to obtain information at the beginning of the ceremony. While it would be wrong to say that the ritual practices are still enshrined in total secrecy (since I had virtually all the information I wanted from the celebrants once they accepted me), I must emphasize that the ritual specialists still view with strong

---

[2] *Phillips' memoirs*, p. 73.

suspicion any visitors who make inquiries into the details of the festival itself. Why did the Ondo people resist so strongly the demand to give up human sacrifice?[3] Why does *Ọramfẹ*, rather than the more widely-known deities in the Yoruba pantheon, command such importance in Ondo? A possible answer will be forthcoming once the nature of the culture hero *Ọramfẹ* is established through the myths and rituals about him.

Next, I shall explain the nature and scope of my field research experience during this festival. Having made two unsuccessful attempts to solicit information on the ritual practice from the priests of *Ọramfẹ*, I approached my host, the high chief Adaja Awọṣika, to seek his counsel on the matter. On the next Sunday morning the chief accompanied me to the priest's house, which I considered an honor, for on other occasions he had sent either his wife or an adult daughter to introduce me to the people concerned. As we approached the *Ṣọra*'s home we stopped at the house of a man who was junior to my host in age but who, as I later learned, was a member of the *Ṣọra* lineage and a very successful and influential man. My host expressed his disappointment at the refusal to allow me access to information on *Ọra*. The three of us then walked across the street to the *Ṣọra*'s residence. It was then that I realized why it was so necessary for my host to introduce me personally to the chief. The first drama occurred when the *Ṣọra* insisted that before we discuss any matter with the high chief, my host must stoop down to say the traditional greetings formally, although they greeted each other when we came in. According to the *Ṣọra*, the high chief had been born in that house in his presence, and therefore he deserved full respect from him. My host tried to by-pass the honorific greeting and gesture by going straight to the purpose of his visit; namely, "to introduce you to a research student, who has come to listen to your own tradition, so that when he finally writes a book on Ondo history, your part of it will not be missing." This sounded very encouraging to me. However, the priest insisted on the proper greeting and my host succumbed. Here we witnessed a conflict between authority based on patrilineage and the chiefly hierarchy, both of which together form a significant social nexus in Ondo socio-political life. It was also a political/mytho-religious struggle in *Ọramfẹ* mythology, as we shall soon see.

My host was eventually able to persuade the *Ṣọra* to give me the information I needed, and we agreed to meet the following day.

When I arrived at his house early in the morning, he had called together all the key members of his lineage to listen to our discussion. This was quite helpful, since they occasionally intruded to remind him of some neglected part

---

[3] One can compare *Ọramfẹ* with the Aztec human sacrifice and its abolition under the Spaniards; in the case of the latter the Christian sacrament became syncretised with the native's religion.

of the story or the ritual details. I realized that we were already in the ritual period since the two-week-long festival had just started. After I restated the purpose of my visit to the gathering of about fifteen elderly people, the priests[4] recounted the ritual obligation I must perform before he could tell the story and the deeds of this deity: "You want to know all these things—yes, I will tell you, for your own sake. Because of your ears, your eyes, and because of the head that you have on you, you will put before us a cock, and when you depart we will slaughter it, and let the blood flow on the ground and we will pour libation (water)."

I quickly made an arrangement for this sacrificial ritual and the story followed shortly after in the priest's sitting room. There was an area marked out on the floor of the room by four cowries and a calabash of cold water placed by his side. He poured out the water onto this area at intervals during the narration. The *Ọramfẹ* myth is unique. The narrator spoke in Ondo local dialect throughout my interview with him. By contrast, younger Ondo storytellers would prefer Yoruba language as they would not be able to tell it in this way. The full story, as I transcribed and translated it, appears below:

The Myth of Ọramfẹ

Ọramfẹ was a human being, a living person who once lived in Ilẹ-Ifẹ. He travelled all around from town to town. He moved everywhere, yet without leaving his seat. He could sit as we are now and be travelling overseas.

Aihọ, the founder of Ondo and the first Oṣemawe, was Ọramfẹ's close friend. Both of them were very intimate and they did many things together. They ate, farmed, and played together. Aihọ then said to Ọramfẹ, "I have tried to establish my town, yet with no success. Would you help me come and establish it?" Aihọ actually asked Ọramfẹ to help him establish Ondo town, having failed to do it by himself. The first person who was installed as Oṣemawe did not live for 17 years, and the next did not live for 9 days (one Ondo week). Then came the third and the fourth. So it came up to six kings within 16 years. (One can see how short-lived the kings were.)

Aihọ then sent a messenger[5] to Ọramfẹ for help in establishing Ondo. Ọramfẹ accepted the invitation and promised his friend that he would assist in establishing the city for him. "The one who is barren will become pregnant, give birth to male and female, and consequently carry the babies on her back; the child who dies young will become a grown-up adult," said Ọramfẹ. Then Ọramfẹ asked Aihọ to bring two hundred kola nuts, two hundred chickens (*ọyẹhẹ*), two hundred goats, two hundred dogs,

---

4 I have suggested in the earlier part of this chapter that it has become evident that it is more profitable to look to priests and ritual experts for information than to literate chiefs and heads of communities, as the latter have converted to Christianity and Islam.

5 He described this messenger as *oniṣe tẹrẹẹ*, a mysterious message bearer that moved with wind.

two hundred sheep and, most importantly, two hundred human beings for sacrificial rites. Aihọ supplied all these items. As Ọramfẹ[6] picked up each of these items, they disappeared. He took a tortoise and placed it on the mouth of Ọṣe river, that river which stretched from Okelisa to Ugelemaroko near Arọwa's residence. [Here he points out in the direction of the street.] "*Apapọọ*, Be gathered together", he said to the river and it did. My father [i.e., Ọramfẹ] then named this river *Ọṣẹ* (the name that it bears to this day). Then he said to us, "The water shall be for your use, drink of it, bathe with it and use it for whatsoever is good and joyful. You will raise your children with it and they will live for you."

(This is what we still do today) and it happened as he has said: our wives became pregnant, the kings reigned a long time, and Ondo world became properly established.

Then Aihọ asked him, "When are you coming back (to complete the job)?"

"Seven days from now," he replied.

"Will you come on your own or should I send for you?" asked Aihọ.

"I will come on my own," replied Ọramfẹ.

When the day for Ọramfẹ's return arrived, Ọramfẹ took his belongings, his yam, his big drum [an Agba drum, also called *ọlọja ilu*, i.e., the head of all drums], and his *ọwẹwẹ* [sliced sticks] and started on his journey back to Ondo. When he was approaching Ondo, the people slowly drifted toward the palace and they debated among themselves whom they should send to meet the man. Finally, they asked the ice man [Lẹhinhin] to meet Ọramfẹ. As Ọramfẹ approached Ondo, his face frowning and very terrifying, he looked up and down, and saw a young boy coming towards him. He beckoned to the boy, saying, "Come this way, my son, what are you looking for at this place?"

"My father, the Oṣemawe, asked me to meet a certain old man who is arriving here, and I do not know him," the boy replied in a frightened tone.

Then Ọramfẹ said to him, "I am the one you are asked to meet; what is the message?"

"You are asked to come to the palace, everybody is waiting," the boy replied. (That is the song we now sing today, *Ọra wa, Ọra wa o, wa o, ole o*, "Ọra come, come quickly like a thief, come into being.")

Then Ọramfẹ asked the boy to stretch forth his right arm and he placed the leather bag he was carrying there. [At this point the narrator pointed to a ritual leather bag on his wall and said, "Like that one there."] The boy fell down because the bag was very heavy. Ọramfẹ, said, *Ajidide gbogbo oriko*! ("Stand still, let all the bush in the forest stand straight.") So the boy got to his feet and they proceeded on their journey towards the palace. They walked and walked and the man suddenly stopped to ask the boy, "What is this place (pointing to an area on the right) called?"

"I do not know," the boy replied. Then Ọramfẹ took his sword, his sacred sword [here my informant pointed to a sword on the wall and said, "That is the one."], and with it he struck a standing tree and the tree collapsed.

Then he said to the boy, "You see that tree, the tree I just cut? Three branches shall sprout up from it in a long time to come, in about three months. One branch will be for Ẹpẹ (that was the way by which he had come), the second branch is for Ijeṣa, and the remaining branch will be facing the Ogun shrine that will be for the Ondo people. That is what they will use to honor me.[7] Whenever it bears fruits, one will be for

---

[6] Here he called Ọramfẹ "my father."

[7] He described this as *ṣe ọdun fun mi* (make festivity in my memory).

Yangede [an Ẹpẹ and culture hero], the second will be for Ijẹṣa, and the third for Ondo. Anyone who steals from the other will perish, but no one is forbidden from stealing from his own fruits."

Then Ọramfẹ and the boy proceeded on their journey until they arrived at Okedoko. There they saw many children playing. There were large sheds and fences [*pakala*]. It was a place where farmers used to grow rice, so he named the place Odeko (the place where farm products were tied to the fence).

Later, they arrived at the road leading to Okelisa (Lisa's farm) and Ọramfẹ asked the people around to try all their might,[8] saying *Dan ka sa upa inu wọn*. This is what we now know as Lisa today.

Later, they arrived at the river Ọyenrẹn.[9] ["Splash! splash! splash!" The priest imitated thus for me the sound of the divinity's feet on the water, "the whole place was filled with water."] Then Ọramfẹ said, "Let the waters come together," and he named the river Ọyenrẹn and also gave the same name to the tree at its bank. [Here the narrator said to me the place name of the tree, *o sanṣọ o o mu ala rosi* ("he tied a cloth around her body and a strip of linen across her left shoulder").] He then commanded that we propitiate it with a white linen cloth tied around her body. "My children and grandchildren and several generations to come shall always be here whenever they eat new yam to wash off their hands." Ọramfẹ and the boy continued their journey until they arrived at a place; he looked toward the right and said, "This place shall belong to Ọbalufọn."[10]

As they walked along, Ọramfẹ noticed heavy smoke coming from afar. "What is going on there?" he asked. "An old man with long pointed fingernails lives there," the boy answered. "What is his profession?" he asked again. "He is a hunter," some people nearby answered him. Then Ọra sent for the old man and when he arrived they hugged and embraced each other and they shook hands (for they were old-time friends). That is why we embrace whenever we meet to this day.[11] It is the old man's fireplace that we use to cook food in Ondo to this day.

And so they continued on their journey. When they arrived at Oreretu the water was up to their knees. Ọramfẹ looked towards his right side and saw Ogun's shrine. "That was where Ogun stood last time he visited this place. That shallow spot was where Ogun placed his foot. You shall call it *Ẹhinmogun* [Ogun's hierophany, or where Ogun was known]." (This is what this place is called to this day.)

Then he addressed the boy who was sent by Airọ to meet him, saying, "From today you will be known as *Akonọna* ('the one that we met on the way') because you met me on the way." This is what we now call *Akunnara* to this day; there was no such title in the Ọba's house prior to that time.

Then he said to Oṣemawe, "The young boy who has been with you for the past three years, your houseboy who runs all your errands, I install him as *Ṣodi*." Thus Ṣodi became the official king's messenger. If the Ọba wants to see anyone today, Ṣodi is sent to call the person to the palace.

---

[8] The narrator presents the situation as if Ọramfẹ was confronting this group of people in a duel.

[9] Another major stream in Ondo town.

[10] Ọbalufọn is another important deity in the Ondo pantheon.

[11] During Ọramfẹ ceremony, the priests shake hands with their left hands.

After several years the people gathered to express their concern about the numerous sacrificial rites Ọramfẹ demanded of them yearly, for they could no longer bear it. "Where shall we get all these things, two hundred of every item?" they complained to Ọramfẹ. "There is no reason to be fearful," he said to them. "Let everyone continue to propitiate his orişa, whether it is Ọrunmila (Ifa), Ogun, or Balufọn. All the gods are my houseboys." The people begged him to have pity on them and take all those sacrificial offerings from elsewhere. So, whenever any of these four divinities is worshipped today, Ọramfẹ takes part of their food as his, and that is the way he claims his two hundred sacrificial offerings.

One evening, as Ọra sat in front of his house, he saw a woman walking on the street wearing four articles of clothing. She wore two as wraps, she had draped the third on her shoulder, and the fourth she held in her hand. He approached her and said, "What do you want here in this place at this time?" "I am on my way to the palace," the woman answered. Ọra then took her home and sent a messenger to Oşemawe to inform him that there was a stranger in his house. The Ondo people then gathered in the palace and asked him to show them the stranger. This woman was installed *Lọbun* and she became the official king-maker. Whenever any man is to be installed Oşemawe, it is Lọbun who performs the ceremony. That is how Ondo became established. Then the king lived a long life, and Şọra lived a long life.

Having described the context in which I recorded the myth, I shall attempt to give an interpretation. Although such a detailed presentation of the myth seems to demand detailed analysis, I shall discuss only a few details here in order not to distort the balance of the work. The rest will become clear as I proceed to describe and analyze the ritual which the mythology generates.

In the course of describing the origin of the festival, the myth also describes the creation of the Ondo universe in very different terms than the "official" version presented in the previous chapter. While the former version of the myth includes cosmogonic elements, this version is primarily a story about the founding of Ondo by the culture-hero Ọramfẹ.

The myth establishes the geographical and sacred landscape of Ondo town as it is known today; the various landmarks, shrines, and sacred hierophanies mentioned actually exist in the respective locations that he mentioned. The myth defines the physical and spatial boundary of the city, especially the limit of Ondo land. This explains why Ondo today with its increased population lacks the much-needed land, a factor that has become an issue in the socio-political context today. Ondo's relations with some of their immediate neighbors, especially the Ijeşa and Ẹpẹ, are established in this myth of origin, perhaps helping us to clarify the boundary ceremony that takes place annually with Ijeşa during the *Oba*'s festival. The myth institutes the chiefly hierarchies in the Ondo socio-political structure but gives elevated status to the Alahoro, the leaders of autonomous groups and a hereditary priestly class representing sources of ritual power independent of the king. An example is the politically-powerless indigenous group, the Iforẹ, which is represented in the person of Ẹkiri, their leader and founder. By identifying the latter as the 'peer of Ọra' himself and also crediting him with the origin of fire, an essential element for survival, the myth brings him under the sacred canopy defined by the new social order. The same principle applies to the Idoko, the largest autochthonous group, which the myth links with farm products, a source of the people's economic well-being. It is equally significant that Ọramfẹ subdued the Okelisa people, who are the residents of *Lisa*'s official place.

Ọramfẹ himself is given a primary place in this story. Within the context of the myth, he is over and above all other divinities mentioned, as indicated by his referring to them as his 'houseboys.' This is significant, for the deities referred to as 'houseboys' are conceived in the general scheme of the Yoruba pantheon as universally higher than any other deities and culture heroes in the Yoruba world view. Pursuing this line of questioning, I asked the old man, "How then did Ọra predate the Ondo world?" He replied, "When the people of the earth were created at Ile-Ifẹ and the Ondo decided to come to this place, they deliberately left Ọra behind. But since all human deliberations are known to the spider (*Tupu tunọsẹ, Ohinu l'antakun*), Sọra knew all their secret plans.[12] As they arrived in Itajamọ, they did not know where to go. 'Where shall we go from here?' asked Ọsẹmawe. It was Akunnara who showed them the way. That is why we call Akunnara *Ogbọni pọn* ('a human carrier'). It was Ọsẹmawe that he carried until they arrived here."

The comments above introduce one of the central themes of the narrative. Not only does the story present the drama of the state of being (chaos) that characterizes early Ondo settlement before the proper establishment of the Ondo world, it also sets in motion the cosmization (to borrow from Eliade) process through which the Ondo religious, social and political order was properly set in place and the Ondo world settled once and for all. Cosmization, or what Peter Berger also referred to as nominization, is a process whereby that which was chaos is incorporated into the cosmos. For Eliade, the ultimate notion of the sacred order is the structure of the cosmos. Hence, the primary function of origin myths in 'archaic' societies is to explain the process whereby primordial chaos is transformed into cosmos.

As mentioned in the previous chapter, when the Ondo people arrived, the aboriginal groups (Ifọrẹ, Idoko, and Ọka people) peacefully surrendered the land. While such a peaceful surrender seems improbable, nonetheless the Ondo people admit that the town was not properly established. There was disorder and chaos. Signs of this chaos included the failure of women to menstruate and to bear children, the short reigns of the *Ọba*, the early death of royal children, and bad harvests. The myth portrayed the land as a swampy

---

[12] The spider in this proverb is not quite clear to me.

wasteland. As in most cosmogonic myths, there is a reversal of the normal order of things. Human acts are portrayed in an inverted form; for example, Ọra, in shaking hands with his old-time friend, used his left hand. The Ekiri, too, was in the state of nature as opposed to culture for he had long, pointed fingernails.

John Middleton brought the same concept of reversal into the domain of mythic analysis of the Lugbara cosmology in a very instructive way. According to him,

. . .before the formation of Lugbara society, the various mythical personages are given characteristics which I have called inverted. They behaved in ways that are opposite of the ways expected of normal socialized persons in Lugbara society today. Before there was an ordered society, there was instead a world of social disorder or chaos. It had been created by spirit, but its human inhabitants were unsocialized, amoral, or neutral. After the advent of the heroes and their begetting songs, order was established and the ideally unchanging pattern of social life came into being. In the beginning there was a time of primordial disorder, and later a time of order. Originally there was no recognized authority among men, only uncontrolled and divine power, but afterward there was the recognition of properly constituted social and moral authority.[13]

Lastly, the Ondo myth attempts to define the roles, obligations and rights of all essential actors, religion and civil-authority, in the Ondo world which Ọramfẹ, the savior culture-hero, was about to construct through his sacrificial rituals. It is this last role that the story tries to emphasize.

The socio-religious institutions and important civil and religious titles such as *Lisa, Lọbun, Akunnara, Ṣodi*, etc. were thus bestowed with sacred status and firmly placed in the Ondo world view. While there is no doubt that the story may favor the narrator and his fellow priestly class, in reality it demonstrates the division of power which had remained the source of tension and conflict in the emerging society. The above story, in my view, accounts for the respect and immunity that Ṣọra and Ọra cult members have in Ondo society today. One Ondo proverb says *Ẹ pa Ṣọra, ẹ mu Ṣurin, ẹ gbe Akunnara de suli Ọba* (It is taboo to beat Ṣọra and to put under arrest Ṣurin.[14] It is totally prohibited to lock up [imprison] Akunnara in the king's palace). The *Ọramfẹ* myth sets the tone for the ritual symbolism and performance which I describe in the festival.

---

[13] John Middleton, "Some Categories of Dual Classification Among the Lugbara of Uganda," in *Right and Left: Essays in Dual Symbolic Classification*, Rodney Needham, ed. (Chicago: Chicago Press, 1973), p. 367.

[14] Ṣurin is another priest who actually precedes *Ṣọra* in Ondo civil hierarchy; however, I did not really see him featured in the festivals that I observed.

Ọramfẹ Festival

The *Ọramfẹ* festival that I witnessed proceeds according to the following sequence of events:

August 26: The end of the Ogun festival and the beginning of the preparation for *Ọramfẹ*.

September 2: *Ọjọ iwọ Ọra* (The beginning of *Ọra*).

September 5: *Uyọ yan* (New Yam feast or expression of happiness for new yam).

September 8: *Opepee* (*Ọra*'s lampooning rite).

September 9: *Imuhọ* (The day of propitiation and sacrifice), and also *Ọjọ Ọra* (*Ọra* day).

Ọjọ iwo ọra: The Beginning of the Ọra Festival

The end of Ogun festival marks the beginning of the two-week long *Ọramfẹ* festival. On this day the king goes into seclusion and will not appear in public until *Ọra* day. The term used for this is *Ọba wọra* ("the king has entered *Ọra*"). One old man noted this by telling me a proverb: *Ọni rọba nigi Ogun, Oitun di gi ọjọ Ọra* ("Whoever saw the king during Ogun ceremony will have to wait until *Ọra* day to catch a glimpse of him"). The king's symbolic invisibility is related to his period of seclusion while being installed. Here, as before, he is in a state of preparation for the ordering of his kingdom through the great sacrifice to the deity.

From this day on, the people prepare for the ceremony. On the third day, the *Ṣọra*, the chief priest of the ceremony, also enters the state of purity. At this time a general state of taboo is declared on secular activities, especially a strict prohibition on drumming. In the morning of *ọjọ iwọ ọra* the king presents the priest with a sheep, a goat, and kola nut at *okeli* (another word for the palace) for sacrificial rites at the *Ọra* shrine.

As the priest and his entourage go along the route, they sing in praise of the god. "It was the practice in the olden days," said *Ṣọra*, "for one man named Elejuwa to ambush me along the path to the sacrificial place in order to collect from me this sacrificial animal which the king presented and to attempt to disrupt the ceremony." This man's appellation, *Apara-lọna, ajọbaju* ("the thunderbolt on the way, the king's most feared man"), supports this fearful view. To prevent this possible interruption, *Ṣọra* must ritually prepare himself to accomplish his pilgrimage to the shrine. Once they arrive at the grove, animals are slaughtered and the carcasses are removed by the children of Ṣọra and taken home for feasting. As they return, they make a high-pitched sound, to warn people to keep indoors:

Heeepa!

Ẹ ma a wo!

Ọni ji wo, oji ku.

It is forbidden to see it!

Whosoever secretly spies on it will die, likewise secretly.

On his way back, the *Sọra* meets the high chief *Jọmu*, and the two exchange greetings. Shortly after this, *Sọra* approaches a shrine towards which he throws a kola nut. Again, the reason for this is located in the mythological past: a man named Owu, also described as *Alajagun janduku enia* ("warriorlike and a hooligan"), would suddenly appear to the procession to disrupt it. "It is because of one single kola nut that he does this," commented *Sọra*. In order to prevent this disruption from happening, *Sọra* throws a kola nut to conquer the intruder. The pilgrimage-journey ends when the group arrives at *Sọra*'s home, and there the sacrificial animal is cut into bits and distributed among the *Sọra*'s household and the other *Ọra* priests.

On September 5, the fourth-day rite, *Uyọyan*, begins when early in the morning the women of *Sọra*'s household cook a great many yams with which they make *iyan* (pounded yam). One man I questioned during the ceremony had this to say concerning the origin of this rite and the likely connection with Ọramfẹ: *Iṣu ti Ọra ko si apo ẹ nijọ yẹn, oun lo di rabata ti gbogbo aiye njẹ loni* ("It was the yam which *Ọra* had in his pocket then [the day he arrived in Ondo] that became the big yam that the whole world eats today"). Thus, according to my informant, the yam itself constitutes good reason for celebration and merriment. In the late afternoon, the entire household of *Sọra* and other well-wishers danced their way to the *Oyẹnrẹn* River to give thanks to the deity in fulfillment of *Ọra*'s injunction that "his children would visit the river to wash off the hands used in eating the celebrated pounded yam." *Sọra* himself informed me concerning this rite: *Iyan e jẹ ninuli, a la wẹwọ ni oyẹnrẹn* ("The pounded yam that we ate inside the house, we wash off the hands in Oyẹnrẹn River"). I have already referred to the position of yam in the economy and diet of Ondo. Unlike the neighboring town of Ilẹ-Oluji, Ondo does not have a separate new yam festival. Nevertheless, yam is such a significant product in Ondo's existence that it is brought under *Ọramfẹ*'s ritual domain. The group returns home after this celebration in the late evening.

Opepee: Personal Insults and Humor as a Way of the Sacred

The rituals of the seventh and eighth days constitute the core of the *Ọramfẹ* ceremonies and the two will be taken as one since they complement each other. *Opepee* starts at about 8 p.m. on September 8 when some of *Ṣọra*'s relations gather in a shrine referred to as *odi*, which stands next to *Ṣọra*'s personal house.

Like a normal residential building, the shrine contains a single room with sacred partitions covered with palm fronds where the god is enshrined. I was not allowed to take photographs of the shrine; however, I noticed that small palm stocks placed across the entrance to the shrine bore red and white paint marks. A man standing nearby told me that the red mark represented woman's menstrual blood and the white represented man's sperm (both symbolizing the procreative power of the deity). Unlike most Ondo deities, *Ọramfẹ* has both a private and a public shrine. This perhaps explains its persistence and continuity in spite of the problems and setbacks its worship has encountered. This also has a major classifactory role in the kingship system as it relates the domestic patrilineage to the outer public sphere and functions of *Ọramfẹ*. Even when the public aspect of the ritual lost its potency, the private shrine was still propitiated throughout this period.

In the early evening before the official start of the rite, children took to the street singing in groups, visiting houses of people and demanding money from them. Some of the people closed their doors at the approach of the unwanted guests, because of the menace which too many visitors often cause. The children then began to sing abusive songs and direct them to the head of such a house:

Baba luli be i	Father, the owner of this house,
o tori ti kọbọ	you lock your door on us
O pẹ kun ẹ	Because of a penny.
	The people inside may sing back:
Wo t'ori ti kobo	Because of a penny
We ramu ka	You are roaming round the street.

The first part of the opepee rites takes place here and this consists mainly of private rites for the deity. The night's ceremony opens with short lyrics first, followed by an invocation of the deity, and then a recollection of his might and power, as follows:

Ṣe mo ma mu j'ogun	It is my inheritance
Ẹ ma rira o	We cannot buy it (in the market)
Ọra wa wa o	Ọra come, come
Ọra wa n'ọra	Ọra come into your shrine,
Ọra wa wa n'oke	Ọra come from above.
Bami lumọlẹ lẹ o	My father, the chief priest
Olumọlẹ yẹ mu g'ọjan wọ	The cult that is propitiated at nighttime.

Next they sang the praise of the deity, especially his myth from the place of its origin:

Ṣọra lade udẹ	Ṣọra, the one with the crown of brass.
Ṣọra lade udẹ	Ṣọra, the one with the crown of brass.
Ṣọra lala n'alẹ ufẹ	Ṣọra is a great man in Ilẹ-Ifẹ.
Bami lala n'alẹ ufẹ	My father is great in Ilẹ-Ifẹ.
O bẹ gi n'oke n'oke	He cuts down the tree from the high
(O bẹ gi)	top.
O wu gi t'egbo t'egbo	He uprooted the tree along with its tap
(o wu gi.)	roots.

Sometimes the songs become a chorus to the long list of the deities' praise names, such as the following:

Opoji mu balawu, Olilubonokun	The mighty one,
Ẹbọ wọn fọ nilẹbe, e dẹn l'unokun	He was addressing people here and at the same time speaking overseas.
Irin oyinbo ṣe rin debe	The way and manner the white people came to this town
D'o sobe, do so d'ulu	And turned this place into a big prosperous city is known by him.
O gbo olu, ẹnikeji, ọba	*Ogbo Olu*, the king's friends,
Gbẹdu Igi igbo n'ọra	*Gbẹdu* [a type of tree], Ọra's tree in the forest.
Abimi n'ọra, me mọra iki	I was born into *Ọra* but I cannot recite his praise name.

Late in the evening the songs focused on the characters present here, detailing their relationship to the god and their taboos as members of the cult group. This can be seen in the following verse:

Okete o ọlọja o	Big rat, the village head [the owner of the market],
Ẹwẹ jẹ, ẹwẹ họ	We are forbidden to eat.
Odu o, ọlọja o	Odu [a kind of green vegetable], the village head,
Ẹwẹ jẹ, ẹwẹ họ	We are forbidden to eat.

In further songs, the *Ọra* is also described as the exorcist god who will expel all disease, sickness, and other malevolent and disruptive forces from the earth's surface:

E sun n'alẹ di tẹtẹ tẹ o	Whatsoever is in the ground let the presser [*Ọra*] press it
Uhun ba h'inalẹ d'ọra ma foo	Whatsoever kind of thing is in the earth's surface let Ọra over-pass it.

As the above songs were repeated several times and the spirit of the singers was flagging, one man, who played the role of the lyric conductor, suddenly remarked to the singing group that the vigor of the song should not decline. Immediately the voices and hand clapping increased in volume and intensity.

Meanwhile, as the home rite continued inside the *odi*, people gathered around Ṣọra's house in anticipation of the night-long street dance. Around 9 p.m., the home rite stopped and the *Agba* drum was taken out and sounded, to the joy and excitement of the celebrants. The drum was propitiated on the street with kola nut, thus signalling the beginning of the second stage of *opepee*.

First, however, it is necessary to describe how the night-dance is organized. The sacred drum is placed in the center and a few young men circle the drum as they sing. As these men are closely related to the *Ṣọra* in whose care the drum is placed, they know much about the cult and they have full responsibility to maintain proper conduct during the night rituals. Next to the ring of men is the general public who surround the inner circle. The dance party makes seven stops throughout the rite before daybreak. The drum is moved from one spot to the next, along the same street. About forty minutes is spent on each spot while the singing crowd moves around the drum. Throughout the ceremony it is the position of the drum that locates the focus of activities. Generally, any person who wants to start a new song may join the closed circle or move nearer and then pass the song on to them. To start a song, the person stoops down beside the drum, making sure that he is covered by the circle of men so as to hide his identity, suggesting that the song sprouts from the drum itself. As he sings the first few verses, the closest men pick up the chorus, and within a few seconds the song is taken over by the crowd. The song is accompanied by the beating of the big drum, some other smaller ones, and also the percussive sounds of what is referred to as *ọwẹwẹ* (small pieces of sticks).

To change from one song to another, either because one has been used for too long or because the singers perceive that a song is in bad taste, the song starter shouts *ofoo* ("by-pass it"). At times the full phrase *Ọra foo* ("*Ọra* by-passes it") is given. While literally this means "let *Ọra* jump over the song," it could also represent a reiteration of the ceremony's general effect on the populace, namely, "that *Ọra* skids over evils and unpleasant things." Once the ceremony starts, the first song is directed at the chief priest himself, a song that recaptures the drama of his first arrival in Ondo as "a thief that comes at night":

Ṣọra ma ole o	*Ṣọra* is the thief.
Ṣọra ma ole o	*Ṣọra* is the thief.

The custodians of the drum did not sing this with much enthusiasm because it was directed at their father. Indeed, they substituted another version for it, though the crowd did not take this up with much enthusiasm:

Bami ma ṣọle o	My father is not a thief.
Bami ma ṣọle o	My father is not a thief.

For the rest of the opepee song rite, I will attempt a content analysis of the songs. However, the songs will not be grouped into any categories since they cover virtually every matter conceivable, from issues of personal and domestic morality to national politics as it relates to Ondo society. I will avoid any artificial subdivisions and simply examine some of the songs as they were collected during the performance I attended.

Most of the songs are abusive, and are directed at the king and high chiefs. At the same time, they contain themes that pertain to Ondo socio-cultural ethics in general. For example, the Ondo are noted for the premium they put on education and the town has the highest rate of literacy in the country. Among the Yoruba it is believed that an educated person (someone with book knowledge) has the will and means to do whatever he wants in life. The following related song is addressed to the king in this fashion:

Ọni a d'aran	He wants to make trouble,
'e ma muwe	But he is not literate (educated).[15]
Ọba wa	Our King
Ọni a d'aran	He wants to make trouble,
ẹ le jẹsẹ o	But he cannot fight.[16]
Ọba wa	Our King.

The public is ever conscious of the power and might of the king and his council of advisors, who were the final arbiters of justice in the old days, especially in cases that dealt with morality.

However, there is also the expressed view that an innocent person need not be afraid of the council's authority:

Me f'aya ọba	I have not seduced the wife of the *Ọba*
me ma fẹ tu joye	Nor have I seduced the wife of the chief.
Ohun a gbe mi kunlẹ Nuha	What other things would make me be summoned before the king's council
o ṣoro o	Are unthinkable.

The position of *Lọbun* was vacant at the time of my fieldwork because custom prohibits the appointment of a new *Lọbun* until the king dies. It will be recalled that the primary function of the *Lọbun* is to install a new king, as we saw in the Ondo myth of origin. The next song urges the king to die conveniently so that a new *Lọbun* may be appointed:

---

[15] Actually, the king is literate. I was reminded of a song used on *Opepee* night several years ago: *Ọba wa leti kogbo, bẹ ba ba fọ, e sọ oyinbo* ("Our king with an inspired ear, whenever we talk to him, he starts to converse in English"). Here we see a change in values. More importance is placed on literacy, the hallmark of which is the ability to speak in English. However, at the time of the late *Ọba*, when illiteracy was more dominant, the fact that as *Ọba* spoke in English to an illiterate audience was interpreted as a sign of his arrogance and pride.

[16] *Jẹsẹ* means 'to box.'

Ọba wa	Our King,
Ṣe duo ku o	Die and let us
Di Lọbun jẹ	Appoint a new *Lọbun*.

The next song is related to the above and its rhythm was adapted from a Christian "folksong" about the parable of the ten virgins. In the opepee context, the song asks the people to be careful:

Ẹ ma ṣ'ọra	Be watchful,
Ẹ si ma kanposi	And get a coffin ready.
Talo le ma igba	For who knows the time and period
Ti o ku	When would die.
Ẹ lọ ṣọra	Be watchful,
Ẹ si ma kanposi	And get ready a coffin.

Some songs voiced personal complaints against the king, and some concerned chieftancy matters in which the king's appointments were questioned. Although the grievance songs are not necessarily true, they nevertheless represent widespread views in Ondo.

It is the custom in Ondo to throw open a vacant chieftancy title, especially that of the high chief, and interested candidates will bring money and gifts to the king and other high chiefs who form the electoral committee. Such monies are referred to as *owo didu oye* (literally, "chieftancy contest money"). When the king and his council decide on whom they wish to bestow the title, the funds belonging to unsuccessful candidates are returned to them. Another *opepee* song suggests that the king has not returned a candidate's money:

Owo jẹnti we mọ tisan	You have not returned Genti's money.
Ọba wa leti kogbo	Our king with the impaired ears.
Owo jẹnti we mọ ti san	You have not returned Genti's song.

I learned that the *Ọba* indeed returned this money, but the *ọra* song indicates the popular view on such occasions.

One or two taunts directed at the high chiefs dealt mainly with their domestic life styles, such as the following:

Wo laya mẹfa	You have six wives,
We tẹba jẹ	You still go out to buy food to eat.

As we noted earlier, the *Lisa*, who is next in rank to the *Ọba*, is referred to as *Ọba ode* (literally, the outside king) and so he is directly responsible for the public welfare. Most public complaints and information about the kingdom are conveyed to the *Lisa* in *opepee* songs.

Ẹ gihan Lisa	Tell the *Lisa*,
Ẹ ẹ yọka nilẹbe	That we are no longer going to Ọka in this town.

| Ẹ gihan Lisa | Tell the *Lisa*, |
| Ẹ ẹ yọka o | No more Ọka. |

The above song could be a protest against the poor condition of the road that leads from Odojọmu to Ọka road, a condition that makes it impassable for commercial vehicles. I noticed that taxi drivers have stopped plying this road and I found that I had to walk most of the time when I had appointments in that area. Another possible interpretation of the song is that it is an expression of the taxi drivers' protests against their arrest and summons to court, since the newly-finished Ondo high court is situated along this road. There may also be a third meaning concerning a more cultural theme. Ọka was said to have been destroyed in the mythic past by the cultural hero *Jọmu* Nla, who ordered that it remain desolate. For quite some time the Ondo did not build around this area even though they had expanded towards other roads on the outskirts.

Public officials are not beyond reproach during this celebration. One critical song was directed at the police. Usually the law enforcement agents are easy targets, especially when the bulk of the singers belong to the lower class working group (drivers, barbers, tailors, etc.) considered by the police to be the prime troublemakers of the society. The *opepee* night rite therefore includes a protest function. It is a protest on the part of the small people against the big men and highly-placed officials who are seen as sources of their oppression. The following song refers to a police officer in the Ondo police division who was punished for an offense he committed against a citizen.

Aluwẹn wẹn o
Aluwẹn wẹn
Inspector we a ṣele o
Aluwẹn wẹn
Aluwẹn wẹn o
Aluwẹn wẹn
Inspector, you will never do this again.
Aluwẹn wẹn

At times, the songs may simply express cultural values and do not in any way involve lampooning. The next three songs deal with the Ondo taboo, and the sense of pride the Ondo express towards traditional culture.

Urogbo ẹ jẹ	We eat bitter nut,
Ẹ jọbi n'Ondo	We don't eat kola nut in Ondo.
Urogbo ẹ jẹ	We eat bitter nut,
Ẹ jọbi o	We don't eat kola nut.
A wẹ pọdunjẹ	We don't miss our festivals,
Akala magbo	Akala magbo [a type of bird].

One more cultural motif can be heard in the burial song below.

Ebiba	Ebiba, [a type of leaf]
Bayi lo da o	This is the way it is.
Bayi lo da hunye lọmọ	This is it for the mother of children.
O digbo sẹ	Bye Bye.

A few of the songs contain obscene and sexual references, and they may be directed at the promiscuous behavior of certain highly-placed individuals and some native 'call girls.'

(I)

Wọn bimọ lana	A child [girl] was born yesterday,[17]
O nsunkun oko	She is [immediately] asking for sex.
Waya waya	Waya waya
weye weye	Weye Weye

(II)

Oko wedo	You are only sexy [promiscuous],
We jale o,	You are no thief.
Oko wedo	You are only promiscuous,
We jale o	You are no thief.

I also recorded an old song that was once directed at a magistrate who was said to be firm and honest as far as dispensing justice was concerned, but who was noted for his sexual misconduct. The song had such an impact on the festival that long afterwards the people still refer to it. This song was effective because it brought out into the open stories that were circulating as rumors, and it led to a widespread reform in the local judiciary. The song is delivered in a sarcastic tone typical of several *opepee* songs in which the opposite meaning of the words was intended.

Otitọ we da	You dispense truth,
We dale	You do not dispense [have] concubinage.
Otitọ we da	You dispense truth,
We dale o	You do not dispense [practise] concubinage.

Implicit ethnic feelings very often come out into the open on *opepee* night. In one song, there is a reference to a businessman still not considered to be an Ondo person even though he has been established in the town for quite a while.

Akinjagunla e s'alẹ n'Ondo	Akinjagunla, there is no more land for you in Ondo;
Akinjagunla e s'alẹ o	Akinjagunla, there is no more land.
A gihan Lisa, e salẹ n'Ondo	Tell *Lisa*, there is no more land.

---

[17] A metaphoric way of saying that the girl is too young.

A few of the songs comment on the state and national political events. At the time of my fieldwork, there was a strong state-wide debate concerning the location of a proposed state university. One man told me that the University located in Ile-Ifẹ had actually been meant for Ondo, and that the people were deprived of it by the politicians. Now that the state was going to establish another one, he felt that it should be located in Ondo. The next song refers to this issue.

Unifasity nẹ	The University,
A fẹ ọ n'Ondo	We want it in Ondo.
Unifasity ne	The University,
a fẹ o	We want it.

National current events were also brought into focus. Ondo is a stronghold of the Unity Party of Nigeria (UPN), which is opposed to the ruling National Party of Nigeria (NPN). The UPN believe that the last presidential election in 1979 was rigged by the NPN. The Minister of Justice was seen by the UPN as a key figure in the controversy that brought the President into power. One song expressed criticism of the last election and another song castigated the President and the Minister of Justice.

(I)

Eru hun mu ṣe	He rigged the election,
E wọli O Shagari	He was not elected, Shagari [the president].
Eru hun mu ṣe	He rigged the election,
E wọli o, he	He was not elected.

(II)

Shagari ṣ'ologbọn ni	Shagari [the president], you [say]
Wa a kọgbọn	you are unwise
Akinjide so logbọn ni	Akinjide [the Minister of Justice], you [say] you are unwise.
Wa a kọgbọn	You will learn your lesson.

I should remark that in retrospect the *opepee* performance accurately forecast the fall of the Nigerian Second republic, as President Sagari's government was overthrown a few years later because of massive corruption and abuse of power.

At about 6 a.m., upon his arrival at Odotu, high Chief Saṣẹrẹ (Akinlami) met the group and presented two kola nuts and a gourd of fermented palm wine to propitiate the earth deity, or what *Ṣọra* refers to as *agbako ori ẹ* (a malignant spirit), in order to avoid unnecessary problems. "This is what Saṣẹrẹ uses to honor Odua," he also remarked. The necessity of this sacrifice, actually directed at the earth spirit, is explained by the Ondo saying:

Saṣẹre, ẹ do ka rubọ Alẹ	Saṣẹre is asked to propitiate the earth deity.
De ba rubọ Alẹ	If he does not propitiate the earth deity,
A juya si	He will be punished for it,
A jude si	He will suffer for it.

This sacrifice formally ended the *opepee* rite and the procession returned to the *Ṣọra*'s residence. The people went home in anticipation of the actual *Ọra* ceremony that would start three hours later.

Despite the forthright manner in which the songs were rendered, there was a great deal of tact in the conduct of the singers and their use of words. I have suggested that *ofoo* is used to put an end to distasteful songs, especially those that do not come from the conductors. Also, some songs, especially those dealing with individual morality, are framed in indirect expressions in the form of metaphors and metonymy. This is consistent with the general Yoruba speech style, which favors indirect figures of speech in non-ordinary language usage when utmost care is needed.

Ọjọ Ọra (Ọramfẹ Day): the Renewal of the Ondo Cosmos

Early in the morning of the *Ọra* day, *Ṣọra* offers at the *Ọra* public shrine the sheep that has replaced the human victim traditionally used for sacrifice. This sacrificial act is called *Imuhọ* (to hang up), which refers to the practice of hanging up the human victim. There is normally a state of remorse among the people following the sacrifice, and this is still remembered by the people to-day, years after the cessation of human sacrifice. An old song refers to this state of affairs thus:

Ọni a muhọ ma ma binu o	The one who is sacrificed should not be an-noyed,
Ẹ muhẹn wa yan o	At another time you will be luckier.

I was informed by a civil servant that in the past it was the custom for *Ṣọra*'s wives to pour ashes on the main entrance of their house so that the ghost of the sacrificed person would leave a trail on their steps when he returned, a theme of reincarnation or resurrection. The above remark helped me to understand certain observations I had taken for granted. During our conversation, I noticed that *Ṣọra* frequently referred to the period of this festival as *igba ajinde* ("Easter time"), which was apparently a reference to the resurrection aspect of the sacrificial rite, rather than a confusion of the celebration with the Christian Easter as I had assumed.

Around 9 a.m., the *Ọra* festival proper began. The ritual drama that follows is a reenactment of the primordial event in which Ọramfẹ arrived to establish the Ondo cosmos. Ṣọra, dressed in his ceremonial clothes (a medicine dress and a brass crown interlaced with green leaves, a symbol of the authority and creative power with which Ọra established Ondo), departs from his house in a procession towards the ritual site, amidst the sounds of a drum and trumpets. En route to the king's site, he makes the mythic stop to embrace the *Ẹkiri*, his old-time friend.

Meanwhile, Oṣemawe and his entourage await his arrival behind Ẹhin-mogun in front of the palace. Akunnara (the messenger sent to meet Ọra in the mythic narrative), circumambulates the city and finally arrives, holding in his hands a sacred object and also an *Idẹn* (two flat brass metal pieces). He reports to Oṣemawe that the 'Ọramfẹ' has arrived and the rites begin. At this stage Oṣemawe, as in the myth, solicits the help of Ṣọra to perform the rites and the latter, placing two kola nuts on the *agba* drum, prays for peace and progress for Ondo.

The following day is the outing ceremony during which Ṣọra dances around the town visiting the homes of chiefs and friends in acknowledgement of the successful performance of the festival. In the late evening a chief, called *Ele-juwa*, fires a gun to announce the end of the ceremony. This final rite is called *jiji okun Ọra* (cutting Ọra rope) and with this the state of prohibition comes to a close.

Interpretation

The interpretation of the Ọramfẹ ritual provided by the participants focused on the *opepee* ritual, especially its social function in the Ondo community. One man stated that the rite was a means of communication between the 'small people' and the 'big men' in the community. Another explained that since there was no newspaper in the olden days to disseminate information and grievances, the festival provided a forum for such matters. My informant added that if I watched very carefully I would see the relatives of the king and the high chiefs "hanging around to listen to what the people were expressing." Not surprisingly, upon arriving at my host's house early in the morning, I found out that he had learned what was said about him in the songs. He jokingly asked what I thought about these songs, and called upstairs to his eldest wife to tell her the town's gossip.

Traditionally, a lampooning festival such as this is by no means peculiar to the Ondo people. It has, however, been an effective method of social criticism and has served as a restraint on forms of socially acceptable behavior for cultures around the world. Harold Courlander comments on Haitian songs of complaints:

Usually an ordinary offended person will not approach an official of prestige and denounce him straightforwardly. Such behavior might involve risks, or even violate social decorum. But an acceptable and effective way to make such criticism is through singing. It carries with it the sanction of propriety, custom, and good manners. The songs of criticism seek to air situations that might otherwise remain local or private affairs, to set in motion public opinion.[18]

The *Ọra* ceremony also displays the characteristics of the ritual type often called in anthropological literature "rituals of rebellion."[19] According to Max Gluckman, in such rituals "commoners temporarily expressed hostility towards the established authorities."[20] He argued that while such rituals demonstrate protests, ultimately they are "intended to preserve and strengthen the established order."[21] Gluckman is saying that what would otherwise have turned into an open public rebellion, with serious disruptive consequences for the kingship, is brought under check in the ritual domain. Gluckman has been widely criticized for overemphasizing social-functional interpretations to the neglect of the symbolic meaning such rituals usually have if examined within their cultural context. Taken by itself, the opepee song rite may not mean much outside the social-functional interpretation traditionally given to such ceremonies. But when considered along with the rites of *Ọra Day* which follow it, its religious and symbolic significance becomes clearer and it complements Gluckman's view.

I propose that the pair of rites, *Opepee-Ọra*, constitutes a reenactment of the transformation of chaos into cosmos, which the *Ọramfẹ* myth amply illustrates. While the *opepee* depicts the upside-down state and disorder that Ondo was in at the beginning of time, a situation that necessitated the invitation of the culture-hero, the *Ọra Day* rite constitutes what Eliade has termed a drama of "cosmization" through which primordial chaos was turned into cosmos. The rest of my analysis will be devoted to elaborating this dimension.

What I suggest here is that the central symbolic purpose of these rituals is to solicit the deity to renew his primordial struggle against the forces of anarchy, chaos, and disorder, and by the same process to reenact his original triumph over chaos.

---

[18] Harold Courlander, *The Drum and the Hoe: Life and Lore of the Haitian People* (Berkeley: University of California Press, 1960), p. 137.

[19] See: Max Gluckman, 1954; Edward Norbeck, 1963; and Barbara Babcock, 1978.

[20] Gluckman, *Custom and Conflict in Africa*, 1965, p. 109.

[21] Ibid.

As we observed in the *Oramfe* myth, the symbols of reversal or inversion that characterize the state of the original chaos in Ondo are implicit in the *Opepee-Ora* ritual complex. By this is meant a broader, all-encompassing concept of inversion, defined by Barbara Babcock to entail "all phenomena of cultural negation . . . an act of expressive behavior which inverts, contradicts, abrogates, or in some fashion presents an alternative to commonly held cultural codes, values and norms, be they linguistic, literary, or artistic, religious, social and political."[22] The rite presents in a very radical way a reversal of "commonly held cultural codes, values and norms" of the Ondo people. As mentioned above, the participants shook hands with their left hands instead of their right hands, which they normally use; the main actors in the drama of recreation, even though they are human, are described as utterly abnormal persons. (*Ora* himself is portrayed in human form, but of gigantic size, and *Ekiri* has long pointed nails.) Also, at the ritual site shortly before the cosmization rite commences, the king patiently sits and awaits the arrival of *Sora*, a situation quite the opposite of the king arriving last in the normal order of rituals which we witnessed in the king's festival.

Once the stage is set, the *Sora* performs the rituals of establishing the Ondo World. Through this symbolic process, the Ondo space and cosmos is reordered. This means, in the words of Eliade, that:

a territorial conquest does not become real until after the performance of the ritual of taking possession, which is only a copy of the primordial act of the creation of the world . . . every territory occupied for the purpose of being inhabited or utilized as *Lebensraum* is first of all transformed from chaos into cosmos; that is, through the effect of ritual it is given a "form" which makes it real.[23]

Conclusion

If the king's festival in Chapter III reaffirms loyalty to the king and provides cultural consensus in the pluralistic Ondo, the *Oramfe* rites illustrate the reality of the social diversities and reaffirm the conflicts and tensions that are part of the daily experience of Ondo life. There are conflicts between the political power of the *Oba* and the ritual power of the Ahoro hereditary chiefs, two independent sources of significant power; there are conflicts between patrilineage and chiefly hierarchy; there are conflicts between the autochthonous groups and the kinship groups; there are conflicts between the

---

[22] Barbara Babcock, *The Reversible World: Symbolic Inversion in Art and Society* (Ithaca, NY: Cornell University Press, 1978), p. 14.
[23] Mircea Eliade, *Cosmos and History*, pp. 10-11.

big men and the small people; and there are conflicts between the *Lọbun* and the *Oṣemawe*. But through the ritual process, these conflicts, tensions, and forms of competition are resolved. The king's supremacy is also reaffirmed, while at the same time acknowledging the rights and privileges of the various subcultural groups within the larger Ondo society.

Chapter V

Ogun: Kingship, Authority, and Order in Ritual Context

Among the Yoruba *orisa*, Ogun is the most popular and revered deity today. More than any other *orisa*, Ogun worship has great diversity within each locality and his following crosses many regional boundaries. As more information is gathered concerning his nature and characteristics, Ogun will no doubt prove to be one of the most significant deities in the history of Yoruba religion. Ogun's complex theological character and multifaceted social roles make it difficult to comprehend his significance in any total sense. The present study will examine Ogun's annual festivals among the Ondo people, where Ogun is worshiped more extensively than all other Yoruba deities.

Mythology and Origin Legends of Ogun

Many myths and origin legends surround Ogun. Much of our knowledge about this deity is based upon the various myths and legends collected by Pierre Fatunbi Verger in Ile-Ifẹ and Benin (formerly Dahomey), where the deity is popular among people of Yoruba descent.

According to Verger, the Ọọni of Ile-Ifẹ, where the oldest Ogun shrine is located, gave the following information:

Ogun was the first born of Oduduwa. He died before Oduduwa, and Oduduwa said, "I have no more sons to keep up my royal line; Ọbalufọn is no warrior, . . ." Then later, Oduduwa regained his sight and then made Ọbalufọn his successor. In Ile-Ifẹ, Ogun is the divinity of Iron and his children live in Ire. He was called, while living, *Ogun Lakaiye dede Igbo*.[1]

Ire is certainly the place where Ogun's appearance was the most important. The oral tradition concerning Ogun confirms that he was the first son of Oduduwa and a great warrior who carried out many military expeditions. He defeated Ara, conquered Ire, gave his son the title of *Ọnire* (king of Ire) and

---

[1] The Ogun myths collected in Ile-Ifẹ and Ilẹsa are summaries from Verger's book, *Notes des Orisa et Vodu*, pp. 141-144.

went back to Ile-Ifẹ. Later, when he returned to Ire, he arrived and nobody remembered him. Thirsty, he saw palm wine, but nobody offered it to him. He became angry, drew his sword, and was about to cut everyone's head off when his son, Ọnire, appeared with food, dogs, snails, palm oil (called *lele*), and palm wine. Then people remembered Ogun and sang his praises. After he was calmed, Ogun regretted his anger, saying, "The courageous should know right from wrong, I am the judge." Then he said certain words which people might use to invoke him. The Ọnire concluded that there is nowhere that Ogun cannot give protection.

In Ilẹṣa, another major Ogun city, a widely-told story is that *Oriṣa* Buku (Ṣọnpọna, god of Smallpox) was the first hunter in the world. When Buku refused to submit to Ogun, the latter was angry and took Buku's bow, arrows, and knife, all of which the hunter had made. Buku went hunting without arms. He threw himself on a wild goat and finally killed it. Buku wanted to cut the animal up, but had no knife. He took a rope and dragged the goat to Ogun's house. Ogun told him to skin the animal. Buku replied that he could not and asked Ogun to return his weapons. Ogun did so, and as of that day the head of any animal Buku killed went in tribute to Ogun.[2]

In the Ondo area, where the cult of Ogun is most widespread among the Yoruba, he is commonly known as *Ogun Nla, Ọlọja Igbo* ("Great Ogun, the paramount head of Igbo village"). Ogun shapes the Ondo identity in several ways. First, a substantial number of Ondo proper names begin with the prefix *ogun*,[3] indicating the deity's significance among lineages and kinship groups. Secondly, the deity has had so much influence on the socio-political structure that every aspect of the Ondo chieftaincy ceremony contains a ritual element traceable to him. In Idanre, for example, one of Ogun's most obvious symbols, a cutlass, is laid on the floor beside the seat of any high chief as his emblem of office. In Ilẹ-Oluji and Ondo, several chiefs must sound the Ogun music for the duration of two weeks preceding Ogun's actual annual festival. In Ondo, the deity is associated with the *Ẹlẹgbẹ* warrior class. A week before the beginning of the Ogun celebration, each high chief takes his turn performing *aisun ogun* (Ogun night vigil).

Whereas it is well-known that several other divinities were brought to Ondo, the reason for Ogun's arrival in Ondo still remains uncertain. Despite

---

[2] Pierre Verger further remarks that the legend is known in Brazil, but there *Omolu* (the Brazilian name for Saponna) claims he doesn't need Ogun to eat this goat.

[3] Examples are *ogunkamisi* (Ogun recognizes me); *ogunyinka* (Ogun surrounds me); *Ogundahunsi* (Ogun intervenes in this matter); *Oguntuwaṣe* (Ogun reshapes character); *ogunṣuyi* (Ogun bestows honor); *oguntade* (Ogun is as great as the crown [Kingship]); *ogunyẹmi* (Ogun fits me); *ogunwọle* (Ogun enters our home); etc.

the aforementioned origin myths collected by Pierre Verger, there are conflict-ing stories about how the deity was established. Leigh suggests that the wor-ship of Ogun was introduced by Ẹkiri at the time the latter inhabited Ondo.[4] This is probably untrue because Ẹkiri does not play the significant role in the Ogun cult that he plays, for example, in the *Ọramfẹ* cult ritual. According to the *Ọramfẹ* myth, Ogun was *Ọramfẹ*'s very close friend back at Ile-Ifẹ and actually arrived in Ondo before him, perhaps even before the Ondo people themselves.

According to the *Ṣọra*, *Ọramfẹ* recognized Ogun's footsteps when he ar-rived in Ondo and called the place *Ẹhinmogun* (where Ogun was known). The chief priestess in charge of *Ogun Aiṣẹrọ* (a neighborhood shrine of the deity) refers to him during an invocation ceremony as *Ogun-abọba* ("Ogun, whom we came to meet here"). We may assume, pending further investigation, that the above version represents the most common Ogun origin myth among the Ondo.

Also, in neighboring *Ilẹ-Oluji*, there is a close affinity between Ogun and Ija. Their shrines are only a few yards apart and are propitiated at the same time during the annual Ogun festival. According to the oral tradition of the town, a hunter called Ija was the faithful servant of Oduduwa, who led the abominable twin children born in Ile-Ifẹ palace into safety. Up until 1901, Ilẹ-Oluji was still officially referred to as *Ẹkun-Ijamọ* (the territory known or dis-covered by Ija). Since Ilẹ-Oluji was the final stop of the Ile-Ifẹ group, this ex-plains why the deity is propitiated there and not in Ondo.

Nature and Form of the Deity

These myths and origin legends indicate Ogun's main characteristics and func-tions. Praise chants and other literary sources highlight additional aspects. Anyone seeing the festival for the first time might be distracted by the appar-ently bizarre and gruesome form of his ceremonies. However, a thorough grasp of Ogun's nature may enable the researcher to understand in a more em-pathetic manner what all these various rites and performances say about the deity and what they represent for the people.

In Ondo, as in similar towns with strong Ogun cults, one gets the impres-sion that Ogun is the religion of the masses *par excellence*. Unlike several other Yoruba *orisa*, whose actual cult directions are restricted to the initiated few, the Ogun cult is practiced by the populace at large. Anyone may become

---

[4] Leigh, *History of Ondo*, p. 4.

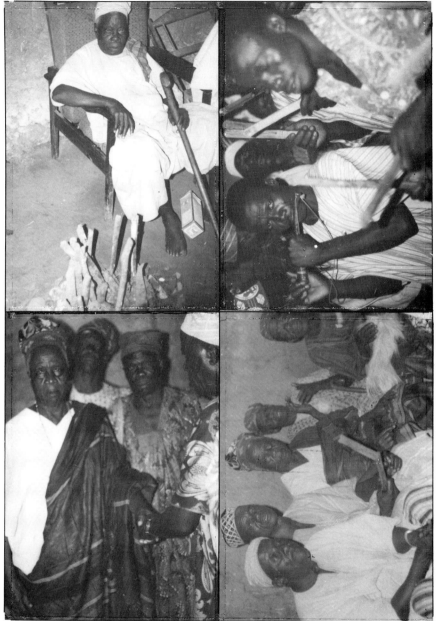

a. Adegbamigbe, the Ṣọra (Ọramfẹ ritual specialist) in the *odi* (domestic shrine of his deity) before starting the Opepe ceremony (7th day of festival).

b. Instruments used in the Opepe ceremony include *ohẹnhẹn* (animal horn) and *ọwẹwẹ* (claves).

c. Left-handed greeting between Opepe participants, symbolizing inversion of social relations.

d. Members of the Sora's lineage gather in the *odi* for Opepe songs.

a. The Oṣemawe of Ondo sits in state before the arrival of the deity's messenger, on the festival's climatic 8th day.

b. The Akunnara, 'fore-runner' of the Savior Deity.

c. "The Deity has arrived."

d. The Sora divines for the ọba to the music of the *agba* drum.

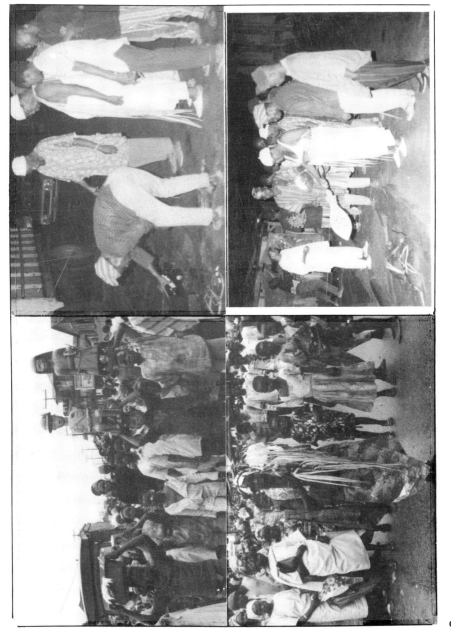

a. *Mimu Ogun boko* (welcoming Ogun from the farm), a rite performed before dawn
   at the old eastern gate of the city by High Chief Adaja.
b. Gesture with sword over shrine symbolizing Ogun's temporal power.
c. Sagun Sisa; Ogun's processional race around the town, includes the *ere* images of
   a soldier and a nun.
d. Female herbalist with her contingent in Ogun's procession.

a. Professional advertising finds a place in the ritual display.
b. Junior *oloogun* in ritual attire.
c. Signposts heralding the arrival of an important *oloogun*.
d. Ogun procession showing hunters and images of soldiers.

a. Ayadi, Chief Priest of Ogun at the ẹhinmogun (Ogun's shrine), prepares for the sacrifice of a dog.
b. Preparation of the ritual site.
c. The ẹhinmogun is hemmed by palm fronds.
d. Offerings of palm wine and a kolanut.

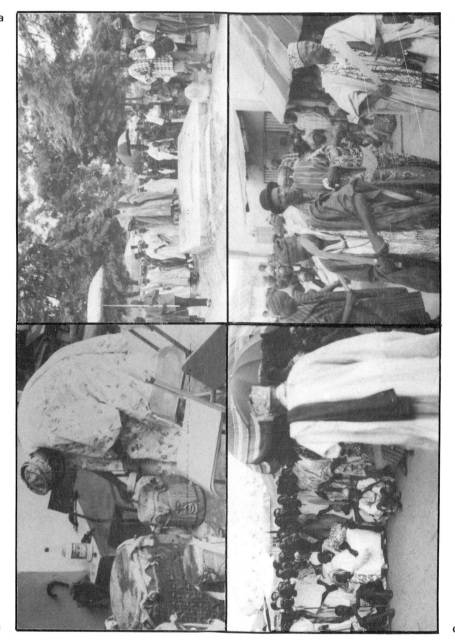

a. Two Otu chiefs pay their homage to the king in the ọdun ọba ceremony.

b. A ritual chief ascends a shrine en route to the 'date fixing announcement' ceremony.

c. In the house of a high Ondo chief, an elder marks his ugbaji drums.

d. The king witnesses the chiefs' approach in the ọdun ọba ceremony.

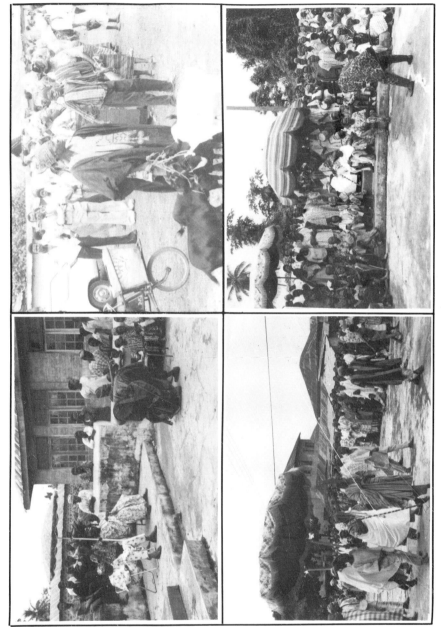

a. Asingba (ceremonial tribute): a set of four goats presented by one group of chiefs.
b. A chief pays obeisance to the High Chiefs.
c. Obeisance in the announcement ceremony.
d. The king on his way to the inner palace after the announcement ceremony.

The Lobun (Woman king). Photographer: Roland Abiodun.

The Lobun installing the new Oba king in Ondo. Photographer: Roland Abiodun.

not only an Ogun worshipper but a full member of the Ogun cult group. In this connection, Wọle Soyinka described him as "essential Ogun."[5] Sandra Barnes calls him "an old god for a new age,"[6] a reference to the ancient god's importance for today. Both the beliefs and the rituals that surround Ogun's cult are closely related to the actual life situation of his worshippers.

Ogun is manifested in various forms in Yoruba religious and secular discourse. His many names refer to his place of origin, his nature, function, and essence as perceived by his devotees. Numerous examples of Yoruba oral literature magnify the power and might of this orisa within the Yoruba pantheon. First his role is often recognized as that of a pathfinder, the one who clears the road for other deities to pass through. Another tradition informs us, that at the time of creation, Ogun was put in charge of matters relating to war and military exploits requiring the use of iron.[7] In this supervisory role he excelled over all the other deities, as acknowledged by the following *oriki* (praise name) recorded by Chief Ayọrinde:

Orisa ti yio ṣe bi ogun ko si mọ
Oju lasan lori inu wọn nya Kiri
Bi ko ba yan, nwọn ko le yan
Bi ko ba rin, nwọn ko le rin
There is no deity that can excell Ogun;
Others are just full of mere affront,
Without his leadership, they cannot move an inch.
Without his company, they cannot march confidently on.[8]

The above text vividly suggests Ogun's worth and the place of honor accorded to him among the other *orisa*.

Recent research on Ogun's association with war, iron, and hunting suggests the probable development of the cult from the ancient past and may also explain why it has such influence on the masses today. The art historian Daniel Williams has suggested that Ogun's association with war dates back to a period before iron was introduced into Yorubaland, a time when the deity became associated with destructive power and the expression of energy and force.[9] This period most probably coincided with the early migration and

[5] Wọle Ṣoyinka, *Myth, Literature, and the African World* (Cambridge: Cambridge University Press, 1976), p. 26.

[6] Sandra Barnes, *Ogun: An Old God for a New Age* (Philadelphia: Institute for the Study of Human Issues, 1980).

[7] Wande Abimbọla, "The Literature of Ifa Cult," *Sources of Yoruba History*. S. O. Biobaku, ed. (Oxford: Clarendon Press, 1973), p. 41.

[8] Chief J. A. Ayọrinde, "Oriki," in S. O. Biobaku, *Sources of Yoruba History*, pp. 69, 72.

[9] Daniel Williams, *Icon and Image: A Study of Sacred and Secular Forms of African Classical Art* (New York: New York University Press, 1974), p. 87.

settlement of the Yoruba people from a far distant place to their present abode. Perhaps this also corresponds to what most oral traditions say about the creation of Yoruba world, that Ogun was delegated to lead the way. Williams further suggests that Ogun began to be associated with and applauded as the god of iron from a time of "an increased availability of the metal"[10] among the Yoruba people, a reference to the ritualization of the objects of material culture such as iron. The association of Ogun with hunting is as old as the creation of the Yoruba world. Hunting plays a significant role in the history and religious practices of Yoruba people,[11] and hunters like Ogun are associated with pathfinding and bravery. They usually "arm themselves with both iron weapons, sacred to Ogun, and magical medicine to allow them to outwit animals, disguise themselves and even make themselves invisible in case of danger."[12] It is under the third category, as hunter, that Ogun has found his most enduring role. Today, Ogun is linked with various elements of the material culture. He is associated with many modern professions and trades in society. This helps to explain why the worship of this *orişa* belongs to both the low and high in the community.

Ogun is also the most amibiguous deity in the Yoruba pantheon. Like the Yoruba trickster Eşu, he is associated with life's destructive and creative powers. In most studies of Yoruba culture featuring Ogun, there is a tendency to associate him with destructive rather than creative power. Thus, Wọle Şoyinka often protests against the violent, destructive image of Ogun that forms the central theme of popular literature and even serious academic studies.[13] Based on the deity's praise-chants and other textual evidence, Şoyinka characterized Ogun as "protector of orphans, roof over the homeless, terrible guardian of the sacred occult. Ogun stands for transcendental, humane, but rigidly restorative, justice."[14]

---

[10] Ibid.
[11] Henry John Drewal and Margaret Thompson Drewal, *Gẹlẹdẹ: Art and Female Power Among the Yoruba* (Bloomington, Indiana: Indiana University Press, 1983), p. 179.
[12] Ibid.
[13] Soyinka, *Myth, Literature, and the African World*, p. 141.
[14] The Ogun praise chants on which the author based the characteristic features of the deity are as follows:
> Rich-laden in his home yet
> decked in palm fronds,
He ventures forth, refuge of the downtrodden.
To rescue slaves, he unleashed the judgement of war.
To aid the blind, he plunged into forests
Of curative herbs; bountiful one,
Who stands bulwark to the offspring of the dead of heaven.
Salutations, o lone being who swims in the rivers of blood.
(Wọle Şoyinka, *Myth, Literature, and the African World*, p. 142.)

Ogun is a paragon of judicial virtues, an area in which he is most powerful among deities; he left no one in doubt about the fearlessness of his judicial decisions, once taken. Whereas most scholars have viewed Ogun from the Judeo-Christian perspective in which justice and violence are mutually exclusive, the two exist together in Yoruba thought. Even among educated Yoruba, those who would easily swear a false oath upon the Bible or Quran would hesitate to swear a similar oath upon Ogun's ritual objects, even a fountain pen, which is indicative of Ogun's adaptation to the contemporary work situation. They would hesitate to swear a false oath on such objects because they have not ceased to believe in the reality of Ogun, even though they now maintain a post-traditional religion or a Judeo-Christian or Islamic world view. There is a strong belief even among the educated Yoruba that while it takes the God of the Bible or Quran a long time to act against sinners and offenders (as both Gods suspend sentences pending a sinner's repentance), the judgement of Ogun is swift and certain.

I have argued previously that Ogun did not take part in the cosmogony as such, but several traditions refer to him as 'providing the cutlass,' 'making the way,' and leading other divinities as they pass through the created universe. So Ogun's history, Şoyinka observes, "is the story of the completion of Yoruba cosmogony."[15]

The incredible intellectual activities purportedly engaged in by Ogun have also earned him a place of honor among Yoruba intellectuals. Şoyinka describes Ogun as embodying: "the knowledge-seeking instinct, an attribute which sets him apart as the only deity who sought the way and harnessed the resources of science to hack a passage through primordial chaos for the god's reunion with man."[16]

In pursuit of the intellectual archetype, a group of Ile-Ifẹ academics formed a research project for cultural studies referred to as *alada* (literally, "possession of the cutlass"), a metaphorical reference to Ogun's cutlass with which the new path of knowledge was to be laid open for others to follow.

The Ogun Festival in Ondo

The festival in honor of Ogun normally occurs in August. Preparation for the festival begins at the appearance of the new moon, seventeen days before the actual Ogun day. In the early morning at a ceremony in the house of *Ayadi*

---

[15] Şoyinka, *Myth, Literature, and the African World*, p. 26.
[16] Ibid., p. 27.

(the ritual specialists of Ogun public worship),[17] the *upe* (a trumpet made from a gourd) is sounded to inform the public of the upcoming events. This method of alerting the public to daily events continues until the end of the festival. As an old man explained to me, "*Upe* is the messenger of the deity and so the sounding of it is to inform all and sundry about the coming event. It can travel far because it is not the voice of a human who speaks in it but that of the deity himself." Throughout this seventeen-day period, Ogun worshippers gather in groups to sing the praises of the deity and their own cultural heroes, especially those who were associated with the cult while they were alive.

Dida ọjọ Ogun: The Announcement Rite

The official announcement of the ceremony is made on the next major market day, nine days before the festival. The ceremony, called *dida ọjọ Ogun* ("naming Ogun's day"), is carried out by the king's emissary. (The market itself is actually held on the previous day so the people can avoid "marketing with Ogun," when no human being gains.[18])

In keeping with Ogun's role as the maker of the new path, the people gather in all the adjoining Ondo villages to clean all footpaths of weeds and to repair old bridges. Ojo observes that in Ondo "this is the only time in the year when public paths were communally repaired."[19]

Five days preceding the actual Ogun day, a ceremony referred to as *Aleho* is performed by a few households and lineages. An early morning meal of pounded yam is prepared and eaten by the members of the household. In the late evening, *Ẹgbẹdi*, an Ogun chief and one-time head of the *Ẹlẹgbẹ* warrior group, dances around the town followed by several children.[20] On the night of the first day, representatives of the king, the *Lisa* and the *Jọmu*, and also the first three *Ẹharẹ* chiefs, take turns observing the night vigil (*aisun Ogun*), and they dance around the town visiting the houses of chiefs and important dignitaries.

---

[17] Ojo, *Yoruba Customs from Ondo*, p. 63.

[18] Akinrinlọla, "Ogun Festival in Ondo," *Nigeria Magazine*, No. 85 (1965), p. 86.

[19] Ojo, *Yoruba Customs from Ondo*, p. 64.

[20] I do not know the special role of children here. Perhaps what has now become *Ayadi*'s praise name formerly belonged to Ẹgbẹdi prior to his demotion by *Ọba* Airọ (see Chapter II for details).

Ogun Alẹ: Night Ogun

The last two days are the actual Ogun festival days, and the *Ogun alẹ* (night Ogun) ceremony fell on the evening of August 25th during my visit.

The Ogun procession constitutes, at least from the point of view of the spectators, the main feature of the festival. Several people I interviewed did not know, nor care to know, about rites other than the procession that takes place either privately or publicly during these celebrations. What, then, does the procession mean for the spectators and the worshippers themselves?

The procession referred to as *sagun* (literally, "to run Ogun's race") derives its name from the fast tempo of the music and warlike-dance. Each individual or group parade is referred to as *Ologun* ("Ogun bearer"). During the procession both traditional and modern-day professionals and guilds join together. Blacksmiths, medicine men and women, drivers, hunters, tailors, barbers, bricklayers, and more modern trading groups such as the associations of printers, painters, fish sellers, and all the other professions combine to form the procession. Every conceivable professional group in Ondo, except for the civil service and white-collar workers, participates in the celebration. Most are dressed in rags and parade through the town with their bodies smeared with blue, white, and black paint. Others, mainly the nobility, wear beautiful multi-colored clothes and still others dress in modern military camouflage attire. They sing in praise of the deity and of their procession. The festival is an occasion to celebrate Ogun's deeds and to display human workmanship. Some of the songs I gathered follow.

These songs are in praise of the medicine man, especially those considered to have great magical power.

(I)

Ọkan ṣoṣo ma t'ogun	A single potent medicine is enough,
To ba ti jẹ	If it works,
To ba ti jẹ o	If it works,
To ba ti jẹ	If it works.
Ọkan ṣoṣo ma t'ogun	A single potent medicine is enough,
To ba ti jẹ	If it works.

(II)

Odidẹ, akukọ	The parrot, the cock,
Ko sẹyẹ bi ọkin mọ	There is no bird like the white eagle.
Ko sẹyẹ bi ọkin mọ	There is no bird like the white eagle.

(III)

Baba wa tan peri	This is our father we have been talking about.
Baba wa re o	This is our father.

Sometimes the chief drummer focuses his attention on the individual Ogun bearer, urging him to display some of his magical power. A medicine man is said to have the ability to change into any kind of animal, and the drummer here asks him to display this power as a proof of his might.

Daun wa da	Turn into whatever you want,
O ma daun wada	Turn into whatever you want,
Kare le	And let us go back home.
Duan wa da	Turn into whatever you want,
O ma daun wada	Turn into whatever you want,
Kare le.	And let us go home.

Ogun's power is shown especially when he manifests his anger. Such anger, which his worshippers fervently pray to avoid, is indicated in the following song:

Me a ri b'ogun sun	I will not witness where Ogun weeps,[21]
E wọ	It is taboo.

Even though the night and day processions are quite similar in form, many people say that this evening parade is a lesser form of Ogun fiesta, as it demonstrates mainly the earthly part of the ceremony.

Aisun Ogun: Ogun Night Vigil

The night of the first day's celebration is *aisun Ogun* ("Ogun night vigil"). The various groups gather in the houses of their leaders or in public pubs where they engage in heavy drinking and different forms of entertainment. Among the guild of hunters, the night is an occasion for *Ijala* recital.[22] *Ijala* consists of Ogun's poetic chants and is one genre of Yoruba oral literature. According to Adeoye Babalọla, *Ijala* is "mythically and ritually associated with the worship of Ogun."[23] Although three songs belong to the hunter's guild, their themes concern virtually all aspects of Yoruba culture; women, animals, and plants. Thus, the *Ijala* chants point to the universal nature of the Ogun deity among the Yoruba. The hunters take turns reciting Ogun's poems in praise of their patron god in this colorful ceremony which extends until dawn.

---

[21] When Ogun cries, it is blood that flows from his eyes.

[22] For a detailed discussion of *Ijala* oral literature, see the following works: Babalọla, *The Contents and Form of Yoruba Ijala* (Oxford University Press, 1966); *Ijala* (Federal Ministry of Information, Lagos, 1968); "The Delights of Ijala," in *Yoruba Oral Tradition*, Wande Abimbola, ed. (University of Ifẹ, 1971), pp. 631-676; and Ulli Beier, *Yoruba Poetry: Traditional Yoruba Poems*, collected and translated by Bakare Gbadamọsi and Ulli Beier (Ibadan), 1961.

[23] Babalọla, *The Contents and Forms of Yoruba Ijala*, p. 1.

Mimu Ogun Bǫko: Ogun Enters the City

Just before dawn on August 27, high chief Adaja proceeds to Idiṣin Street at Ondo's old eastern gate, to perform the ceremony referred to as *mimu Ogun boko* (bringing Ogun from the farm). As this rite must be performed in the utter darkness before dawn, two young boys precede the group with shouts of *mama woo* ("it is forbidden to see it") to warn oncoming vehicles to shut off their lights. At the ritual site, Mr. Taiwo Akintewe (son of the deceased Adaja Akintewe) offers a sacrifice of kola nut and palm wine on behalf of the high chief to appease the god and welcome him into the town for the annual celebration. The following prayers are then recounted.

Ogun, ko mu ẹsẹ tutu wǫle	Ogun, enter the house with a cool leg;
Ko mu ẹsẹ obinrin wǫle	Enter it with the leg of a woman.[24]
Ogun ma ma ja l'ǫdun yi o	Ogun, do not cause any havoc this year;
Ko rǫ gbogbo Ondo l'ǫrun	Let it be a year of peace for Ondo.
Ẹharẹ, Ẹlẹgbẹ, Ekulẹ, Opoji	Ẹharẹ, Ẹlẹgbẹ, Ekulẹ, Opoji,
Ko jẹ ki ǫba pẹ lori oye,	Let the king reign long.
Ko rǫ ǫkunrin lǫrun	Let it be peaceful for men,
Ko rǫ obinrin lǫrun	Let it be peaceful for women.
Ma jẹ ki Oluwaiye wǫlẹ yio	Do not let the god of smallpox[25] enter this town.
Ma ma jẹ ki a ri ija ẹ o	Let us not witness your anger.
Bami Laniyi yi, o jẹ Adaja	Our father, *Laniyi*, who became the Adaja,
Ma ma jẹ ko mu aisan joye o	Do not let him spend his chieftaincy in sickness.
Emi lami yi me baṣe lǫdun yi	I, myself, who am celebrating with him this year,
Kin le ba ṣe lǫdun tonbǫ	May I live to perform this function next year.
Onilu, ko le lu fun lǫdun t'onbǫ	Let the drummer be alive to drum for him next year.

On his way home, the chief branches off at another Ogun shrine called *Ogun Aiṣerǫ*, where he offers a kola nut sacrifice. From there, he visits his titled house, and ritually sits three times on the doorstep to renew his title.

Ogun Owuro: Morning Ogun

In the early morning, at 6 a.m., the king starts the annual Ogun procession in the ceremony called *Ogun owurǫ* ("morning Ogun"). He wears a beaded crown that covers his whole face and a white sheet tied on the left shoulder

---

[24] The feminine represents the soft, cool, and tranquil, while maleness represents the exact opposite. A New Year wish, for example, is that "it be a female born" (*ǫdun a yabo*), thus signifying peacefulness and a year free from disturbance and turmoil.

[25] A synonym and respectable name for Ṣǫnpǫna (god of smallpox).

over his *agbada*. This is the second festival occasion when the King wears his full regalia, *Ọdun Ọba* being the first. He dances to the tune of the *ugbaji* drum. One of the stopping places is at *Ogun Aiṣẹrọ*, and there he is met by a priestess.[26] She propitiates the deity for the king in the following manner. Taking a kola nut, she invokes the deity first:

Ogunlade aburo Oṣhin	Ogunlade, Oshin's brother,
Iyan kan bi ogi	The pounded yam,[27] sour like corn porridge;
O pọn mi sule fẹ jẹ wẹ	He has water at home yet bathes with blood.
O di ugba uli hi daka mu yẹ ẹ si	You asked that we propitiate you, With the calabash in the house.
Awo uli hi da ka mu yẹ ẹ si	You asked us to propitiate you. With the dish in the house.
Dede ahere hi da ka yẹ ẹ si	You ask all the hamlets to propitiate you,
Di igba ẹ san ulu	Let his reign be peaceful for the townspeople.
Do jẹ pẹ	Let him reign long,
Do ma r'ogun le nini	Prevent evil doers from reaching him.
Emi kẹ, ma dun ṣe awọn ọmọ mọ mi	And for me, do not let anything happen to my children.
Ma dun ṣe awọn ọmọ ọkọ mi	Do not let anything happen to my husband's children.
Ogunlade abọba	Ogunlade, one that we met here;
Ibe a ba ẹ hin	We met you here when we first came.

After this invocation the priestess presents the king's offerings of kola nut divination.[28] A four-lobed kola nut is split open and thrown on the elevated floor of the shrine. At the ritual I witnessed, two lobes faced down and two faced up; this is considered a good omen for the coming year. Following the divination rite, the priestess faces the king and conveys to him the good wishes of the deity:

Kabayesi	Kabayesi
Wa jẹ pẹ	You will reign long.
Igba uli ẹ e a fọ	The calabash in your household will not break.
Awo uli ẹ e a fọ	The dish in your household will not break.
Ẹ a sun a ṣe	No evil thing will happen to you,
Ẹharẹ, Opoji, Ẹlẹgbẹ, Ekulẹ	Ẹharẹ, Opoji, Ẹlẹgbẹ, Ekulẹ [Ondo grade of chiefs].

---

[26] The impression is often given that women play a lesser role in the worship of Ogun. This is hardly the case in Ondo, where a woman is in charge of *Ogun Aiṣẹrọ*. Also, several Ogun bearers in Ondo and Ilẹ-Oluji are women. I noticed in particular a medicine woman in Ilẹ-Oluji referred to as Lakọmọla. She is fairly popular and is responsible for circumcising newly-born children.

[27] Perhaps, a yam pounded the previous day.

[28] Divination by kola nut performed by women in Ogun shrine is not peculiar to Ondo. Verger observes a similar practice during the ceremony of the installation of a new Alase of *Odun Edeye* at Ilodo, a Dahomean (new Republic of Benin) town. There, an important priestess, *Iyafero* (the one whose function it is to calm Ogun's violent temper), performs the divination by kola nut to see if the offerings made to Ogun on behalf of the new chief are acceptable.

The *Ugbaji* music follows this chant, and the king dances around the shrine three times. From there he proceeds to Okedasa Street, where he collects gifts from various well-wishers who have come out to meet him. Then he goes to pay homage at the late *Ọba* Adeuga's burial place, where he knocks his sword on the floor three times. At *Ọba* Fidipọtẹ's burial place he repeats the same rite; both dead *Ọba* come from his lineage. Both performances appear to have overtones of ancestor worship.

The king then proceeds to *Lisa*'s house. Upon arrival *Lisa* meets him in front of his domicile. *Lisa* points the drum he carries at the *Ọba* and pays him obeisance. With this completed, the king proceeds to the palace, thus completing his own personal worship of Ogun. The king's annual Ogun worship takes several forms, from a direct propitiation of the deity to ancestor worship and rites of renewal of authority.

Ogun Sisa: Ogun's Ritual Dance

The king's Ogun dance is followed by other processions. First come the high chiefs, then the medicine men, and finally all of the other tradesmen who had participated in the previous day's celebration. This procession is the most spectacular part of the whole festival. It proceeds counter-clockwise around the town with *Adaja, Ayadi*, and the king dancing clockwise. Spectators from far and wide gather to observe the groups. The procession breaks into separate performances, each group demonstrating its professional skills, despite dilapidated and worn-out instruments. For example, I observed a bricklayer pretending to map out the ground on the street as if he wanted to lay a foundation for a new building. A hunter held an empty gun and aimed it at the audience nearby. The most revered group of *Ologun* is that of the medicine men, referred to as *Oloogun* ("medicine people"). They wear medicine garments decorated with different kinds of herbal substances, and they have more followers than other *Ologun*.

Most medicine men engaged young schoolboys to carry signposts displaying the name of the Ogun bearer, his lineage, his praise name, a warning coded in proverbs, and a metaphor of the magico-medical prowess of the *Ologun* which signals the public to watch out. An example of such a signpost is reproduced below.

Ẹniti o ba fi oju ana wo oku	He who looks upon the today's dead with the same eye that saw the living
Ẹbọra a bọ lasọ. Ati pe	Will have his cloth removed by the spirit.
Ẹni ti oju ẹni ti ju ẹni lọ	He who is above one is above one.
Bi iya nla ba gbenisanlẹ	When one is overpowered by big trouble,
Kekeke a ma gun ori ẹni	Smaller problems come up too.

Opẹkẹtẹ ndagba	As the little palm tree grows up,
Inu Adamọ nba jẹ	The harvester of palm leaves grows sad.
Milo kaabọ	Milo, Welcome!
Aṣeyi ṣamọdun o	May we perform this and the next one also.
Ogun ye moye	Ogun lives and so do I.

Another signpost carried by the same *Ologun* advertises his job: "Fawẹhinmi Commercial Institute Ondo, Milo! Typing is our business. *Aṣeyi ṣamọdun, gbogbo ọmọ Fawẹhinmi* ("Congratulations, all the Fawẹhinmi and Company, Limited").

Of all the sacrificial objects, the dog is considered the major food of Ogun. In fact, in an annual Ogun festival, several dogs are killed in various ways in different rituals. These animals are called *ẹran ogun* ("Ogun's favorite meat"), which can be taken at will by the deity. To kill a dog by accident is considered a good omen, as this is interpreted as an unsolicited sacrifice to the god. Additionally, the dog is taken to stand for an otherwise human victim whose life has been spared by the god.

It is believed that Ogun does not require any special shrine for propitiation, as his presence is felt whenever anything made of iron is visible.[29] However, this presence is given a central focus through a public shrine located on a hill within an area referred to as *ẹhinmogun*. The high point of the celebration is the public sacrifice performed at this shrine. I was present when the morning sacrifice was made. The shrine is decorated with palm fronds, and a fence surrounds the sacred tree at the shrine to further separate the spot from the surroundings. The ritual specialists, called *Ayadi*, arrive with a dog, a tortoise, and palm wine in a small gourd decorated with palm fronds. The priest saw me standing by with a camera and beckoned me to move closer for a better angle. This enabled me to follow every step of the rite. First, the tortoise was cut into two halves and thrown at the base of the tree. Then one man held the dog by a rope tied around its neck while another man held the hind legs. The animal was then pulled at both ends and suspended in the air, at which point *Ayadi*, with a very sharp sword, severed the animal's neck with a single stroke, in accordance with the Ondo saying, *ẹkan ẹ b'aja Ogun* ("Ogun's sacrificial dog must be cut once"). The success of this sacrifice is determined by *Ayadi*'s ability to decapitate the dog in one stroke. Failure to do so might lead to calamities for him and society. The carcass is then cut longitudinally to allow the intestines to be opened. It is then tied to the tree. The palm wine is poured all over the base of the shrine, which completes the sacrifice.

So far, I have stated that the Ogun ritual, like the rituals discussed earlier,

---

[29] Akinrinlọla, *Ogun Festival*, p. 75.

conveys an ethos of hierarchy and royalty which is deeply rooted in Ondo social structure. This was observed in the pre-Ogun dance where the high chiefs take turns in performing the night vigil in order of their rank. Also, processions often reveal the social order most fully. In the Ogun procession, the priest-chiefs connected with Ogun such as the *Adaja*, the *Jọmu*, the *Ayadi*, and the king himself, who all belong to the *ọtunba* (literally, "the right side of kingship") classification in the Ondo social-cultural structure, dance in a clockwise manner (what I called the side of honor), while the rest of the Ogun bearers dance in a counterclockwise direction.

Furthermore, it is obvious that the procession implicitly contains a warrior ethos. Of the many faces of the Ogun, it is this aspect for which the god was most famous. I shall illustrate this further in a discussion of the Ogun parades in Ilẹ-Oluji where the warrior motif dominates the ceremony.

In Ilẹ-Oluji the Ogun bearers dance in a counterclock-wise direction, the normal dance pattern for any social activity in the town. However, an Ogun bearer and highly-respected, famous medicine man, Lọgọ, dances clockwise, like the *ọtunba* group in Ondo. As a result, he is most likely to meet every other *Ologun* on the way. The procession becomes entertainment with symbolic meanings characteristic of Ogun. It is the practice that whenever two *Ologun* meet, especially on a narrow path that would hardly accommodate one group conveniently, a struggle or a challenge ensues over the right of way; one *Ologun* wins a symbolic victory. The ceremony becomes an opportunity for a show of force by the individual medicine-*Ologun* and often creates a temptation for them to test their medicinal power in public and to confirm their superiority. This aptly illustrates Ogun's attributes as "the embodiment of challenge, the Promethean instinct in man, constantly at the service of society for its full self-realization."[30]

I witnessed such challenges and displays of magical power in several Ogun festivals, especially between Lọgọ and another popular *Ologun* called Oyinbo.[31] Very often the two groups had to wait until the police officials who accompany the processions moved up and down between them to negotiate a peaceful manner of passage. In these situations the drummers and the followers and 'fans' of each *Ologun*, mainly school children and middle-aged adults, made the situation more difficult and an actual conflict more probable. The individual drummer feeds the flames of challenge by asking each one to show his true self, as the following music for Lọgọ indicates:

---

[30] Ṣoyinka, *Myth, Literature, and the African World*, p. 3.
[31] I learned that Oyinbo has since converted to Christianity and so has ceased to participate in the Ogun parade.

Lọgọ ṣe buwoti ṣe	Lọgọ, do as you always do.
Lọgọ ṣeun ba ẹ ṣe	Lọgọ, do as your father used to do.
Bamatula ṣe buweti ṣe	Bamatula [Lọgọ's surname], do as you always do.
Ologun mo bẹru rẹ	The medicine man, I am afraid of you;
Da wayiwayi jo	Pour the medicine on him.

The song could also be this:

Kilo ko, kilo ko, l'ọna	What do you meet on the way, what do you meet on the way,
Lọgọ lo ko.	It is Logo that you meet on the way.

Two latent or covert meanings appear to be involved. On one level, the apparent struggle between the two *Ologun* characterizes the ancient warfare situations to which the god himself is well-accustomed. On another level and beyond this apparent state of violence, the subtle nature of the god is brought into focus. To avoid the destruction to which a blind display of power could lead, a mediating force comes between the two *Ologun*. There may also be conflict between two or more areas of Ondo social strata: economic, political, sub-ethnic, residential, and generational variables. I once witnessed an occasion where a high chief, a symbol of the high political status, and an *Ologun* met on a narrow path, and a violent conflict would have occurred but for the guide's intervention. To avoid a stalemate, the drummer changed the tune of the *Ologun*'s music from "Do as you always do" to a more subtle song of appeal to the high chief to exercise patience, perseverance, and statesmanship worthy of the deity himself:

Baba maja o, Baba maja o	'Father,' do not fight, 'Father,' do not fight.
Ogun binu	Ogun does not get angry.
Ogun maja o	Ogun does not fight unnecessarily.
Baba maja o	Baba, do not fight.

By appealing to the statesmanship of the elder high chief, both parties dispersed peacefully without anyone's being accorded victory.

Ogun's Ritual Process: Meanings and Functions

Next, I shall present an analysis of the ritual processes. A careful examination of the structure and nature of the festival shows that Ogun rituals revolve around three significant persons: the high chief *Adaja*, the *Ayadi*, head of the warrior chiefs, and the King. The position of *Ọdunwo*, the priest-chief normally linked with Ogun celebration, was vacant during my field work. His designated ritual was either performed by someone else or omitted entirely during this festival. I shall examine the ritual functions of the three as illustrated in the festivals described above.

The *Adaja*, the fifth of the *Ẹharẹ* high chiefs, is designated to be in charge of the East gate at Idiṣin, the place where Ogun would enter the town. Two previous rituals symbolically herald Ogun's approach: the clearing of the farm and village paths several weeks before the festivals and the local bugle being blown daily for two full weeks. As *Adaja* ushers in Ogun through the ritual *mimu Ogun b'ọko*, Ogun is asked to step into the city via the "feet of a woman" (*ẹsẹ obinrin*). This indicates a cool, calm, and nonaggressive posture, a stereotypical image of womanhood in Yoruba culture. The Yoruba normally describe and pray for a peaceful and tranquil year as *ọdun abo* ("female year"). The essence of *Adaja*'s ritual is to soften the aggressive nature of the deity before it unleashes terror onto the civil community. The sacrifice must be performed before daybreak, a time when no one would accidentally encounter Ogun and aggravate his hot temper and unleash his violence and harm. In the modern period, vehicles are forbidden from plying their trade in the city or performing regular services during Ogun's rites. Those who must perform essential services tie palm fronds, Ogun's cloth, in front of their vehicles as a sign of respect and honor for the deity. It should be noted that the only other occasion when palm fronds are tied to vehicles is in conveyance of corpses from one place to another.

Once Ogun is reverently ushered into the city, the *Ayadi* must perform the required sacrifice of dog (*aja*) and tortoise (*ahun*) and pour the libation of palm wine (*ẹmu*) at Ogun's central shrine. The sacrificial elements are related to the nature of the deity in several ways. The tortoise, the first sacrificial animal, is close to the humans. In several Yoruba myths and legends it is recounted that the tortoise once shared the same physical space and habitat with humans. He is renowned to be stubborn, wise, and cunning. The tortoise is an essential ingredient for powerful human medicine. A human who is thick-skinned, stubborn, and unmoved by pain and affliction is presumed to have consumed tortoise head. Moreover, it is a liminal animal, mediating between forest and city life.

But the most significant aspect of the sacrifice is the immolation of a dog, a domesticated animal often used in hunting expeditions. The dog is not in any way regarded as a pet, as in Western societies.[32] Ondo people do not normally eat dog meat, but because of its frequent use in sacrifice their neighbors make fun of them as dog-eaters (*Ondo ajaja*). The sacrifice of the dog is the climax of the ritual, and by this means blood flows onto the shrine. It is believed that Ogun takes delight in drinking blood, and in Yoruba society

---

[32] Stanley J. Tambiah, *Culture Thought and Social Action: An Anthropological Perspective* (Cambridge: Harvard University Press, 1985), p. 188.

violent death such as a fatal motor accident is presumed to be the handiwork of the bloodthirsty deity. He is often described as one who has water at home and yet "prefers to bathe with human blood" (*olomi sile fẹjẹwẹ*). It is assumed that once enough of the animal's blood is shed, since it is the domestic animal closest to humans, Ogun's bloodthirsty instinct will be quenched. Several Ondo people I interviewed saw this as a substitute for human blood, "the destruction or surrender of something for the sake of something else normally of higher value."[33] Once the sacrifice is performed and declared acceptable to the deity, *Ayadi* and his associates (*ẹgbẹ ayadi*) are filled with joy. As he performs his own warlike dance around the town, the lyrics that accompany his dance refer to his role as the great sacrificer: "May the *Ayadi* who performs the sacrifice live long" (*Ayadi yo ṣe tutu, a ko wọn pẹ*).

The central role of the king is amply demonstrated in the ritual process, both in communicating an awareness of the significance of kingship in Ondo society and in demonstrating his relation to the deity. Ogun's full name is "ogunlade," the crowned one, and he is regarded as the first son of Oduduwa. Thus Ogun shares royal blood and kinship with the *Ọba*. The *Ọba*, in turn, performs sacrifices to invigorate and nourish this bond of common kinship and kingship with Ogunlade. Yet, the *Ọba* also recognizes Ogun's dual character, with benevolent and malevolent powers. The *Ọba* asks for the deity's favor for himself, to maintain a peaceful reign during his time, and he also pleads for nonviolence in his domain in the ensuing year, a request only Ogun can grant. Note that in the prayer said on his behalf at the Ogun Aiṣẹrọ shrine, Ogun's contradictory nature is acknowledged when he is described as "the pounded yam sour as corn porridge." Pounded yam, the favorite Ondo food, is here described as having a sour and unpalatable taste. But at the same time, the *Ọba* is asked to honor Ogun with all his earthly possessions in order to secure the deity's much desired favors. As the festival proceeds, the king's power and authority over both social and religious spheres is maintained and recognized. He was the first to perform Ogun's dance; it is taboo for any chief to dance before him or meet him on the path so that there is no temptation to challenge his right of way. The *Ọba* stops in the *Lisa*'s house are also significant, for *Lisa* is the person to whom the *Ọba* often delegates civil authority. The *Lisa*, on behalf of the chiefs and Ondo people, publicly pays homage to the *Ọba* and acknowledges his authority over his kingdom. As the palace servants dance around the town in the late evening, carrying the *Ọba*'s

---

[33] M. F. C. Boudillon and Meyer Fortes, eds., "Introduction," *Sacrifice* (London: Academic Press, 1980), p. 10.

symbols of authority, the big umbrella and the bugle, they sing the well-known song lyric, "The King is the greatest" (*Oba nlao, ee iwo*), which further confirms the king's authority. The king, in theory and in practice, is now placed in a position to mediate between rival authorities and to prevent any act of violence from erupting through an unrestricted display of power.

Hierarchy and Status

In addition to the roles and functions of the three persons discussed above, the demonstration of hierarchy and status in Ondo society is an important motif. As I observed earlier, the high chiefs take turns dancing in the early morning of the second day of Ogun's festival. Each *Ologun* devotee also dances around the city. Trouble starts when prestige and power acquired through chieftaincy titles on the one hand and the medicinal knowledge of the *Oloogun* (medicine men) on the other confront each other. This, as we noticed, normally takes place in narrow pathways where Ogun is thought to show his presence regularly. Although both the chiefs and the *Oloogun* are highly placed in the Ondo society, the latter are less frequently noticed, except during processions like this one. Ogun's festival provides the opportunity for the *Oloogun* to celebrate and the townspeople to recognize their significant but silent source of authority. As one of the signposts reads, *Ologun mo beru re* ("I am afraid of you, the medicine man"), an indication of the dread and fearful feeling that the common people show to the medicine men's and Ogun's devotee. The Ogun festival provides an opportunity for the *Oloogun* to challenge physically and symbolically the more recognized and visible authority of the chiefs, who make decisions in Ondo daily life.

If Ogun's procession often results in the demonstration of authority of the chiefs and the medicine men, it also involves a display and test of superiority among the *Oloogun* themselves. In a sense it is a re-creation of the old Yoruba ethos of warfare and conquest, when bravery and gallantry were rewarded, and it is an opportunity to test the combat readiness of those who in wartime would be the leaders of the warrior groups. It is significant to note that this is the only period in Ondo festivals when medicine and magical power, both of which are ordinarily considered harmful and dangerous to civil life, are openly displayed.

Ogun Worship as Popular Religion

Earlier in this chapter, I described Ogun as the *orisa* of the masses. Ogun is the focus of Ondo's popular religion for several reasons. In Ogun festivals every segment of society is represented. This is the only festival where children, domestic servants, foreigners, artisans, circumcision doctors (*alakọmọla*), and religious and political authorities perform as Ogun devotees. Since the deity is linked to professionalism, every conceivable person participates: warriors, blacksmiths, traders, etc. Women, who are less frequently seen in Ondo festivals, play very prominent roles on these occasions. Indeed, it is a time when women-dominated professions, such as traditional medical pediatrics (*alaagbo ọmọde or olomitutu*) and women's market associations display their wares and advertise their profession.

The festival also recognizes humanity's indebtedness to Ogun as the founder of metals, the essential ingredient for technological development. Therefore, through Ogun, iron and steel become the link between the ancient and modern civilization. Above all, the Ogun festival is an occasion to commemorate the memory of deceased ancestors and cultural heroes. The exploits and deeds of old warriors and medicine men, passed on in legends and stories, are remembered and celebrated in a special way. It is not uncommon to find old photographs of recently-deceased great-grandfathers brought out and carvings of long-deceased soldiers on display in windows overlooking the main streets. Descendants of deceased chiefs and *Ologun* bring out the Ogun of their deceased fathers. The women dress in their father's oversized garments and dance around the town. In a sense, Ogun's shrine represents the local cenotaph where sacrifices and offerings are made to the community. Ogun vividly symbolizes the deeds of known and unknown local warriors. The motifs of ancestor veneration in Ogun's festival are presented in an idealized form so that the present-day patriots are unlike the past heroes. One *Ologun* dance group, holding the picture of a famous deceased high chief, indicates in its lyrics: "Be it parrot, or the cock, there is no bird like the white eagle" (*odidẹ, akukọ, ko si ẹiyẹ bi ọkin mọ*). No one is insignificant or without a ritual part to play in the Ogun festival.

Finally, a dominant feature of the festival is the display of violence and molestation of the public. Once in a while an Ologun charges into the crowd to display the destructive might and power of the deity, while blue and black powder is freely sprayed on onlookers with the intention of provoking a fight. At times these clashes lead to serious violence and accidents. The manner and form in which the animals are sacrificed also illustrate this same motif. Several scholars of Ogun's tradition have touched upon the occurrence of violence in Ogun's worship[34]. The themes of challenge, combat and violence that resonate in Ogun's myths and rituals reflect as much the nature of the deity as of the society; yet violence is resolved and brought under control

---

[34] Ṣoyinka, 1976; Barnes, 1980; Pemberton, 1979, 1986.

through recognized higher authority within the society itself. Commenting on similarly-structured rituals of violence in Ogun's festival of the Ila people in Western Yoruba states, Pemberton aptly remarks that "the entire Ogun festival is an acknowledgement of the reality and ambiguity of violence in human experience and that it is also an affirmation of the potential interpretation of Yoruba social life. . . the Yoruba acknowledge that life is not without conflict and that it entails death, but that life is not simply or essentially a project to death or a flight from violence."[35]

In conclusion, Ogun's festival has transcended time and space in the Ondo imagination. I believe that the festival will remain long after several aspects of Ondo traditional religion have disappeared.

---

[35] John Pemberton, III. "Sacred Kingship and the Violent God: The Worship of Ogun Among the Yoruba," *Berkshire Review*, Vol. 14, 1979, pp. 102-103.

Chapter VI
Women's Rituals of Reproduction and Wealth

In this study I have referred on several occasions to the importance of women in Ondo myths, history, and rituals. In this chapter, I shall examine two central and related ceremonies that focus essentially on females. The first is *Obitun*, the girls' puberty rite, and the second is *Ọdun Aje*, a festival devoted to the Ondo goddess of wealth and prosperity.

Obitun: Girls' Puberty Ceremony

The Setting

Among the Ondo people, an initiation ceremony referred to as *Obitun* (literally, "maiden") was performed for girls at puberty prior to marriage. In the Ondo view, it was a social stigma for a girl not to be initiated when she reached puberty. As one informant put it, it was derogatory for a girl to be told: *we ṣobitun, we ṣ'apọn, ki we ṣe* ("You did not perform *Obitun*, neither did you perform *Aapọn*, what did you perform?").[1] This was tantamount to being told that she had achieved nothing in life.

Another informant said that it was no longer necessary to perform the ceremony since most Ondo have become christian, and Christian baptism had replaced it. This remarks suggests that *Obitun* was still widely-practiced until the 1920s, the early years of Christianity in Ondo, when it was considered no longer necessary and therefore became extinct.

If *Obitun* as a puberty rite is completely extinct today, it survives in another fashion. In major cultural shows in the country, groups of college-aged dancers perform dances that are replicas of the ancient puberty ceremony. The popularity of these groups and their award-winning shows indicates the prestige and value of the ceremony in the past.

I interviewed several older women who had taken part in the Obitun rites. Two other main sources proved quite helpful in reconstructing the stages of this elaborate ceremony. The first source is the account given by the Ondo

---

[1] *Aapọn* refers to the male initiation ceremony that is also extinct.

historian Chief Ojo, whom I interviewed on several occasions and who has given a detailed description of each day's celebration in his book.[2] A sizeable part of my description of the ceremony relies on this account. The second source is a tape-recorded interview by the Yoruba Historical Research Group with a man credited with laying the foundation for the contemporary dramatization in which the ceremony once existed. The timely recording of this ceremony was remarkable, and I will comment briefly on it.

During the visit of the Ifẹ research team, led by Professor A. Akinjọgbin, to Ondo, the members had been informed of a local expert on *Obitun*, and the group went in search of him. The 78-year old man was seriously ill when they arrived at his house and his wives told the group that he was not in (a not-unusual way of turning away unwanted guests in Yoruba society). However, the man overhead this discussion, shouted from inside that he was home, and gladly agreed to give the interview. His account of the rites focused upon its dramatic action, the elaborate songs and mime which the ceremony often includes. At the end of this interview, the team promised to return sometime in the near future. The man died in the evening of the day after the interview. When I was engaged in my fieldwork in Ondo five years later, many people to whom I spoke still referred to this man's knowledge of the *Obitun* rites, but with a note of pity directed at me since he would have been the best possible person to consult.

In the distant past, the *Obitun* rite was organized during important family ceremonies, especially at the death of the most senior members of the *ẹdili* (patrilineage).[3] But in the more recent past, the ceremony assumed greater importance and became associated with chieftaincy installation ceremonies, before dying out.

Any number of girls could perform the ceremony jointly, so whenever there was an occasion for this ceremony those girls who had reached puberty, within and outside the lineage, would be informed and their parents would start to make elaborate preparations. These preparations included, among other things, assembling plenty of foodstuffs, the necessary clothing, and ornaments for the various ceremonies.[4]

---

[2] Jerome Ojo, *Yoruba Customs from Ondo*, pp. 52-60.

[3] In Ondo today, installation ceremonies are marked by what is referred to as *peto*. Here, young girls (far younger in age than girls who participate in the *Obitun* ceremony) are dressed and adorned with ornaments and they accompany the initiates out in the ceremonial dances.

[4] Ojo, *Yoruba Customs from Ondo*, lists the necessary food items for the ritual: forty-four kola nuts, nine coconuts, the hind leg of a Colobus monkey (*edun*), palm wine, salts, and yam. In addition, expensive traditional woven cloths (*aṣọ oke*), red coral beads, beads from palm nut shells, blue tabular beads, cowries, and different types of ceremonial drums were assembled. (cf., p. 53)

The ceremony normally started on the day of the *Ugha Nla* (the assembly of the council of chiefs), which also corresponded to the major market day. The advantage of holding the ceremony on this day was twofold. First, most members of the lineage and the larger community would be at home and able to take advantage of it to witness the admission of new members into the adult group. Second, the market day is an auspicious day for women when most of their activities are performed. Moreover, it is a favorable time when the malignant spirits or shades, which the rites are meant to exorcise, are thought to be most prone to attack the initiates.[5]

The day before the ritual, the bodies of the initiates were marked with a black substance called *ani*. They would later add red marks of *osun* (camwood, *Pterocarpus tinctorus*). On the morning of the first day, the *Obitun*'s hair was plaited in a special hairstyle called *agbe*;[6] those who wished to also decorated their hair with big beads made of palm nut shells. From then on, they could not carry loads on their heads until the end of the ceremony. The *Obitun* were dressed in an elaborate ceremonial outfit of initiation: an initiate would tie a white wrapper of *sanyan* (a locally-woven brown or white silk cloth) around her waist on top of which she would wear an expensive *alaari* (also a locally-woven cloth of scarlet color). The initiate would be further ornamented with brass bangles placed on her ankles and coral beads on her neck and arms.

Accompanied by their relatives, the initiates would then proceed to the house of the nearest *opoji* ("female chief") to propitiate *aje* ("goddess of wealth and fertility"). Each woman chief has a movable shrine of *aje* in her custody. This goddess is propitiated with two kola nuts, the hind leg of a Colobus monkey, salt, and one penny-cowry. From there, the initiates would proceed to the house of their ritual female sponsor, usually an elderly woman, who would make an offering of two kola nuts and one penny for fertility by touching the breast of the initiate with these objects.

In the evening of the first day, all the *Obitun* and their relations would gather in the house of the person organizing the ceremony, where they would dance and sing to a special type of drumming referred to as *esi*. These songs consisted of lyrics in praise of prominent chiefs and important people in the town. The head of the household, normally a male chief, would then conduct a ritual invocation of the sacred drum in preparation for the next rite. As we

---

[5] In Yoruba religious belief, the malignant spirits of *abiku* (children who die young only to be born again to their original mothers) could appear in any place and at any given moment. However, the market days are the most probable time for them to attack their victims.

[6] *Agbe* literally means calabash, which means that the hairstyle is made in manner resembling a calabash.

saw in the previous chapter, this drum rite consists of offering kola nuts and placing a thigh of a Colobus monkey on the face of the drum, and prayers are said on behalf of the *Obitun*.

Eyegbe: Mock Betrothal Ceremony

A mime-rite, called *eyegbe*, followed this invocation. Since the *eyegbe* was also dramatized by this highly-knowledgeable informant, I shall first give a summary of what happened in it and then reproduce below the text of the ritual drama. Here, a mock betrothal negotiation took place between the *Obitun*'s father and a man representing the family of a fictitious spouse (selected to stand in for the would-be husband of the *Obitun*).

The bridegroom came in and prostrated himself on the floor in front of the father-in-law and asked for the hand of the maiden in marriage. The father-in-law requested two gourds of palmwine, the traditional gift of betrothal in Ondo society. In the second stage, the bridegroom returned with two gourds for the father-in-law. At the same time the father invoked blessings upon the maiden and especially prayed for the blessings of children and long life for the *Obitun*. The father then promised to give the maiden to the man but with a warning that once given she should not be deprived of the good things of life, nor should she be maltreated. The third time, the bridegroom came in to renew his request. The father-in-law then accepted the proposition for his daughter's marriage.

The text of the ceremony, which had three stages, appears below.

(Part I)

(The fictitious bridegroom came in while the audience sits.)

Bridegroom:	Bai lẹ o.
Father-in-law:	Hee.
Bridegroom:	Mo ri ọmọde kan n'ode
	O wu mi,
	Mi ma mu ṣ'aya
	A fi iwọ obi hun
	Oun mo ti wa e yẹn.
Father-in-law:	Otitọ wo wu mi kẹ ọmọ mi
	Mo dẹn a mọ mọ ni kẹẹ
	Ṣugbọn, la fẹ ago jẹ jẹ jẹ meji
	Duo rọ ẹmu si wa
	Duo rọ sinu ugo
	Duo ko si nọ ẹ wa
	Un yẹn mu bere ọmọ
	Ni pẹ muṣẹlẹ 'e yẹn.

(Part II)

Bridegroom:	Oun mo gbe wa o bai.
Father-in-law:	Otitọ ma mọmọ yi kẹ o
	Ee kan, Ee bajẹ
	Ma dẹn pa ọmọ mi nupa kupa
	Ọmọ ma mu kẹ yi
	Ọmọ mẹsan han bi kẹ in
	Ọ kọ kan họn dẹn a ka bi hun.
	Oriṣa majọ da mulogbo, damu latọ,
	Aṣẹ ẹ.

(Part III)

Bridegroom:	Mo ma dẹn tun wa o bai.
Father-in-law:	Eee, ọmọ ma mu kẹi, ma mebi pa
	Ma mode ji
	Adiro Kan aṣọ iṣi e in
	Bo ṣe ọmọ mẹsan o hi nu ẹ
	O dẹn a bi kẹẹ
	Oriṣa majọ, damu logbo, damu latọ
Bridegroom: (Facing the initiates)	Lẹ o Obitun
	Ẹ mẹ lọ, wo ma ṣo bitọn
	Ati bẹ gẹlẹ o
	Si bẹ nko, un yi a gi han dede po
	Oun wo ma
	Mu ṣọkan in o

TRANSLATION

(Part I)

(The fictitious bridegroom arrived and prostrated himself before the father-in-law)

Bridegroom:	Hello, father.
Father-in-law: (responding)	Hee.
Bridegroom:	I saw a girl outside,
	whom I like,
	and I wish to marry her.
	I was told that you are the father so
	I decided to come.
Father-in-law:	Truly, I admire you my son
	And I will truly give you the girl in marriage.
	However, go and bring two gourds.
	Fill them with palm wine,
	And bring them for me.
	That is what we used in the olden days from
	the beginning of time to ask for the hand of
	the maiden in marriage.

(Part II)

(The bridegroom returned with two gourds for the father-in-law.)

Bridegroom: Here they are, father

Father-in-law: Speaking truly,[7] I will give you this daughter of
                                       mine.
                                       No one must tamper with her, she must be
                                       taken care of.
                                       Don't maltreat [beat] her.
                                       This daughter that I am about to give you
                                       Will give birth to nine children.
                                       And she will give birth to them in succession
                                       [one by one].[8] (Hereafter, the father-in-law im-
                                       plores the goddess *majọ* for long life and pros-
                                       perity.)
                                       And so it shall be.

(Part III)

(The bridegroom returned to renew his requests.)

Bridegroom: I have come again, Father.

Father-in-law: Yes, this child that I will give in marriage,
                                       Don't starve her; don't allow her to roam
                                       about homeless, and don't lock her out.
                                       A hearth once molded is never removed[9]
                                       If it is nine children that she has in her, she
                                       will surely give birth to them for you.
                                       (Hereafter, he continued begging the goddess
                                       majọ for prosperity and long life for the bride.)

Bridegroom: (now facing the
Obitun)   Hi! bride.
                                       We are about to go,
                                       You are about to be initiated
                                       However, what we are going to tell you
                                       tonight,[10] you must keep in mind.

---

[7] Here the father-in-law would make a firm promise to his daughter's suitor and ensure that
he was making an honest deal. This is an indication of the controversy that often surrounds
betrothal periods before marriage. It is not uncommon for would-be fathers-in-law to make false
promises to several suitors in an attempt to collect several gifts from them or to ensure that their
daughter is given to a very rich bidder. At times it may be a desire to screen a series of men who
have shown their interest so as to ensure that the best of them is finally chosen for their daughter.
See for example the old Yoruba play: *Adukẹ Ọpẹlẹngẹ and Her Seven Suitors*.

[8] An attitude towards twins in Ondo culture is expressed here. Perhaps it confirms the
recently-held view that, unlike the people in other parts of Yorubaland who see the birth of twins
as good luck, the Ondo show less appreciation for multiple births. Audrey Richard's account of
puberty rites among the Bemba records a similar attitude in the initiation song called "Cen-
tipede"; see her *Chisungu: A Girls' Initiation Ceremony Among the Bemba of Northern
Rhodesia* (London: Faber and Faber Ltd., 1956), p. 105.

[9] This means that once she is married she should not be removed from her husband's house
(i.e., divorced), like a hearth which once made remains there permanently.

[10] This refers to the moral lessons in the *Egbee* songs to follow.

Ojo records a role-reversal rite that takes place in the course of this mock betrothal rite, called *Eyegbe*:

A woman, dressed as a man by tying a wrapper across her shoulder, gets up to dance around three times in place of the man who has just spoken (the bridegroom). On the third occasion, she seizes the hand of the *Obitun* to show her as his wife and the onlookers applaud.[11]

Egbee Songs Ceremony: Counseling the Initiates

When this ritual drama is over, the group gathers together to sing and dance for the initiates. The songs contain explicit instructions to prepare the bride for her new role as wife. Part of the *egbee* ceremony is reproduced below.

Egbe mọ ṣe yọhọ yọhọ
Logboṣẹrẹ ọmọ
Ọmọ ehe ipẹ ju
Oun iye me ipẹ ṣe
O da titun ọla, ojoye seipẹ
Awa dede a hi ka kọli
O Ya hun mato do ma ku
A ma gbohun s'oke nalẹ yi o
(Chorus) Egbee o loye loye o obitun
(Singer) Obitun lẹ ẹ o ọran nṣo mi
Due johe, jue mu j'ẹdon, mẹ mọ mugbẹ ẹ.
Duẹ lẹ ẹ o, e e ọran m'ṣomi
Due loṣe lẹ hẹ lẹ hẹ non ẹni o
Me ma mugbẹ ẹ
(Chorus) Obitun lẹ o e e ọran mu ṣo mu
(Singer) Mo bẹku lọ o. Ẹku kẹẹ mo bẹ ku odo
Mo baye lọ o aye kẹẹ
Mo baye odo
Alaye gbe yegbe, awa yoko, awa bọ
Osanyin baa, ọsanyin baa mara gbodo
Oludegbe Oludegbe o mu de
Opa Oheogunjo, dee o mude o mude
Onibuka goi dee o mude o mude
Ẹdọn ma yan, ọgọhẹ ma d'ẹdọn yan
Ẹdọn ma wẹ, ọgọhẹ ma dẹdọn wẹ
Obiri po, obiri po, obiri po
Oluku mi ndi ṣe sa a koun n'ori igi
Eyiyi o o hi origi
Oluku mi ndi ṣe sa a ko hun n'ọrọta
Oorun e ho n'ọrọta
Oluku mi ndi ṣe s a ko hun nibi gbigbẹ,

---

[11] Jerome Ojo, *Yoruba Customs from Ondo*, p. 56.

Ekuku o hibi gbigbẹ
Oluku, mi ndi se ṣa a koun n'etomi
Eera o hi etomi
Oluku mi ndi se ṣa o ko hun nibo ti yẹn
Mo rin rin, nko fubo ti yẹn.
Ọkọ ẹ ja koko,
Ale ẹ ja lọbẹ
Ṣu o ka toi l'ọbẹ waiya
Eeeee eeee eee eee
Ṣuku, ṣuku lẹ kẹ rẹ
Gbagi, gbagi lẹ kẹ rẹ
Balogun, ajaja maji o he[12]

TRANSLATION

Let the chorus ring out loud.
Logboṣẹrẹ [his title], the bricklayer,
Who builds with perfection
Out of the use of mere mud.
He brings inovation into bricklaying and became a chief among bricklayers.
We all started to build;
He gave way for the vehicle to pass, so as not to run down and be killed.[13]
We must all raise our voice [be ready to sing] tonight. Egbee [the chorus] the wise[14]
knows better than the maiden.
Hello, maiden, the cynosure of all eyes,
When you were eating donkey I did not know.
Listen, maiden, the cynosure of all eyes,When you were relaxing on a mat [sleeping]
I did not know.[15]
Hello, maiden, the cynosure of all eyes,
I have gone to the village
Ẹku that leads to a stream.
I have gone to the open road,
The open road that leads to the stream.
We have gone to the farm and we have come back.[16]

---

[12] These are vocables of not much significance in the song.

[13] The first seven lines are devoted to the acquired praise names of the singer. According to evidence I gathered, he was the late president of the Ondo bricklayers association, and so was responsible for certifying a house after its completion. The young man who informed me about this said that he used to go around with a piece of charcoal chalk and write '*Eyi, dara o Dudu*' ("This is certified, signed Dudu") on any newly-completed house. This job earned him these appellations and praise names contained in what he himself records as part of the *Obitun* song.

[14] This line refers to the elderly people present. They are wise, having been through the rites themselves, and out of the experience of life they know better than the newly-initiated.

[15] By now the maiden is assumed to have been courted by some men and perhaps to have a fiancé already. The song refers to the fact that courtship or affairs before *Obitun* ceremony take place secretly.

[16] Since it is a public ceremony, most townspeople would be back from their farm to watch this celebration.

The Ọsanyin [oracle of medicine] is very good-looking.[17]
Oludegbe, Oludegbe.
Broom sticks are not equal.
An amputated hand cannot reach the head.
The monkey wants to match but his buttocks prevent him from matching.
The monkey wants to swim but his buttocks prevent him from swimming.
Obiri po, obiri po, obiri po[18]
My paramour asked me to bring food for him on a tree
But ants are on the tree.[19]
My paramour asked me to bring food for him on a rock
There is sun on the rock.
My paramour asked me to bring food for him on a dry place;
There is sand on the dry place.
My paramour asked me to bring food for him at the river bank;
There is mud on the river bank.
My paramour asked me to bring food for him in a far distant place;
But I never found the far distant place.
Your husband is plucking cocoa;
Your paramour is plucking something else.
You did not come to earth for the sake of this one who is plucking something else.
Eeee eeee eee eee
(deleted verses)[20]

On this day, when the egbee song was over, the guests feasted on food, usually *iyan* (pounded yam), prepared exclusively by the *Obitun*; it was regarded as a test of her maturity and a foretaste of her duties at home.

Rites of Exorcism

On the third day, a rite of exorcism took place; a girl referred to as *Kumasi* (literally, "let there not be death") was chosen to attend to the needs of the initiate during the period of her seclusion. She tried to expel the malignant spirit *ọgba* or Abiku, believed to be common among maidens in the prepuberty stage, from the body of the *Obitun*. In doing so, *Kumasi* would touch her head with the ritual objects, three kola nuts, three *akara* (fried bean balls), and the hind leg of any bush animal, and would recite the following formula:

---

[17] Ọsanyin, the god of medicine, is usually portrayed as a one-legged man; here he is seen as beautiful and fleshy.

[18] A type of drumming or dance.

[19] Perhaps the most important lesson for the maiden and would-be wife is to avoid the temptation of developing relationships with male friends (as paramours); the song shows that making food for an outside friend is an undesirable thing and something to be discouraged. Here, an excuse is given that makes the illicit love affair impossible.

[20] These verses are composed of vocables which vaguely suggest abusive words. They are translations of the connotations and not explicit translations of the text.

We remove the *ogba* from your flesh,
We remove the *ogba* from your bones,
May the *ogba* leave you forever.[21]

Afterwards, a stand-in spouse[22] selected to play the role of the ritual bridegroom for the occasion placed kola nuts and an *akara* (bean cake) on the *Obitun*'s palm and blessed her so that she would have along life and many children. In return the obitun blessed her would-be husband. To carry out this blessing, she knelt down and poured some palm wine from one of the three gourds standing by into a basin (in fact only one of the gourds contains palm wine). She also covered the man's face with an *abebe* (fan), an important woman's symbol in Ondo, and made him sip palm wine as if she were feeding him. She then poured out the rest of the palm wine into the basin.

In the evening, the attendant girl took a piece of pounded yam, dipped it into melon sauce, and threw it out into the open yard while again reciting this formula:

Ogba, this is your pounded yam.
Do not bother us anymore.
Accept this and go away.[23]

She also added a cracked walnut and a kola nut to this offering. The third-day rite would be repeated on the seventh day with the number of ritual objects having been increased to seven.

Throughout the period of her seclusion the initiate would be properly fed. This custom reminds one of the often-reported 'fattening ceremony' that accompanies initiation rites among the Calabar people of the Cross River state of Nigeria.

Special feasts were arranged for the *Obitun* and her friends on either the seventh or eighth day, depending on which day was more convenient for the planners. For the celebration, a large tortoise (among other things) was cooked and, unlike the annual *Odun-Oba* where nursing mothers were given primary roles of participation:

. . . a nursing mother may not partake of the food used during *Obitun* celebrations because it is believed to bring ill fortune if mother and child both partake of these meals. Any mother may, however, eat of the food if she has a child who is old enough and refuses to take part of the food.[24]

---

[21] Ojo, *Yoruba Customs from the Ondo*, p. 57. Ojo suggested that any child in Ondo generally has three names and for those girls who do not have three, their *Oriki*-praise names would be substituted.

[22] If, however, the initiate has a fiancé, he would play the role of the ritual husband.

[23] Ojo, *Yoruba Customs from the Ondo*, p. 57.

[24] Ibid., p. 58.

This reveals an important aspect of Ondo thought. Since the ceremony is meant to aid fertility, a nursing mother could not benefit from it. The internal logic is that by abstaining she would open up the way for her children to receive the blessing of fecundity. I have heard of men who refused to marry a particular woman because the mother of the woman had many children and so by indication had given birth to all the children allocated to her line by the divinity, including those of her daughters. The same popular belief applies to kingship situations. Whenever a king stays too long on the throne, it is believed that the next king will not reign very long, since the previous king had added to his part of the assigned reigning period.

On the morning of the ninth and final day, the final expulsion of the spirit (*lile ọgba*) was performed. A coconut was cracked and the milk used to make a trace of the malignant spirit trailing from the inner room through the door to the outside open yard. The coconut was left outside for whoever desired to eat it there. The girls then proceeded from the inner room to the street outside until they reached a crossroad,[25] where they carried out the final rite of exorcising their *ọgba*. On their way they sang the following song:

Ọgba gbobi o
Ọma gbohosa
Duo lọ
Ọgba gbobi o
Ọgba, accept this kola nut.
Accept this walnut, too,
Accept whatever thing you want to have
And depart.
Ọgba, accept this kola nut.

As a preamble to this final rite, the maidens were warned not to look back once the final rite was performed. As they arrived at the sacrificial place, the ritual specialist split open the offerings of kola nut and walnuts and placed them on the intersection of the roads. The initiates then returned home without looking back. In the late afternoon, their sponsors would once again offer two kola nuts and one cowry-penny on their behalf to the deity of the 'breast' of the initiates; this offering is referred to as *bibọ aya* ("propitiating the breast").

---

[25] There is some contradictory evidence as to the actual place where this final rite is performed, since another informant told me that it is performed in a place called *Lagbogbo*, the eastern gate of Ondo town.

Outing Ceremony

The same evening, an outing ceremony was performed. The *Obitun* dressed up in a fashion similar to their first-day attire. Although it was uncommon for initiates to be pregnant, those who had already shown signs of it added a new set of necklaces called *abǫn*. Few "special" maidens among them (like the daughter of the king, or *sǫra*, the custodian, and chief priest of *Ǫramfẹ* deity) added coral beads to their hair as a show of their special status. These newly-initiated women danced around the town as a public demonstration of their new status and initiation.

The dance followed the structure of an adult ceremonial and ritual dance. It was the first occasion for the initiates to act like adults. They danced to *kekege* music and moved in a counterclockwise direction. The dance procession stopped at various shrines in Ondo, such as Ogun Aiṣẹrǫ, Ogun Lẹi, and Aje, where they would offer two kola nuts and a cowry-penny. In the late evening, each initiate returned to her own home where her parents offered a sacrifice of a chicken to the guardian spirit represented in the peregun tree (*Dracaeana fragrans*), which she had already planted in their backyard at the beginning of the initiation rites.

Interpretation

Obitun as an Aspect of Ondo Religion

The purpose of the *Obitun* initiation ceremony is clearly religious. Its function is to exorcise and appease the malignant spirits (*ǫgba*) that pose a threat to the young women at the time of puberty, when they were most vulnerable to attack. The girls" first menstruation indicated their physical maturity and showed them to be a "potential source of danger to the community . . . ."[26]

Since menstruation involves the emission of blood and feelings of pain, the Ondo believe that this is the time when the uninitiated girls can be snatched away by their *ǫgba*. To prevent this, they must be set aside and purified to assure a peaceful passage. On more than three occasions, the *ǫgba* is exorcised and the girls purified. Offerings are made to *oriṣa* Aje and other deities to ensure their fecundity, and verbal appeals are directed at *oriṣa* Majǫ (as we saw in *Egbee* rites) to look upon them favorably, especially in childbirth. Above all, each *Obitun* plants a 'tree of life' to be propitiated by her for life. This

---

[26] Audrey I. Richards, *Chisungu: A Girls' Initiation Ceremony Among the Bemba of Northern Rhodesia*, p. 19.

is expected to mystically guarantee her a lasting sustenance in her new role as wife and mother.

In the Yoruba four-day cycle the special days for the rites are the first, third, seventh, and ninth days of the ceremony.[27] Every social rite, be it naming, burial, or chieftaincy title-taking, must adopt these days for special offerings and public outing dances, as they are considered to be the days when the gods are most visible for propitiation. Once the ceremony is concluded and the *Obitun* has become a full-fledged member of the adult group, they propitiate all the major divinities located all around the town. Henceforth, the initiates may participate in all the religious rites prescribed by custom for adult female members. They can be elected into *opoji* (female chieftaincy) and thereby become the custodians of Aje, the goddess of wealth and fertility.

The Stranger Spirit and the Origin Myth of the Obitun Ceremony

Since the focal point of the *Obitun* ritual is to exorcise the *ogba* in the *Obitun*, it is necessary for us to examine this phenomenon as it relates to the total ceremony. At first glance, it is difficult to find the internal logic between the ceremony and the malignant spirit, or shade, which the rites purport to exorcise. All the people I interviewed told me that every child is susceptible to the influence of the spirit. But in the neighboring town of Ile-Oluji, where the *Obitun* ceremony also forms a strong part of their belief system, a myth of the ceremony's origin is told which credits its beginnings to a 'stranger spirit'.

According to Chief Adegbamigbe, the Ile-Oluji local historian for many years, the origin of the *Obitun* ceremony is as follows:

There was a male slave who sojourned in Ile-Oluji for quite a long time. After some time, the slave left Ile-Oluji for Ipogun (a nearby town) and carried with him his idol [i.e., a god], but unfortunately he did not reach Ipogun, for he died on the road in the jungle and there was nobody to remove either his dead body or the idol.

The incident coincided with a period when the *Obas*, chiefs, and important people in Ondo and Ile-Oluji districts were dying in rapid succession. When the people consulted Ifa divination as to why their leaders were dying like this, they were told that the cause had something to do with an important stranger. They investigated throughout the district and later detected that it was the lack of care for the idol left by the dead slave that resulted in the death of the *Obas*, chiefs, and important people. They

---

[27] The reason for adopting these days of the weekly ritual is not quite clear. However, Reichard's comment on the importance of the first day of ritual ceremony among the Navaho may also be true of the Ondo: "So much importance is attached in myths and practice to beginning an event or to the first time an act takes place as to make initiation a major symbol. Apparently the first day has power because it signifies the purposes and predicts the outcome." Gladys Reichard, *Navaho Religion*, p. 248-249.

were later advised by their oracle to take the idol to the *afin* [palace] of *Ọba Ọṣemawe*. When the idol was to be brought from Ilẹ–Oluji on Ipogun road, it was not to be taken through the heart [center] of Ilẹ-Oluji town; hence, the carriers passed from Okedoko through Otapọtẹ to Ṣamọlọgbẹ from where they took it to Ondo (sic).

Then the *Ọṣemawe* was advised to propitiate the god with a tortoise. After this, the district was no longer plagued with death. Then, as a mark that they had overcome their difficulty, the men shaved their heads and made great feasts. The women were dressed in beads and proclaimed that they were then free from evil spirits. Later on this evolved into the *Obitun* rite of the people.[28]

The narrative certainly refers to what has often been called, in the history of religions, "the dead without status."[29] In the literature, the term often refers to children who die young without undergoing the necessary status-giving rite or to those who are old but have been deprived of decent mortuary rites that guarantee them a peaceful passage into the afterlife (i.e., the ancestor world). Juha Pentikainen aptly describes this situation:

An individual who has undergone a bad death is not believed to succeed in reaching the community of the dead. It is feared that he will only get halfway and remain in an eternal transition phase and haunt the living in one form or another.[30]

Although it is not clear how the propitiation of the stranger deity was transformed into a rite of passage in the Ondo story, we do know that the belief in a reappearance of children who die young, referred to as *abiku* or *ọgba*, is quite common in Ondo. It would appear from the above myth of origin that the permanent liminal status of the stranger spirit (represented in his neglected god) became associated with the *ọgba* phenomenon which constantly threatens children before they reach puberty.

The Social Dimension of the Ceremony

The major social consequence of the ceremony was that it afforded the family of the initiated an opportunity to declare the availability of marriageable girls in their lineages. If the *Obitun* already had a fiancé, a betrothal rite was actually contracted between the girl and the would-be husband. This public announcement was possible because the ceremony coincided with the big market day and a chieftaincy ceremonial period when a broad cross-section of the community was in town. The publicity implied in the ceremony itself was supported by the reference to the initiate as "the cynosure of all eyes" in the *egbee* song rite.

---

[28] A. Adegbamigbe, *History, Laws, and Customs of* Ilẹ-Oluji, p. 22.

[29] Juha Pentikäinen, "The Symbolism of Liminality," in *Religious Symbols and Their Functions*," Heralds Biezais, ed. (Stockholm: Almqvist and Wiksell International, 1969), p. 162.

[30] Ibid.

The *egbee* song contains instructions on family and societal ethics, related to the new marital life the girl was about to enter. She was warned, among other things, to resist extramarital love gestures from male friends, to maintain good relations with her in-laws, and to show respect and tolerance for her co-wives, especially the senior wife.

The ceremony also provided an opportunity to honor the note-worthies in the town and surrounding communities. The *egbee* is filled with lyrics that resemble the song rite of Ondo, "let us now praise famous men." It is no wonder then that up until the time the Obitun ceremony died out,[31] the rite was held at the same time as other important community ceremonies.

Obitun as a "Rite of Passage"

Van Gennep's analysis of rites of passage and Victor Turner's elaboration of it provide a useful framework with which to interpret the *Obitun* puberty ritual. But first, let me examine the concept of the rite of passage.

In his book *Rites of Passage*,[32] Van Gennep argues that all rituals dealing with passages from one state to another have three rite sequences: *rites de séparation* (separation), when the previous state of things or status is left behind; *rites de marge*, when the initiates are in a state of becoming and the new state of life aspired to is still being fashioned; and *rites d'agrégation*, when the initiate is incorporated into the new state of life. Turner,[33] following Van Gennep, argues that the most important state in the threefold ritual is the transitional or "liminal" phase. He goes on to elaborate on the symbolic content of this middle phase, basing his discussion primarily on the Ndembu rites that he has studied. This theoretical framework of the ritual can be applied to the *Obitun* ceremony.

---

[31] This probably took place in the early years of Christianity in Ondo.

[32] Arnold Van Gennep, *Rites of Passage* (Chicago: University of Chicago Press, 1961). Other valuable analytical models that I have found quite helpful in looking at the same phenomenon are: Jane M. Shaughnessy, ed., *Roots of Rituals* (Grand Rapids, MI: Grand Rapids Press, 1973). According to Shaughnessy, "The three elements that have traditionally been associated with the religious and social process of acceptance into adult society are first, a period of *enforced retreat* from society; second, a personal *interior revolution*—the recognition by the initiate of something in herself that has to be purged away; and third, a *public rite* or ordeal to symbolize society's acceptance of the new purified individual." p. 24; and Bruce Lincoln (*Emerging from the Chrysalis*), who also suggests as a substitute for Van Gennep's three-tiered pattern "metamorphosis," 'magnification," and "emergence."

[33] Victor Turner, *Forest of Symbols* (Ithaca: Cornell University Press, 1967), p. 98.

Rite of Separation

As the initiation ceremony begins, the Obitun are separated from their normal daily routine. Their bodies are marked in black chalk, thus symbolically making them what Turner would call "structurally invisible" (though physically visible).[34] Perhaps the most visible sign of the separation rite in the *Obitun* ceremony is that the hair of the initiate is braided in the special manner referred to as *agbe*. As a result, she is prohibited from placing anything on it for a period of three months. Although the hair is not shaved, as in some other African rites of passage, the initiate's new hair style expresses the same symbolic meaning. We will explore this meaning further.

It is remarkable that in the extinct *aapọn* rites, the male initiation ceremony of the Ondo, the boys were required to have their hair shaved prior to any further initiation rite as a sign of their separation. In fact, the puberty ceremony is referred to as *fifari aapọn*, "shaving off the bachelor's hair,"[35] which suggests the significance of the hair-shaving rite in the total ceremony. It is the belief among the Yoruba that one's "outer head" (*ori ode*), on which the hair grows, is a replica of a more important "inner head" (*ori inu*). This is the source of an individual's destiny and the driving urge in life. The inner head is responsible for a man's performance and well-being, so to alter the shape of the outer head in ritual context is to make a break with the old and to signify the passage into the beginning of a new state of being.

As Droogers has pointed out, for the Wagenia of Central Zaire:

. . . shaving of the head was pre-eminently suitable as a symbol of a break in this phase. The novice was leaving something of the old phase behind him, and was re-entering a new period as a tabula rasa in this respect.[36]

What then can be made of the braided hair that replaces the shaving of hair observed in the Obitun ceremony? While it remains the custom among Yoruba males to shave off their hair both in ordinary situations and in life crisis rituals, by and large it is considered socially indecent for women to do so. However, changes in a woman's hair style are taken as a substitute to denote transition both in religious and social contexts. A recent study carried out on Yoruba hairstyles by Marilyn Hammersley Houlberg[37] has provided ample evidence to show that there exists a connection between hair style and

---

[34] Ibid.

[35] In the girls' puberty rites among the Nandi of Kenya, the hair is shaved off also.

[36] Andre Droogers, *The Dangerous Journey*, p. 109.

[37] Marilyn Hammersley Houlberg, "Social Hair: Yoruba Hairstyles in Southwestern Nigeria," in *The Fabrics of Culture*, Justice M. Cordwell and Ronald Aswarz, eds. (The Hague: Mouton Press, 1979).

life cycle and, moreover, that the different facets of the socio-political and ritual process of the Yoruba could be studied through an analysis of their hair styles over a period of time. She remarked:

Hair is especially appropriate as a ritual focus and social indicator since it is so highly visible and as a medium is capable of being modified in an endless number of patterns or entirely removed. It can be dressed in elaborate sculptural styles or it can be totally neglected. In a sense, hair can be considered a "process" symbol involving the element of time, since it is capable of growth and regenerating. Because of all these characteristics, hair is particularly suitable for indicating temporary changes.[38]

The *agbe* hair style signified the *Obitun* initiate's sacredness. It thus separated them from other uninitiated girls in Ondo.

In a recent important study Bruce Lincoln has questioned whether Van Gennep's imagery of the rite of separation as a movement from one social position to another along the line of territorial passage is applicable to women's puberty rites, which he believes lack any change of residence.[39] Lincoln's analysis of female puberty rites in several societies allowed him to state that "while this may be a time of isolation . . . it cannot be rightly called a separation: the initiand is not removed from the space she normally inhabits. Only the nature of her activity is changed, not her spatial locus."[40]

He further suggests that "although there are of course examples of male initiation in which true separation does not occur and examples of female initiation in which it figures prominently, it [separation] seems to be much more closely related to the men's rite."[41]

The theoretical significance of Lincoln's hypothesis, as he himself puts it, is that:

the lack of any true separation from one's former dwelling space is due, I submit, to the fact that women do not have open to them a variety of socio-political statuses through which they may pass by means of initiation. . . Rather than changing women's status, initiation changes their fundamental being, addressing ontological concerns rather than hierarchical ones. A woman does not become more powerful or authoritative but more creative, more ontologically real.[42]

---

[38] Ibid., p. 367.

[39] Lincoln, *Emerging from the Chrysalis*, pp. 100-101.

[40] Ibid., p. 101.

[41] Ibid., p. 100. The custom of separating pubescent girls from their normal habitat or homestead for the purpose of initiation into adulthood is not an exception to a general rule as Bruce Lincoln would argue, as such separation does take place in many African girls' initiation rites. Notable examples are the girls' initiation ceremony of the Sande society of the Mende people of Sierra Leone and the girls' puberty rites of the Nandi of Kenya.

[42] *Emerging from the Chrysalis*, pp. 101-104. I agree with Lincoln that initiation rites affect the ontological reality of the initiates.

It must be pointed out that the Ondo are an exception to the first part of the above hypothesis, namely, that women do not have socio-political status. As noted in the previous chapter, they possess not only socio-political status and ritual power, but also a stratified chieftaincy structure attained through ritual ceremonies just as their male counterparts. While not diminishing the heuristic value of Lincoln's hypothesis, what is more important in the Ondo context is the purpose for which the ceremony is carried out. If the ultimate aim of initiation is to make a pubescent girl a full-fledged member of the adult group, with the rights and privileges pertaining to it, the rite must reflect the social ethos of the people with whom she is to function.

A careful look at the Ondo social organization suggests a different picture than that which Lincoln has painted. For the Ondo people the dwelling house has generally remained the locus of women's activities, since they are more concerned with domestic duties. By contrast, the farm, the bush (in the case of hunters), or an outside location is the operating locus for men to carry out their duties as farmers, hunters and warriors.[43] The purpose of initiation is to make a child into an adult male or female. It is likely that the men in undergoing initiation will be put to a test, at least in a symbolic manner, in farming techniques, hunting disguises, and military techniques in appropriate contexts. The same applies to the pubescent female whose assigned duties are the upbringing of the family, trading, and general domestic duties.

The initiation lessons contained in the *egbee* rite deal precisely with those areas that are directly related to the dwelling house, i.e., the private domain of the society's life.

In view of the above I would propose, contrary to Lincoln, that the rite of separation need not necessarily relocate the residence of the initiate in order to be valid.[44] Rather, what is important is the ritual symbolic act of segrega-

---

[43] Jules-Rosette explains the continued persistence and revitalization of female initiation ceremonies in urban cities in contrast to the relative decline in male initiation ceremonies in terms of the defined roles of each sex in the community. She observed that whereas "men's initiation rites have a political focus in training males to assume permanent leadership responsibilities in their respective communities, they often entail instruction in the group's lore and oratorial skills. In contrast, women's initiation rites focus on domestic responsibilities and are structurally linked primarily to the family rather than to the community at large." Since the traditional role of males has been taken over by modern political structures, boys' initiation ceremonies, Jules-Rosette would argue, have become less common. See Bennetta Jules-Rosette, "Changing Aspects of Women's Initiations in Southern Africa: An Exploratory Study," in *Revue Canadienne de Études Africaines/Canadian Journal of African Studies*, 13 (1980), p. 390.

[44] I am in agreement with Bruce Lincoln in taking seriously Van Gennep's emphasis on "territorial passage" in the separation rites of *Rite de Passage*. However, one must point out that virtually every author who has adopted Van Gennep's scheme has modified it in one form or another, since Van Gennep did not address all the pertinent issues that would make his often-quoted theory thoroughly universal.

tion itself that makes the experience of transition possible in the most sacred environment. Turner's exposition of the rite of separation emphasized this symbolic aspect of the passage when he said in his recent study:

> The first phase of *separation*, the phase which clearly demarcates sacred space and time from profane or secular space and time (it is more than first entering a temple—there must be in addition a rite which changes the quality of *time* also, or constructs a cultural realm which is defined as "out of time," i.e., beyond or outside the time which measures secular processes and routines), includes symbolic behavior—especially symbols of reversal or inversion of things, relationships, and processes secular—which represents the detachment of the ritual subjects (novices, candidates, neophytes, or initiates) from their previous social status.[45]

On this note let me recall, once again, my experience with my informant on this aspect of the *Obitun* ceremony. The woman had informed me that the black paint is applied to the body of the *Obitun* on the first day and that only on the third day when the initiation was already in process would red paint be added. I wanted to make sure that both colors were not actually applied the first day, so I asked her again to explain the ceremonial process stage by stage. I was impressed by the clear picture she gave of this aspect of the ceremony. She was quick in telling me the essential purpose of the black paint: "It is to make her look different from the others. Only on the third day can we treat her as a royal person," i.e., apply red colored paint, since red signifies royalty.[46]

Liminal Phase

Having been symbolically separated from their ordinary daily-life routine, the initiates then entered the liminal phase of the initiation ceremony.

Again my informants expressed the 'ordeal' through which the initiates go: "They are kept awake morning and evening to participate in the *Egbee* song rite." They are referred to simply as *Obitun* and individual names are not mentioned. All are considered equal (though hierarchical roles of instructor and initiate still exist between the ritual elders and the *Obitun*) while undergoing the experience that Turner calls "*communitas*."[47] This is the state where

---

[45] Turner, *Process, Performance and Pilgrimage: A Study in Comparative Symbology*. Ranchi Anthropology Series, No 1 (New Delhi: Concept publishing Company, 1979), p. 16. Among such symbolic acts or rites of separation in secular rituals which Turner cited above is, for example, a sergeant who, in taking his first order after his passing out passage, moves a step forward, stands at attention, and salutes his superior officer. Such a movement from a profane to a sacred space would be regarded by Turner as a rite of separation.

[46] Field notes, July, 1980.

[47] Victor Turner, *Ritual Process* (Ithaca: Cornell University Press, 1969), p. 96.

the initiates exist in a uniform condition of equality akin to what Martin Buber termed the I-Thou relationship.[48] The initiates temporarily put behind them the social structure of normal life, i.e., "the patterned arrangements of role sets, status sets and status sequences consciously recognized and regularly operative in [Ondo] society,"[49] and they entered the life of anti-structure where the distinctions of rank and status become blurred.

Symbols of Liminality in the Obitun Ceremony

I will further analyze below the symbolism involved in the liminal phase of the *Obitun* rite: the ritual elements (objects and acts employed during this middle phase) are highly symbolic phenomena which aid the initiates' process of transformation. First of all, I want to explain the use of "symbols" in this context.

Anthropologists in general define symbols as the universal unit for human communication. Turner suggests in his study of the symbolic aspect of Ndembu ritual that symbols are polysemic or multivocal, i.e., they have many referents or multiple meanings at the same time. As he points out, "certain dominant or focal symbols conspicuously possess the property of multivocality which allows for the economic representation of key aspects of culture and belief."[50]

An important focal symbol, for example, the sacred drum, is encountered in the Obitun rites. We observed that the *Egbee* song rite was preceded by the ritual blessing of this sacred drum by the head of the homestead where the initiation took place. We also saw in the preceding chapters that the ritual blessing of the drum precedes all rites of renewal in the Ondo civil-religious system. In the *Obitun* context, the drum also functions as a liminal object, as it possesses in its very nature the mediating powers of the in-between.[51] This mediating role is derived from the drum's capacity to give utterances that are multivalent. As a Yoruba proverb points out, *Ko si ẹniti o ma ede ayan afi ẹniti o mu ọpa ẹ lọwọ* ("No one but the drummer himself can decipher what the language of the drum is"). In explanation of this proverb, an informant told me a story that points to the origin of the proverb and sheds light on the liminal nature of the sacred drum. An ancient gate once led to the Yoruba city

[48] Ibid, p. 136.
[49] Victor Turner, *Drama Fields and Metaphors* (Ithaca: Cornell University Press, 1971), p. 231.
[50] Victor Turner, *Forest of Symbols*, p. 50.
[51] N. Ross Crumrine, "Mediating Roles in Ritual and Symbolism: Northwest Mexico and the Pacific Northwest," *Anthropologica* N.S. XVIII (1976), p. 142.

of Ibadan, called *Bode lalupọn*, where a notorious gatekeeper always stood as a guard. A man playing a drum approached the gate, which put the gatekeeper on the alert. The rhythm from the drum could have been interpreted in two opposite ways: the first, in praise of the gatekeeper, and the other, in condemnation of him. The gatekeeper interpreted the sound as a condemnation and took offense at the drummer's behavior. The drummer got to the gate and, without giving him any chance to explain himself, the gatekeeper started flogging him. After much beating, the drummer managed to free himself and he explained to bystanders that he had intended the rhythm of his drum as a praise for the gatekeeper. The notorious gatekeeper was ashamed of himself for behaving in such a way to a drummer who was singing his praise. He apologized and freed him.

The ambiguity which the drum manifests enables it to function as an in-between symbol in many transitional rites. Riddles play similar roles in some folk cultures. Ian Hamnet's similar observation of the mediating power of riddles may also throw some light on this interesting phenomenon:

An ambivalent word, concept, or item of behavior can be considered as belonging to any of two or more frames of reference, according to the interpretation brought to bear upon it, or indeed to several or all such frames at once. It can therefore operate as a point of transition between these different frames of reference or classificatory sets. It can, indeed, mediate between sets that are not only different, but in many aspects opposed, and in this way it can form the basis for a differing system of classifications, or allow contrasting classifications and conceptual frameworks to co-exist at the same time. . .inconsistency, ambiguity, or ambivalence may be thought of as simply 'vague' or, what is not quite the same as *indeterminate*. It is the second aspect that is important here. A reference is 'vague' if it points to an insufficiently specified area of discourse; and this is perhaps a kind of ambiguity. But it can be ambiguous not only because it is vague for lack of specification but also because it fails to indicate which of two (or more) references is intended, though each possible reference may be fairly specific in itself.[52]

The drum, like the riddle, possesses multiple characteristics, as the proverb illustrates. As a result of its liminal or ambiguous nature, it mediates between two opposing states of being between which the initiate is caught and, as such, helps to hasten the process of transformation which the ritual aims to accomplish.

In addition to the blessing of the sacred drum, the *egbee* song rite also features clapping, shaking of *ṣẹkẹrẹ* (gourd rattles), and beating of *agogo*

---

[52] Ian Hamnet, "Ambiguity Classifications and Change: The Function of Riddles," *Man* N.S. 2 (1967): 381-383, quoted from N. Ross Crumrine, "Mediating Roles in Ritual and Symbolism," Ibid., pp. 142-143.

(metal gongs). Building on Needham's hypothesis that there is a connection between percussion and transitional rites, Vogt has argued that when used in a ritual context, percussive sounds transmit symbolically meaningful messages that are vital to the passage that is being experienced.[53] If Vogt is right, what then is the message that is transmitted in the percussive sounds that surrounded the *egbee* rite? The songs are largely secular, dealing with the mundane activities of the woman in her home, but they possess a 'sacred' quality through the medium of the sounds. The percussive instruments are the communication medium between the supernatural and man, and the sounds are the voices of the gods.[54]

Another focal symbol in the liminal stage of the *Obitun* ceremony is the tortoise, the main ingredient in the communal meal taken in the last phase of the liminal passage. The use of the tortoise in Ondo ritual is not, however, limited to the *Obitun* rites; it was a tortoise feast that was prescribed for the Ondo people at the critical moment of their origin and, as we observed in the Ogun festival, it was featured in the sacrificial rite performed for the deity. One may ask why the tortoise became such an important ritual animal in Ondo rites of transition. My interpretation is derived from the symbolism of the tortoise contained in a version of the Yoruba origin stories collected by Ulli Beier. According to the myth:[55]

Stones, men, and the tortoise were created by God. Life was given to men and the tortoise but not given to stones. Man and tortoise could not have children, nor could they die. When they became old, they became young again [*ajidewe*, i.e., rejuvenation]. The tortoise asked God for children and was told that in order to have children one must die. The tortoise decided he would make the switch; God endowed the tortoise with the ability to have children and at the same time made him suffer the throes of death as a result. Man became jealous because he wanted children, so God then endowed man with children. The stone never made the requests of these two so it remained truly immortal.[56]

Silverstein has also argued that the tortoise represents a liminal object. The myth shows that the tortoise is endowed with the qualities of death and life (fertility). It is also an amphibian and could live on dry land and near watery

---

[53] Evon Z. Vogt, "On the Symbolic Meaning of Percussion in Zinacanteco Ritual," *Journal of Anthropological Research* 33 (1977), p. 233.

[54] See my discussion with an informant on the importance of *upe* (the gourd trumpet), a commonly-used percussion instrument in Ondo rituals, in Chapter IV.

[55] I have taken this story and interpretation from Stella Bobbie Silverstein, *Structural Analysis of Ifa Divination of the Yoruba People of Nigeria* (unpublished paper).

[56] Ulli Beier, *Tortoise, Man and Stone*, 1966, pp. 58-59, quoted from Stella Bobbie Silverstein, cited above.

places.[57] It also represents an intermediary stage between man (who is absolutely mortal) and rock (which is completely immortal).[58] Thus, the tortoise functions as a mediating symbol that aids the initiatory process.

Food and Color Symbolism in the Obitun Rite

Two aspects of food usage can be observed in the liminal phase: (1) the provision and preparation of large quantities of various food items for the initiates; and (2) the offering of sacrificial food for the gods, especially the malignant spirits. The provision of food items is very significant in this ceremony. For one thing, it contradicts the understanding of the liminal process as presented by Turner, who argues that liminality is characterized by a process of frugality and perhaps even fasting or deprivation. However, an abundance of food is made available in the liminal phase of the *Obitun* rites of passage.[59]

As indicated earlier, the purpose of excessive eating is to make the initiate robust (to "fatten" her) so that she will be an admirable bride at the end of the ceremony for her future husband. Perhaps the most important meaning implicitly conveyed in this act is the education motif, as Turner's liminal theory suggests. The girl had the opportunity to learn by participating in the preparation of the meal itself, comprised of the traditional foods of the Ondo people. It is not a coincidence that many older Ondo women, when probed, complain that the younger ones no longer know how to prepare most of their traditional menus, especially *ọbe ase*,[60] the special stew for various ceremonies.

The foods offered to the deities in the course of the ceremonies are mainly kola nuts, coconuts, walnuts, and baked beans. They are all staple fruits that are featured in many ritual sacrifices. All the items are used for ritual purposes, and they possess significant symbolic meanings in Ondo cultural contexts. In the *Obitun* context, their purpose is to exorcise the malignant spirit. As we have seen, the coconut water is used to draw out the malignant spirit from the homestead to the outside. Those who would like to partake of the

---

[57] Ibid., p. 30.

[58] The tortoise possesses a rocklike shield which protects it from danger.

[59] A suggestion made by Droogers may help explain that such a phenomenon is not uncommon in anthropological research: "Rather obviously, eating, drinking, dancing, singing and dressing up are all indicative of the festive character of a given occasion. We should not lose sight of the fact, however, that such activities might at the same time be symbols of transition and point to the abnormality of the situation. Large-scale eating and drinking certainly represented a reversal of the usual order where normally the way of life was frugal." See Droogers, *The Dangerous Journey*, p. 333.

[60] See my description of this special food in Chapter I above.

remaining fruit must do so outside, for to take it inside the house is to bring back the bad spirit. The kola nut is used for the same purpose: to remove the malignant spirit from the initiates' bodies (chest).

The color symbolism portrayed in the *Obitun* ceremony centers on black, red, and white. These are the three primary colors in Ondo cosmology. While the white and red color combination dominates the liminal rites, at the beginning of the ceremony the *Obitun* are marked in black to delineate them from their previous locus and to "mark their profanity which through exorcism and ritual must be transformed to acquire favorable power."[61] The initiates then wear their white underwear and red royal native clothes on top of it. Both colors are interpreted as signs of purity, nobility and royalty, the status to which the *Obitun* are temporarily elevated. From then on until the end of the liminal process, they will be treated as such. The two food sacrifices represent these two primary colors (coconut and walnut are white; kola nut and baked beans are red). The two colors combine to symbolize the reproductive life force (white = semen, red = blood) that will now be part of the newly-initiated.[62] That is why at the end of the initiation ceremony it is assumed that conception has taken place and pregnancy has occurred, as if it were the end product of the ritual itself. As mentioned earlier, those initiates who were actually pregnant at the time of the ceremony were treated with special honor by adding a special form of coral beading to their hair style during the final outing ceremony.

Post-Liminal Rite

The third and final phase of a rite of passage (reaggregation or incorporation) includes symbolic phenomena and actions which represent the return of the subjects to their new, relatively stable and well-defined position in the total society. "For those undergoing life-cycle rituals this usually represents an enhanced status, a stage further along life's culturally prefabricated road."[63] This is true of the final outing dance. When the *Obitun* makes her reentry into the life of structure, she publicly propitiates the gods and culture heroes in the

---

[61] Gladys Reichard, *Navaho Religion*, p. 187.

[62] As fertility is a central focus of several Ondo rituals, we can conveniently assume that this is the meaning attached to the symbols in the absence of any native exegesis of it. In another ritual context (Ǫramfę festival) where both colors were in a similar combination, an informant gave me this same interpretation.

[63] Victor Turner, *Process, Performance, and Pilgrimage*, p. 16.

Ondo pantheon. As the procession stops on every public sacred hierophany, she gives her token offerings to the deity.

As a further sign of the return into the life of structure and of the "anti-communitas" stage of this post-liminal stage, those among these newly-initiated who are of royal or noble birth dance to a special drum in a clockwise manner, as in other Ondo festival dances. The rest of the participants, the freeborn, dance in a counterclockwise direction, until they reach their homes.

The final rite of incorporation, the propitiation of the sacred *Peregun* tree (*Draceana oleracee*), raises another issue entirely. The tree represents for the initiate her *axis mundi*, i.e., her point of orientation in her new life situation. The symbolic meaning and use of the plant in its cultural context, however, suggests a different motif. Pierre Verger, in his survey of Yoruba medicinal leaves,[64] suggests its symbolic significance. The leaf is used in making an aphrodisiac, or "love potion." Thus, we can assume that the plant would normally symbolize or form the main ingredient in a potion for a woman seeking a special favor from her husband, especially when married into a polygynous home where there may be rivalry among co-wives. Also, the plant secretes a semen-like juice that suggests a close association with procreation. But the most pertinent question is that if the woman is to live in her husband's home, why should a tree of such importance be planted on her own homestead? It suggests that in an earlier period, residence was actually matrilocal, or at least a woman retained close contact with her own home. These observations would lend further weight to our earlier hypothesis that Ondo was formerly a matriarchal society. Further research may produce evidence to explain the powerful social roles for women contained in this patriarchal society. As the *Obitun* completes her initiation, she may now participate in the religion and social life of the community as an adult and a full participant. She is now entitled to a decent burial at death (she can be buried in the home instead of the forest), and she can be made an *opoji* or can act as a sponsor in other subsequent girls' puberty rites.

Ọdun Aje: The Festival of the Goddess of Wealth and Fertility

The role of women in the Yoruba economy, especially the market economy, has long been recognized by scholars.[65] In Ondo township, it appears from

---

[64] Pierre Verger, *Awọn Ewe Ọsanyin* [Yoruba Medicinal Leaves] (Ifẹ: African Studies Institute, 1967).

[65] Bernard Belasco, *The Entrepreneur as Cultural Hero*, N.Y. Praeger, 1980.

all the available evidence that women play even more significant roles than in most Yoruba towns. *Odun Aje*, the festival celebrated to honor the Yoruba goddess of wealth and fertility, is an extension of the *Obitun* initiation ceremony. Once the *Obitun* is performed, the Ondo woman takes up the significant roles of wife, mother, and trader. She produces children to perpetuate the lineage and guarantee its immortality, and engages in the reproduction of wealth through market trade. Aje is by right in charge of these well-defined functions in Ondo social and religious life. The adult female, through the Ondo women chiefs, must regularly propitiate this deity.

My concern here is to examine the festivals and the two central roles, economic and human reproduction, as represented in the rituals.

As I observed in Chapter I, Ondo is a patrilineal society, but it has a central female focus, and perhaps was initially a matriarchal community before the change to a male-dominated one. In addition, Ondo women play central religious and socio-political roles, several of which have also been discussed. The women have an equivalent of the male political structure and they participate in *Ugha Nla*, the major traditional council. As I also pointed out, the *Lobun* is referred to as a woman king, and she has ritual influence over the entire Ondo society.

Although *Aje* is a minor deity in the Yoruba pantheon of deities, and indeed her celebration is purely the affair of women, *Aje* has wider ramifications beyond the women's sphere for the larger society. The apparently low profile that the deity maintains made it difficult to learn much about her, since she was hardly mentioned by most of the male priests that I interviewed. It was not until 1985, when I undertook additional fieldwork,[66] that I was able to gather more detail about her nature and the *Aje* festival in general.

In the *Aje* festival, two main groups of people are involved: the Ondo women and the leaders of the Idoko priest-chiefs, one of the autochthonous groups in Ondo. The involvement of the Idoko priest-chiefs should be explained here. First, as I pointed out while discussing the rituals of the installation of the *Oba*, the *Oloja Idoko*, who maintains an avoidance taboo with the king, promises to perform the rites necessary for the well-being of the Ondo people. These include the economic well-being that Aje symbolizes.

In addition, the Idoko people promise to perform the ritual purification of Ondo after sudden death, for example when women die during pregnancy and labor. It is in fulfillment of this pledge that the Idoko comes up to assist in the Aje celebration.

---

[66] Olatunde Lawuyi and Jacob K. Olupona, "Making Sense of the Aje Festival: Wealth, Politics and the Status of Women Among the Ondo of Southwestern Nigeria," *Journal of Ritual Studies*, 1, 2 (Summer 1987), pp. 97-109. I thank Lawuyi for allowing me to make use of our field materials on Aje Festival.

Ọdun Aje is a one-day festival performed in November every year. Early in the morning of the festival day, each *Opoji* or female chief prepares and dresses up her assemblage of Aje for the evening festival. Aje's movable shrine consists of *Igba Aje*, a big clean bowl usually of brass, in which several items symbolic of wealth and fecundity are placed. The items are usually *owo ẹyọ* (cowry money) *lyun* (coral beads), *aṣọ oke* (native woven cloth), *awo* (china plates) and a white doll.

In the evening, Aje is placed on the head of a prepubescent girl who is dressed in the manner of an *Obitun* undergoing the initiation rite. The *Aje* assemblage is carried in a procession of the chief and her women supporters and children, who dance to the tune of *Aje* music. They go to a chief's house overlooking the *Ọba*'s palace and sing in praise of the goddess. I recorded the following lyrics.

Aje ṣu le mo ri	Aje excreted on my head;
Ẹni aje faraba lo ṣoni	Whoever Aje touches is made human.
Aje sun le mo ri	Aje slept on my head;
Ẹni Aje faraba lo sọ mọ	Whoever Aje touches acts like a child.
Aje gbemiloke bi ọba	Aje elevates me like a king;
Ngo ma yọ	I shall forever rejoice.
Aje yọ mo yọ	Aje is happy, so am I.
Aje yọ mo yọ	Aje is happy, so am I.

In the song Aje symbolizes success in trade and plenty of wealth. The songs idealized market gains and profit made in trade and business. All these are made possible by this deity. Aje is compared to the state of childhood: in Yoruba culture a new child is considered innocent and a good thing of life. Nor is the image of fecundity and human reproduction absent from these lyrics. In Yoruba culture, it is considered a good omen for a baby to excrete on the person who is carrying it. This is a sign of fecundity and reproduction of life. Finally Aje is placed in the context of the king's status. It is only Aje that can elevate one to the status of a king.

Whenever a chief arrives at the festival place, her Aje is removed from the girl and placed on a long table set out for the deity. The conductor of the festival announces their presence and the chief takes her seat, while the songs and dances continue.

In the late evening, the Idoko chiefs, led by the *Saṣẹrẹ Idoko*, arrive for the celebration. They offer prayers for each of the chiefs for profit in women's trade and for the fecundity of Ondo women. After this long prayer, the Aje is touched with the Idoko's staff of office, a magical-ritual staff conveying *aṣẹ*, the vital power that makes things happen. The final rite concludes this brief festival. The Idoko return to their quarter, while the women chiefs dance to their different homes to continue the celebration with their followers.

Several of the items in Aje's bowl symbolize wealth and fertility in Ondo culture. The cowries were the medium of exchange for goods in the Old Yoruba kingdom before the British introduced their currency; today they have ritual and religious potency related to wealth, acquisition, and profit-making. The beads, traditional cloths and china plates are Ondo's most prized possessions. To possess them in large quantity is to be affluent. While the red beads symbolize royalty, the cloths and china plates are white and symbolize purity. The girl who carries the Aje assemblage also embodies purity as she has not started menstruating. More significantly, the white doll resembles a living bird (*eiye*), which signifies women's association with witches. "Witches are known as *eleiye* ('one with birds')." It is believed that one with birds (a witch) has the ability to alter one's fortune in life. It is indeed an important fact that the Idoko's magical powers are solicited to check the dangerous power of witches that may harm Ondo's quest for both the economic profit and human reproduction that *Aje* festivals seek. The medicine man, it is believed, provides the only effective check against such malignant female powers of witchcraft (*Oloogun lo le soko aje*, "Only a medicine man can be husband to a witch"). *Oko*, husband, here means not only a spouse but also a controller, one who has the power and authority to control or direct the purposes to which the witch puts her vital power.

The song in praise of Aje indicates the position of honor accorded this deity in the Ondo pantheon. The faithful worshipper and the one who finds favor with the deity becomes rich and is elevated to the status of a king.

In conclusion, both *Obitun* and *Odun Aje* point to the significant role Ondo women play in Ondo religious and social life, as the Ondo myth of origin suggests. Both celebrations convincingly demonstrate women's place in the human and economic production in Ondo society.

Chapter VII
Religion, Kingship, and Social Change

In the preceding chapters, I have attempted to describe and analyze the festival calendar of Ondo people. A central theme running throughout this festival cycle is the articulation of the sacred power of kingship. By means of the centralized power and symbolism of kingship, the various social and religious groups within the city-kingdom transcend their differences and affirm their shared allegiance in Ondo society. Drawing on rich ethnographic data, this study has sought to understand the symbolic meanings involved in this ritual process and to gain insight into the relationship between the rituals and the political and social networks that shape Ondo life. By examining the tensions within Ondo society which arise from the realities of the mythic background and the complex cultural networks, I have tried to show the role the festivals play in containing and/or discharging these tensions.

Today, three major religious groups exist within Ondo: the traditionalists, the Christians, and the Muslims; each group exists as a source of potential cleavage within Ondo society. Here, I shall examine (1) how the kingship and kingship rituals have acted as a major means of accomplishing social integration across these potential cleavages, and (2) how conversion and social change have affected Ondo kingship and religious life in general.

Ondo's Conversion to Christianity

The second half of the nineteenth century was a very significant period in Ondo history, and the events that occurred during this period had a profound impact on the conversion process. First, there was a protracted Yoruba civil war in the nineteenth century which, although Ondo was not directly involved, nevertheless severely affected the people of Ondo. An internal crisis erupted at this time in Ondo and led to a total breakdown of law and order. This crisis exposed Ondo to the warlords in Ile-Ifẹ who joined hands with the town's dissenting forces and brought an end to Ondo's autonomy. The Ondo people fled the town and scattered to different places, remaining dispersed until 1872 when the British government stepped in to restore peaceful government.

At the insistence of Governor Glover, the chief British representative in

Lagos, Captain Goldsworth was sent to Ondo in 1872 with a mandate to put an end to the incessant civil strife and to restore order to the city. Captain Goldsworth successfully completed the mission. He encouraged the people to return home and restore the *Ọba* Jimẹkun to the throne.

The primary motive for the British was the creation of a trade route by sea and by land from Lagos to the Yoruba hinterland through Ondo, thereby avoiding the western routes made dangerous by the escalating Yoruba civil war. The hostilities had put the British government at the mercy of the Ijẹbu people, another Yoruba subgroup.[1]

Ondo was, as far as the new religions were concerned, virgin territory, and Captain Goldsworth conceived of the idea of a Christian mission to Ondo in the wake of his own political mission. On arrival in Lagos, he persuaded the Church Missionary Society (C.M.S.)[2] to open up a new mission frontier in the Ondo area. The C.M.S. quietly responded to the call and sent the Revs. J.A. Maser and E. Roper to survey the prospects for a permanent missionary enterprise.

The two missionaries arrived in Ondo on Christmas Day, 1873, as the guests of *Ọba* Jimẹkun, who had been briefed in advance of their visit. The missionaries were housed with an Ondo high chief, *Jọmu* Operusu. On their return to Britain, Maser and Roper spoke favorably of their visit and ardently supported the move for a mission post. Thus the road was opened for the C.M.S. evangelization.

When Reverend David Hindrer and his two assistants, Hunsi Wright and William Dada, arrived in Ondo on March 29, 1875, to open the new mission post, they were hospitably received by *Ọba* Jimẹkun, who gave the missionaries a place to live. Rev. Hindrer returned to Lagos in December of 1876, and his place was taken by the Reverend (later Bishop) Charles Phillips, a Yoruba, who would later be called "the Apostle of Ondo missionary enterprise."

Reverend Phillips arrived in Ondo in January, 1877, for a familiarization tour, settling there permanently with his family in March of the same year.[3] Almost immediately, Phillips put into work all the necessary evangelical skill and machinery at his disposal in order to convert the Ondo to the Anglican fold.

---

[1] The route which was established in 1870 is referred to simply as "Ondo Road." For an excellent analysis of the influence of Ondo road on the Eastern Yoruba sector, see S.A. Akintoye, "The Ondo Road Eastwards of Lagos c. 1870-1895," *Journal of African History* 10 (1969), pp. 581-598.
[2] Anglican mission church.
[3] Ibid.

Phillips started morning prayer meetings and vigorous training of catechumen on May 18, 1877, with an initial membership of 5 men and 1 woman. He also enlisted some men to be trained as church agents and sent to the neighboring villages to spread the Gospel. It would appear that these people were Ondo indigenes who had already been converted to Christianity in Lagos during the dispersion occasioned by the civil war and thus quickly identified with the new church leadership. Phillips utilized open air services and public preaching as a means of reaching the people. He preached in the palace of the *Ọba* and in the open compounds of the Ondo high chiefs, especially the *Lisa*. Phillips' memoirs, in a passage dated July 4, 1877, describe in detail his vigorous attempt to convert those of high status in Ondo. The memoirs bear witness to the Victorian style of evangelism that characterized his apostolate in Ondo. He was concerned from the outset to ensure his converts' strict obedience to Church doctrines and would not tolerate even minute lapses into their former "paganism." For example, he recorded that one church member was suspended for selling her dove (ẹiyẹle) for sacrifice in the worship of a traditional Yoruba god (*oriṣa*).[4]

In spite of the openness with which *Ọba* Jimẹkun received the missionaries, the early years of the mission were filled with bitter conflicts between the Church and the town's political authorities. The major problem was the uncompromising attitude of the new religion to the traditional religion and social customs. Other Ondo customs that were at variance with Christian practice were attacked with the same vigor as were religious beliefs. One such custom was polygyny, especially levirate marriage, whereby a brother married his deceased brother's wife. Based on scriptural authority and the practices of the C.M.S., Phillips condemned levirate marriage as unchristian. In 1885 Phillips intervened in the case of a convert named Christiana Akinde and her late husband's brother who wanted to take her as wife. Characteristically, Phillips settled this dispute according to strict Christian principles.

Other areas of conflict centered on land issues. Phillips had applied for a parcel of land on which to build a permanent place of worship. This request was rejected by the chiefs in July, 1877. It appears that the townspeople at this time were beginning to feel the negative impact of the Church, especially its uncompromising attitude towards their traditions,[5] and they denied the land grant.

---

[4] Ibid.

[5] The uncompromising attitude of Rev. Phillips would perhaps explain the impact which Christianity has on the Ondo area today. David D. Laitin suggests that the lack of a resident Victorian-type missionary in Ile-Ifẹ is responsible for the Anglican Christian mission's lack of a vigorous anti-traditional religion posture there. See Laitin, "Conversion and Political Change:

Phillips, however, displayed superb diplomatic skills in handling this matter. He renewed his campaign, but this time sought to persuade individual high Chiefs, especially those who appeared to be attracted to the new Christian church.

Impressed by Phillips' missionary zeal, high Chief Odunwo, the fourth in rank to the *Oba*, advised the missionary to ask for a piece of land near his own home, since this would not create a problem once the town agreed to Christian land traditionally placed under his jurisdiction. A large piece of land was consequently granted to the Church at Oke-Aluko on November 4, 1880. The Church was built and publicly dedicated on May 3, 1881. However, it does not appear that Phillips' troubles with the Ondo chiefs were over, for in February, 1882, he mentions in his diary an unsuccessful attempt to extradite him from Ondo at the instigation of the *Adaja*, the last and sixth of the Ondo high chiefs.

Phillips' style of church administration made a significant contribution to the success of the mission. He encouraged a strong lay leadership in order to support his small crew of Church workers. Thus, in February, 1888, Church chiefs (*oloye–ijo*) were elected. Among them were Joshua Talabi, J. Peters, I. Fawehinmi, and David Fadase. The first meeting with church agents occurred in February, 1877, and comprehensive plans were made for the growing church, including evangelism to the surrounding districts.

In the years that followed, the mission was preoccupied with putting up church buildings and with training personnel for further expansion. Oba Osemawe Jilo laid the foundation of the new church on November 19, 1891, and Bishop H. Tugwell consecrated it on August 18, 1892. In the congregation were several British officials. The Church was named St. Stephen because this apostle's life was said to resemble that of the early Ondo missions.

Phillips persuaded the Lagos mission to establish elementary schools alongside the mission churches, so that western education and Christian instruction would be taught to the children of the new converts. A school was opened for Ondo behind the church building, and a teacher named T. Ogunbiyi was appointed. As evidence of the British support of the mission programme, Major Swart paid the first official visit from Lagos to the school on June 12, 1889.

The early missionary endeavors in Ondo engendered several social, politi-

---

A Study of (Anglican) Christianity and Islam Among the Yoruba in Ile-Ife'', a seminar paper delivered at the Department of Political Science, University of Ife, June 12, 1980, p. 6. It would be helpful to look at the effect of missionary types on matters of conversion among the various Yoruba subgroups. This would perhaps explain the unevenness in the continuity and discontinuity of traditional religion among the various subgroups.

cal, and economic developments within the region. By 1898 Ondo had become a relatively strong mission center, so much so that it was in a position to start other mission outposts outside Ondo district. In this same year a small delegation from Ile-Ifẹ, the sacred city of the Yoruba people, arrived to solicit C.M.S. for recognition and also to request a church agent to cater to the small gathering of Christians[6] in Ile-Ifẹ. The Ile-Ifẹ Christians became aware of Rev. Phillips'' presence in Ondo during the latter's visit. Along with the Rev. Samuel Johnson, he visited Ile-Ifẹ to settle the disputes between Modakẹkẹ and Ile-Ifẹ on behalf of the British governor in Lagos. This was indicative of the role and influence of the Christian mission in the internal politics of Yorubaland at this period.[7]

It was, however, in the sphere of economic development that the mission made one of their most significant contributions. As has been suggested by Sara Berry,[8] the Christians in the early years of the church played a most important role in the introduction of cocoa. Cocoa, which later became the chief export product of Nigeria, may actually have been introduced to Ondo by Rev. Phillips.[9] Phillips encouraged the Ondo people to engage in agricultural endeavors, especially in growing crops such as cocoa, coffee, and palm oil. Foreseeing the future expansion of the Church and increased financial expenses, Phillips suggested that the Church acquire crop land for economic purposes.

The Church elders took Phillips' advice and started a cocoa and coffee plantation to raise money for church expenses and for mission expansion.[10] Individual farmers also benefitted from Phillips' counsel. For example, the first cocoa plantation in Ondo district was said to have been started by an Oke-Igbo man named Kọlajọ, who accidentally discovered cocoa while hunting on a farm very near Ilẹsa.[11] Kọlajọ reported his discovery to Phillips,

---

[6] The small Christian group was started by John Adelaja, an Ijẹbu businessman dealing in rubber and stationed in Ile-Ifẹ and Daniel Amodu Lawani Ọlọgbẹnla, an Ifẹ indigene who had been educated in Lagos. For the history of the origin of Christianity in Ile-Ifẹ, see M.A. Fabunmi, *Ẹsin Kristi ni Ile-*Ifẹ *ati Agbegbe* (Christianity in Ile-Ifẹ and district) (Ile-Ifẹ: Kosalabaro Press, 1970).

[7] The information in this section largely follows Sara Berry's work, "Christianity and the Rise of Cocoa Growing in Ibadan and Ondo," *Journal of the Historical Society of Nigeria*, 14 (1968), p. 443. See also her *Cocoa, Custom, and Socio-Economic Change in Rural Western Nigeria* (Oxford: Clarendon, 1975).

[8] Sara S. Berry, *Cocoa, Custom and Socio-Economic Change in Rural Western Nigeria* (Oxford: Clarendon Press, 1975), p. 4.

[9] Here, Sara Berry was quoting from E.M. Lijadu's Diary, April 10, 1898; see "Christianity and the Rise of Cocoa Growing in Ibadan and Ondo," p. 443.

[10] Ibid.

[11] Ibid.

who was said to have advised that, should Kọlajọ plant cocoa, "he and his children would never suffer."[12] Taking Phillips' advice, Kọlajọ obtained some cocoa seeds from Ilẹsa, planted them, and became a successful cocoa farmer in the district. From this beginning, Oke-Igbo became a major center from which cocoa farming spread to other parts of Ondo district.

Phillips also encouraged people to start small farming businesses to improve their economic lot. This perhaps was the basis for the founding of Ajebandele, an Ondo village first inhabited by a group of Ondo entrepreneurs who had previously lived in Lagos. Encouraged by the prospects of the Yoruba trade in Lagos and Abeokuta, this group obtained land from the reigning *Ọba* and started a joint farm and business involving cocoa, coffee and kola nut. This village, known as Ajebandele ("I return home bringing prosperity"),[13] derived its name from its early economic success (an indication of the affluence that followed their initiatives). These young entrepreneurs were encouraged by Phillips, who helped them acquire rights to the land. The success of this farm settlement led Phillips to encourage the Ondo church to take up farming and trading businesses in the village. However, the references to "*Aje*" should not be missed. *Aje*, which refers to the deity of wealth, acquired a new meaning, signifying a new market economy and prosperity.

Islam in Ondo

Having shown how Christianity arrived in Ondo, I wish to describe how Islam entered the area ten years later. Unlike the Western Yoruba region where Muslims form more than sixty percent of the population, the Eastern Yoruba area has a small number of Muslims. In Ondo, Muslims constitute a minority, albeit an influential one, among the total population. In the 1952 census the population of Muslims in Ondo district was 13 percent while the Christian population was 73 percent.[14] It is the small but penetrating influence of Islam in Ondo which makes the study of Ondo Islam important both for the understanding of conversion to Islam and for the understanding of Yoruba religion and society as a whole.

As early as 1880, there were indications of the presence of Muslims in Ondo. An interesting story is told about the activities of one such early

---

[12] Ibid.
[13] Ibid., p. 447.
[14] See also Ogunṣakin, *Ondo*, p. 9.

Muslim, Abu Bakr Ajao, a migrant trader and weaver from Isẹyin in Ọyọ district in western Yorubaland. He excited the curiosity of people by his "strange" habit of constantly bowing up and down and touching his forehead to the ground (*rak'a*). Since the people did not understand what this meant, he was presumed to have epilepsy and people gathered around him to see how best to help him with his infirmity. Thus the religion of Islam was said to have had its modest beginning in Ondo.

Abu Bakr, we are told, took time to explain to the inquisitive audience the meaning of this *salat*. Ondo's receptivity to change and openness to new religious teachings were important factors in enabling Islam to make inroads in the Ondo area. Reportedly, Abu Bakr's first painstaking efforts to explain Islam were not viewed with suspicion but with the hope that his endeavors would be accepted by God. As my key informant, Chief Fawẹhinmi, the Seriki of Ondo Muslims, put it, "*A jẹ iṣe o, Ọlọrun a duo le ṣe o*" ("May you accomplish your aims. May God help your endeavors"). As a result, Islam did not suffer the same kind of initial hostility as Christianity did.

The sudden growth of Islam in Ondo was similar to that of Christianity, and the development of both must be seen against the backdrop of the opening of trade routes through Yoruba country in the latter part of the nineteenth century. As was mentioned earlier, in 1870 the British administrator J.A. Glover established a new trade route between Lagos and the Yoruba hinterland. When this route finally opened, a sizeable number of Lagos traders, many of whom were Muslim, settled along it, especially in Ondo. Ondo became the most important place along the route and the focus of Christian and Muslim proselytizing activities for the entire Eastern Yoruba country.[15] In this manner Islam gained influence among the Ondo chiefs and nobles who were the main benefactors of the new commercial activities.[16]

The first record of Muslim presence in Ondo is contained in Phillips' diary, November 26, 1880.[17] Phillips refers to his frequent contacts with Lagos

---

[15] There is no doubt that Ondo continues to be the major Christian and Muslim center for the entire Eastern Yoruba country.

[16] This is an important factor in the imprint of Islam and Christianity in Ondo community. In spite of the small number of Muslims, both religions are equally represented among the most prominent lineages in Ondo today, as for example among the Awoṣika and Fawẹhinmi, perhaps the two largest lineages in Ondo. The Awoṣika family is largely Christian, but the present missioner of Oke-ọtunba central mosque, and the grandson of Alfa Alimi, the man credited with the establishment of institutional Islam in Ondo, descend from the same (Awoṣika) lineage. During my fieldwork the Muslim cleric called "missioner" showed me the roster of Awoṣika lineage meetings and told me that it was his turn to host the next meeting.

[17] CMS G2 A2/01, Annual letter of Charles Phillips, 26 November, 1880, cited from T.G.O. Gbadamọsi, *The Growth of Islam among the Yoruba: 1841-1908* (London, 1978), p. 85.

Muslims residents in Ondo with whom he debated matters of Muslim and Christian belief. He also states that among his early converts to Christianity was an old Ondo Muslim returnee who had been converted to Islam while in slavery.[18] His account, coupled with Islamic oral tradition, suggests that by at least 1887 there were a sizeable number of Muslims in the area and that active proselytizing was occurring. Islam's entrance provided Christian interests with a powerful competitive force.

In fact, it was not until the period 1883-1885 that institutional Islam became established in Ondo. The person credited with this accomplishment is Alfa (later al-hajj) Muhammed Alimi. He came from *Erinmo in* Oyo State and is said to have been a relation of the prominent Ondo high chief, Saserẹ Ayotilerẹwa Awosika. According to my informants, Alimi's generous personality helped him gain converts, especially among the Ondo elite who formed the earliest nucleus of the *Ummah* (Muslim community). My informants noted that Alimi was fond of wearing traditional Yoruba garb. The Ondo people's identification with his dress made them more secure in their new religion. It was due largely to the proselytizing efforts of Alimi that the first Muslim congregation was established. Through the help of the Ondo high chiefs he secured a piece of land at Oke-otunba street for his newly-formed group. The present central mosque now stands on this site, where the Muslim *Ummah* first gathered and prayed in 1888, marking the official beginning of Ondo Islam.

Ondo nobles and chiefs supported the growth of Islam and encouraged the general tolerance of their people toward this new religion. Two Ondo high chiefs in particular are remembered as significant in directing the course of Islam at its very beginning. These were Saserẹ Ayotilerẹwa Awosika, already mentioned as a relation of Alfa Alimi, and *Lisa* Anjanu Fawẹhinmi. Although neither man embraced Islam, they laid the foundation for the cordial relationship that later existed between Islam and the traditional political structure.

Some Observations on Christian and Muslim Conversion

The early Christian mission had a significant impact on Ondo society. E.A. Ayandele, a Yoruba historian who seldom uses appreciative language to describe Christian missionary success, observes:

In Ondo district a large number of people became Christians partly because the missionaries were associated with the restoration of peace and national rehabilitation of

---

[18] CMS G3 A2-01 Charles Phillips' Journal, 1887 (4th March, 1887), cited from Gbadamọsi, *The Growth of Islam*, Ibid.

the Ondo. Christianity was also associated in this area with the wealth brought to the people by timber concessions and the growth of cocoa. As in many parts of the Yoruba country, it was becoming fashionable to be described as a Christian.[19]

Conversion to Christianity in Ondo must be viewed within the social milieu of the time. There was no doubt that Ondo people thought of the coming of Christianity as an important watershed in their history and a turning point in their lives. Their thirty years of forced exile caused a depressed national psyche and low morale, and it made traditional ways of constructing reality increasingly implausible. The social restoration therefore provided a much-needed opportunity for a cultural rehabilitation. The British missionaries helped both to provide an alternative religious world view and to establish a lasting peace.

It is no wonder, then, that what is generally called *Orin Ondo* (the Ondo national 'anthem') expresses this unique experience in Ondo history. Unlike the 'national anthems' of other Yoruba subgroups, which tend to be based upon folk beliefs and traditional experience, Ondo's anthem is grounded on the Christian encounter and conversion experience; an experience interpreted as a new life under the Christian missionary banner:

Bi ọla, Bi ọla, Bi ọla o	Luxuriant, colorful and majestic,
Adodo fusi s'eti omi	Like the flower growing by the river bank.
Jesu ma fusi S'Ondo	So did Jesus (Christianity) flourish on Ondo soil.
Ọla ti bọkan wa'iye o Eee	Our prosperity has come from above,
Bi ọla, bi ọla, bi ọla o	Luxuriant, colorful and majestic
Adodo buyi s'eti Omi	As a flower growing by the river bank.
Jesu ma buyi S'Ondo	So Jesus (Christianity) has become the pride of Ondo town.
Ọla mi toke waiye o	Our prosperity is from above,
Aiye wa ṣ'ẹṣẹ w'agun o.	Now, we lack nothing.

The activities of the Rev. Phillips are crucial to understanding the conversion process. The significance of Phillips lies in his mission strategy which enjoyed appreciable success when compared with mission works in western Yoruba country. The nucleus of the Ondo early church were the Ondo returnees, mainly traders from Lagos.[20] We can assume that as traders they were semi-literate persons whose experience was of a larger world of relationships and interests. These migrant traders formed the basis of Phillips' new congregation, having converted to Christianity prior to their return to Ondo. In com-

---

[19] E.A. Ayandele, *The Missionary Impact on Modern Nigeria 1842-1914*, p. 156.

[20] J.D.Y. Peel, "Religious Change in Yorubaland," *Africa*, Journal of the International African Institute, 37 (1967) p. 300.

parison with Western Yoruba country, which did not enjoy the benefits of native returnees to the same degree, large numbers of people in the Eastern Yoruba region, and in particular Ondo, converted to Christianity.[21] Ondo people reacted more positively to the Christian message propagated and spread through these Christian migrant traders. As Peel rightly observed, "The greatest attractiveness of Christianity to aliens, and the fact that evangelization of an indigenous population went more easily if some of them had already converted elsewhere, can also be illustrated from the Ondo district."[22]

Now I shall comment on the significance of authority and chieftainship for Ondo Christian conversion. Phillips no doubt recognized the enormous authority which Ondo chiefs exercised and their influence over the *Ọba* and the townspeople. He himself had clashed with them on several occasions, and he had to persuade them to allow the mission to stay.

While Phillips was busy persuading Ondo high chiefs, he also developed strategies to improve the social and political status of the new converts. He moved quickly to appoint some of the returnees as 'church-chiefs' *oloye Ijọ* in 1888, perhaps the first instance of such a practice in Yorubaland. By so doing, Phillips employed the Yoruba practice of conferring honorary status titles. But unlike Ondo titles, these were borrowed from Western Yoruba political structures.[23] They were mainly war titles to which Phillips attached significant religious roles. While these 'Warriors of God' or church-chiefs were not perceived as identical to or rivals with town chiefs, they nevertheless had similar social status and received honor and respect from their fellow Christians. They followed church law by being monogamists, and they functioned as models of the ideal Christian manliness.

As cocoa cultivation became the focus of Ondo economic life, several new villages were founded and new farms established in Ondo district. This gradually led to the establishment of new C.M.S. village congregations. The nucleus of these villages, made up of the village heads, male elders and alien laborers hired from distant Yoruba towns, also constituted the nucleus of the new worshipping community. They met weekly on Sundays for services at the cocoa plantations. As the congregation grew, lay readers were appointed to take care of spiritual needs and to collect church dues for the parish work. Not surprisingly, the most significant period of the C.M.S. festival cycle was the harvest season. Once a year on this occasion, the parish priest and his

---

[21] Ibid.

[22] Ibid.

[23] Some of these titles are Balẹ, Seriki, Balogun, Ọtun, and Osi. They are all war titles similar to the Ibadan chieftain hierarchy.

church elders returned to the village church to celebrate the harvest thanksgiving with the local congregation, usually under the cocoa trees. This was the only period when it was obligatory for the priest to visit the village churches. In addition to blessing the harvest, he performed clerical functions such as baptism and administering the Eucharist, which the appointed layreader could not do.

The place of cocoa cultivation in the propagation of the new religion in Ondo is also quite noteworthy. As Berry points out, Christianity and cocoa growing were historically linked in Nigeria, and, certainly with Phillips' encouragement, cocoa cultivation became closely associated with the Christian church in Ondo. Berry's work is a revision of Max Weber's classical thesis on Christianity and the rise of capitalist entrepreneurship. Unlike Weber, Berry does not see specifically Protestant "moral and theological sanctions" as significant factors in Ondo's economic growth. Rather, she argues that Yoruba religion has traditionally been linked to improving one's lot in life and that Christianity only advocated a more rational system through conversion from traditional belief systems.[24] Phillips saw the new economic opportunity that could provide access to status and power and encouraged his followers to take advantage of it. They became wealthy and increased their status in town.

When compared with the phenomenal rise of Christianity in Ondo, conversion to Islam was less successful. Perhaps the most significant contribution to Islam's growth in Ondo was made by the Muslim traders. The eastern route made Ondo easily accessible to Muslim traders, and Islamic ideas and doctrines in turn were disseminated by them. The primary purpose of these traders was business. However, a Muslim trader considered himself an instrument of conversion, a missionary of Islam in addition to his daily vocation. That this phenomenon is in no way peculiar to the Ondo situation is suggested by A. Mukti Ali's observation:

Islam does not preach an exclusive, magical charisma - to borrow Max Weber's term - belonging to the priest alone, as Christianity teaches, but is by its nature a missionary community. Because of the expansive missionary nature of Islam, every Muslim is a propagandist of the faith. That is why the trader from the Muslim world was the most common missionary figure beyond the confines of his own land, and that is why the faith was sure to follow trade routes.[25]

Another major factor was the important role played by the Ondo high chiefs. A striking observation in the Ondo religious population is that, in spite of the

---

[24] Sara Berry, "Christianity and the Rise of Cocoa Growing in Ibadan and Ondo", p. 443.
[25] A Mukti Ali, "Islam in Indonesia," in *Religionen* (Handbuch der Orientalistik) (Leiden: E.J. Brill, 1975), p. 73.

numerically small number of Muslims, Christians and Muslims are almost equally represented in the chieftain class because they embraced both religions. An interesting area of research would be to trace the genealogy of these major lineages to the family heads and chiefs whom Phillips first met, but who did not convert. This would enable us to understand when and perhaps why their descendants made the choice between Christianity and Islam.

Islam, unlike Christianity, did not conflict with prevailing socio-cultural ethics and norms of the traditional Ondo religion. One looks in vain for accounts of such open confrontations between Islam and traditional religious values in Ondo like those recorded between Christian missionaries and proponents of traditional religion (see the case of Phillips). Indeed, the Muslims proudly refer to the fact that the land which the Muslims were allocated to build the central mosque was a 'sacred grove' once referred to as "Igbo-ajaka", where smallpox victims were ritually buried. The symbolic significance of this in the eyes of the local populace cannot be missed. The Muslims inhabited a place that was polluted. Hence, Alfa Alimi, the first Imam, ritually cleansed the site for Muslim worship.

Religious Change Among the Ondo-Yoruba People: A Comparative Perspective

Having pointed to the factors that aided the establishment of Christianity and Islam, I shall examine the conversion process from a comparative perspective. A good starting point is Robin Horton's important work on conversion.

In his review of Peel's *Aladura: a Religious Movement among the Yoruba*,[26] Horton proposes what he calls an "intellectualist approach" to examining the conversion process. He postulates that there exist two spheres in the typical traditional (African) religious world view: the microcosm and the macrocosm. In the microcosm, lesser deities, i.e., ancestors and spirits limited to the local communities, take charge of the daily affairs of people. The *orisa* complex provides a meaningful relationship that informs and shapes

---

[26] J.D.Y. Peel, *Aladura: A Religious Movement among the Yoruba* (London: Oxford University Press, 1968), was reviewed as part of an article in Robin Horton, "African Conversion". Robin Horton's paper has generated several responses and debates including the following: H. Fisher, "Conversion Reconsidered: Some Historical Aspects of Conversion in Black Africa"; Caroline Ifeka-Moller, "White Power: Social-Structural Factors in Conversion to Christianity, Eastern Nigeria, 1921-1966"; R.W. Whythe, "On the Rationality of the Devout Opposition," *Journal of Religion in Africa* XI (1980), pp. 81-82. Horton expanded his theory in response to Fisher in his "On the Rationality of Conversion." *Africa* 45:2, 19—235, 373—399.

the lives of people in a particular locality. The concept of the supreme being, underpinning the 'macrocosm,' is not well-developed. However, as a society's world view is broadened in response to heightened international interaction through increased trade, communication, and social, educational and political changes, people become increasingly aware of and involved in the macrocosm, and the microcosm becomes progressively less important. Simultaneously there is a shift in religious focus from lesser "spirits" to the "supreme being," which becomes much more prominent in the affairs of the community. This more inclusive symbol provides much-needed moral guidance, which is consonant with the emergence of a new cosmopolitan world view. It is quite possible that if Christianity and Islam had not been present, African traditional religion would have responded to modernization by emphasizing the High God tradition latent within it.

While several scholars have argued that changes in traditional religion were due to the presence of Christianity and Islam, Horton argues that this conclusion is wrong and suggests that traditional religion was already actively responding to ongoing social change at this time. This thesis reduces Islam and Christianity to mere catalysts, stimulating and accelerating social and religious changes that had already begun.[27]

Horton's conversion theory argues that traditional religion has the potential to adapt on its own, in response to changes within its environment. Horton may be right in emphasizing the fact that there was a mechanism with which the Yoruba world view enabled people to make this accomodation, namely, the larger ideational framework relating to the Yoruba concept of a supreme being. It was this concept that the Yoruba could have appealed to, and often did, that provided the larger view in terms of which they adapted to the rapidly changing world in which they found themselves. This confirms the observation made in Chapter III[28] concerning the development of the king's cult into an independent civil religious system, quite apart from the *Orisa* worship complex, in which the king's cult forms the focus for a plurality of religions. It can be argued that the relationship between the supreme being and the lesser deities in the microcosm is analogous to the relationship between the king and his chiefs. Just as the remote supreme being is the overseer of the macrocosm, the king-priest, often hidden in the palace, designates his chiefs to take charge of the daily affairs of the town. If my interpretation of

---

[27] Robin Horton, "African Conversion," p. 104.
[28] Jacob K. Oluọna, "Some Notes on the Religion of the Ondo People: A Phenomenological-Anthropological Study" in *Bulletin of the International Committee on Urgent Anthropological and Ethnological Research*, Nov. 27, 1985:47—58.

the king's festival in Ondo is correct, it is the king's cult rather than the supreme being, as Horton has suggested, that has actively taken over the affairs of the "macrocosm." I have argued that the king's (civil religious) cult probably developed in response to social changes in Ondo society, such as the introduction of Christianity and Islam.

The ultimate issue, in relation to Horton's conversion hypothesis, is that "acceptance of Islam and Christianity is due as much to the development of traditional cosmology in response to other features of the modern situation as it is to the activities of the missionaries."[29] In this sense Horton has dissociated himself from the mainstream position that conversion is due primarily to religious "change agents," i.e., Christianity and Islam. In my view, it is doubtful that these changes would have occurred at all without those contacts which Horton regards as mere catalysts. Evidence from Ondo neither proves or disproves Horton's thesis in this aspect, because from the time of the Ondo's first contacts with the "outside world," there was a simultaneous contact with missionaries and later with the Muslim traders from Lagos. Thus, the evidence suggests that Horton's conversion thesis begs an important question, namely, the degree to which the economic and social changes of the early colonial period can ever be separated from the presence of Christianity and Islam.

Another implicit issue in the debate over the conversion phenomenon in Ondo-Yoruba society is 'world view'. Fortunately, world view analysis is an important new extension in the scientific study of religion.[30] When studying "conversion," the nature of which is a *process*, a tool that allows for understanding *dynamic change* such as world view analysis is required. It can provide insight into how and why cultures change, and it incorporates the sacred as well as the secular, functional and substantive ideas of religion. As Charles Kraft remarked, "world view may be understood to consist of thousands of complex constructs (perceptions) of portions of reality," which he labelled "paradigms".[31] Conversion then "would ordinarily involve changing one or more paradigms within a group's world view."[32] In the African context what

---

[29] Ibid.

[30] In this context, the use of Religious Studies (employing the history of religion and the phenomenology of religion) as a tool is inadequadate. It is too narrow, relating specifically to religious data. It is also incapable of interpreting or predicting change. See Ninian Smart's work on *Worldviews*, (New York: Scribner's, 1983). Also in his *Religion and the Western Mind* (NY: State University Press, 1987), pp. 93-4, Smart speaks of world view analysis (its construction and evaluation) as a kind of *dynamic phenomenology*, much to be preferred over the static typology approach of Van de Leeuw, etc.

[31] "Conversion: Shaping our Reality," *Theology, News and Notes*, June, 1986, p. 13.

[32] Ibid., p. 14.

this means is that the old world views are not entirely destroyed as whole systems and replaced by other complete world views. It is better to say that elements from the world views that "make sense" are added while those which have proven inadequate are deleted. The process occurs in all cultures, for world views themselves are dynamic organisms. Conversion, then, represents both a continuity and discontinuity with the old traditions.

The significance of this methodology is that in any study of conversion, the nature and forms of the old traditions themselves are as important as the new religions. Herein lies the significance of J.D.Y. Peel's works on Yoruba relig-ious change. In a very important paper, "Syncretism and Religious Change" (1968), Peel provides a basic rationale for explaining the change phenomenon from the point of view of Yoruba religious attitude. He informs us that the change is definitely *not*, as some missionaries would say, toward taking on "a veneer of Christianity," nor is it adequately called "acculturation," a favorite term of sociologists and anthropologists. He urges us to recognize that relig-ious change within Nigeria is more than "movement along a continuum." Such faulty methodologies (Linton, Wallace, Lanternari, etc.),[33] he feels, create wrong and artificial impressions which avoid the realities of life and history in that country.

We see that Peel is moving away from the very limiting approaches previ-ously used. The article, written about 20 years ago, calls for a more com-prehensive methodology and analysis. Again, if not in terminology, but cer-tainly in methodological approach, he seems to suggest something like world view shifts as the cause of religious change.

Peel aptly observed that in the nineteenth century, developments within the Yoruba religious world view encouraged change. Among these were the fact that individuals could choose their cult-group, that the Ifa system of divina-tion - the most sophisticated thought form of the Yoruba people - was not a threat to prophetic "truth," and that the *Ọba* operates in relationship to all religious systems. All of these developments provided functional autonomy at the individual level, and made for a high level of religious tolerance among the Yoruba people. Lastly, he argues, the individual followed the form of religion which offered the best conditions of living in this world.[34]

As a result, "[The Yoruba] did not understand the unique claims made by [Christianity and Islam], and tried to soften their uncompromising out-lines."[35] The nature of Yoruba religion outlined above enabled the world

---

[33] J.D.Y. Peel, "Syncretism and Religious Change," p. 121.

[34] Ibid., pp. 123-4.

[35] Ibid., p. 125.

religions to make many inroads once they were seen as providing plausible alternatives to the old traditions that were already undergoing a stressful period in the nineteenth century.

All available evidence seems to suggest that the beginning point of new changes was the introduction of Christianity and later Islam. As such, the term conversion is synonymous in the Ondo person's imagination and interpretation of reality with development and adaptation. Conversion represents a shift of religious affiliation in new situations to ease "the conditions of living in this world."[36] This is why the conversion experience forms the basis of the Ondo civil anthem, an historical and musical reflection upon Ondo's experience in the nineteenth century.

In conclusion, I should remark that historically Yoruba religious practice has historically placed no emphasis on what might be called doctrine, dogma, or belief, which is one reason it could be so eclectic. There was no sense of exclusivity, therefore there was no insistence upon adherence to a particular dogma in order "to join" a religion; there was no "conversion," so to speak. On the other hand, there was a strong concern for the efficacy of a given religious system. In my view these characteristics are very evident in Ondo's conversion to Christianity and Islam. This emphasis on non-exclusivity and efficacy is partly responsible for the high degree of interaction and accommodation among the Ondo Muslims and Christians and traditionalists. This openness is greatest at the non-institutional level, in the daily activities of the people in which they bring to bear much more of their beliefs and faith.

My first observation in this regard occurred in the house of one of my Muslim informants during a visit that coincided with the annual festival of Ogun. An *Oloogun*, a traditional healer and Ogun priest, lived very close to my informant. The *Oloogun* came to confer with him because he was about to slaughter the animal for the ritual sacrifice before he set out for the Ogun procession, and he wanted my host there for prayer. My host wished him good luck and God's blessing on his celebrations. After the *Oloogun*'s departure he commented that despite this man's religious affiliation (an *orişa* worshipper), he was a person of good character and a respected gentleman in the area who would not make harmful medicine (*Oogun buburu*). What just transpired between the two men was a case of religious accommodation, a frequent phenomenon in Ondo society. In spite of the minority status of Islam in Ondo, a revered Muslim man commands the respect of his neighbors, whether Christians or traditionalists. His fervent prayers can be counted on for such festive occasions. A similar situation occurred in my second month of fieldwork in

---

[36] Ibid., p. 124.

Ondo. I had accompanied a friend to an *asun* (goat barbecue) ceremony given by one of his peers, a Christian, to celebrate his new Peugeot car. As the goat was pulled out of the back yard to be slaughtered, it was handed over to a Muslim who was standing by. He was asked by our host, a Christian, to say the prayer (*ad-du'a'*) and slaughter the animal, which he did according to the Muslim rite. Such behavior on social gatherings is considered perfectly normal.

For the average Ondo man there is nothing wrong with harnessing the resources of any of the religions in his daily pursuits, be he an auto mechanic or a taxi driver. The insignia displayed on a commercial motor vehicle during the annual Ogun festival illustrates this point. As a sign of his participation in the Ogun ceremony, the driver tied palm fronds, the sacred symbol of the deity, to the front of the car. Close to the front seat, hanging over his head, this man had a small wrap of medicine in a gourd as a prophylactic against accidents and bad luck. At the back of the vehicle, there was a sticker on which was written in Arabic script, *Allah Akbar* (God is Great), and in front there was the expression, *"se amọna mi oluwa"* ("Be my keeper Lord"), obviously a Biblical reference.

Conclusion

This study is based on several periods of field research spread over five years. Most of the research data came from Ode-Ondo (Ondo-city kingdom). The study focuses on the city-kingdom context, since Yoruba personal, political, social, and cultural identity is essentially tied up with membership in an ancestral city. Hence, the focus on Ode-Ondo has enabled me to define and come to a better understanding of Ondo-Yoruba religious culture at the local level.

In general, this work is concerned with the forms, content, and symbols of Ondo ritual life as it is articulated and shaped by the city's most significant festivals. I have paid particular attention to the oral and performative aspects of these rituals—the songs, the chants and dances, and the use of ritual space—in order to understand the relationship of the festival cycle to the social and ecological circumstances in which Ondo-Yoruba culture has developed.

This work presents new material as well as a new perspective for understanding Yoruba religion. It addresses issues in Yoruba religious studies such as the importance of religious ideology, the role of cultural symbols, and the significance of ritual in mediating potential political and religious conflict. The work argues that deeper understanding of African religion must be based on a sensitivity to the local structures of specific cultures. This requires an interdisciplinary perspective, involving both phenomenological and sociological methods of analysis.

This study differs from the general subject matter of the history of religions which usually focuses on texts. It is an ethnographic study based upon participant observation. The nature of my participation was to elicit through questions the Ondo informants' own interpretation of the meanings of the ceremonial symbolism. Both the participant observation and the informants' interpretations of the rituals give us the additional perspective that is otherwise missing from a purely observational and textual approach. I have added and used concepts drawn from the phenomenology of religion and anthropology.

This study therefore aims at providing new insight into Yoruba religion. Unlike previous works on Yoruba religion, which often start with theistic concepts (a list of deities with Olodumare, or God, at the top) I begin with the royal rituals and the *orisa* festival cycle, that is, religion as it is lived and practized in the public domain. In this sense, we see how the Ondo people define their place in the cosmos at the important corporate level and the religious significance of life in the public context.

The work centers on five principal festivals in the Ondo festival calendar: *Ọdun Ọba*, *Ọdun Ọramfẹ*, *Ọdun Ogun*, *Ọdun Obitun*, and *Ọdun Aje*.

Chapters I and II provide the mythic, historical, and ethnographic background for this study. In Chapter II, I describe the Ondo myth of origin and the historical traditions. This chapter also highlights the special roles and the symbolic significance of twins in Ondo religion, and by extension in Yoruba religious culture. The theme of aboriginal inhabitants, tamed and civilized by the newcomer cultivators for Ile-Ifẹ, also emerges. It illustrates the significance of the "aboriginal priests" who play an important role in the royal cult. The chapter also examines the composition of the various historical groups in the city as well as the structure of kingship. The account of Pupupu, the first Ondo female ruler, also conforms to the common African mythic theme in which women serve as primal generative beings. A male culture hero (*Airọ*), on the other hand, appears to be related to the symbolic, upside-down and reversed nature of the primal beings and to the era of chaos which characterizes Ondo's mythical origins. Although the origin story reflects more on the present male dominance and its symbolic inversion myth, rather than on an historical period of matriarchal authority, it provides a background for the continued significance of women in Ondo ritual life. The chapter also examines the place of magic and medicine in Ondo legends. Magical deeds are often associated with the rule of early kings, they constitute a paradigm by which later rulers are measured, and they serve to shape the kingship cult. Finally, the chapter discusses the incessant civil wars in early Ondo history, a normal reversal of the kingship ethos, which provides stability against schism and disintegration. To a large extent it is this anomaly in the Ondo social system and history that the kingship festival sets out to correct and control.

Chapter III focuses on *Ọdun Ọba*, the kingship ritual, first describing it, then analyzing its meaning. Several important motifs in the Yoruba religious culture and history are emphasized, among which are the structures in Ondo symbolic classification, ritual color symbolism, and the significance of boundary rites as a means of delineating space. The purpose of the festival is to renew Ondo kingship and cosmos; the royal rite links the kingship to the primal time through the ritual recitation of the kinglist. The role that civil religion plays in the entire cycle is another very significant finding. The ideology and rituals of kingship, I argue, provide a coherent drama through which the center can continue to hold.

Chapter IV presents the mythic and ritual aspects of *Ọramfẹ*, the culture hero who saved Ondo city from total extinction in the beginning. Here I examine the details of the *Oramfe* cult, the role of the *Sora* group (*Oramfe* priests), and the overall structure of Ondo religion. Although the *Oramfe* story represents a myth rather than authentic history, it serves as a link with the Yoruba's ancestoral city kingdom (Ile-Ife) and thus points towards its significance in Ondo history and culture. Another important aspect of this ceremony is the ritual of *opepee*, songs of reproach against the *Oba* and chiefs and "obscene" songs about the social life of the Ondo people. Here I suggest that these rituals fit into the pattern of "rituals of rebellion." The *opepee* ceremony also serves as a medium of communication between the big people and the small people in the Ondo community. Chapter V presents the festival of Ogun, a famous *Orisa* in the Yoruba pantheon. I describe Ogun's overall significance in Ondo and Yoruba religion, examining who he is mythically, his attributes, what role he plays, and how he related to other *Orisa* and to the kingship. This background provides the basis for the interpretation of the complex annual festival, *Odun Ogun*.

Next I examine in Chapter VI the women's rites and thereby present the role and significance of women in Ondo's religious culture. Two important ceremonies, the *Obitun* puberty rites and *Odun Aje*, are analyzed in detail. The Obitun rites fit into Van Gennep's tripartite scheme and reveal the significance of "territorial shifts" in the social/symbolic space. My discussion of the *Aje* festival presents the role of women leaders in the economic rituals and analyzes their symbols of power in the festival.

Lastly, in Chapter VII I examine the process of religious conversion to Islam and Christianity, pointing out continuity and change in Ondo traditional culture.

While each of these festivals is analyzed in detail, the overall purpose of the study has been to examine the interaction and interrelatedness of the five festivals in the Ondo liturgical calendar. In this regard, the study reaches several basic conclusions. First, ritual symbols link the five festivals together in a meaningful sequence and in doing so give shape to the ritual process. Second, the important aspects of the ritual process uniquely express Ondo-Yoruba identity. Third, the authority of the king is expressed as a political and religious center of Ondo cultural existence in a changing context. Fourth, the kingship and its rituals have responded to the inevitable changes in Ondo religion and cultural life produced by conversion to Islam and Christianity.

Appendix I
Oral Sources

1. Informants' List

High Chief Adaja Ọlaniyi Awọṣika (Information on History and Religion of Ondo), July 1980.
Chief Jerome Ojo (Information on History and Religion of Ondo).
Chief Adegbamigbe, The Sọra of Ondo (Information on Ọramfẹ Cult), June 1980.
High Chief Jọmu Ogunye (Information on Ọdun Ọba), August 1980.

2. Yoruba Historical Project

Tape recordings of interviews (Tapes deposited with the Obafemi Awolowo University, Ile-Ifẹ).
Chief Adedeji Ẹlẹja Baminusen — 19 August 1975
Chief Fadaṣe — 19 August 1975
Chief Lọbun Ọbabinrin — 19 August 1975
Chief Jerome Ojo — 16 August 1975
Chief Sama Akinlami — 15 August 1975
Chief Logboṣẹrẹ Duudu — 16 August 1975
Chief Bajulaiye Akiapa — 16 August 1975
Father Macphee — 16 August 1975
Chief C. Ọlaniyi Awọṣika — 14 August 1975
Chief Saṣẹrẹ Idoko — 13 March 1975
The Oṣemawe Elect, Ọba Adekolurẹjọ — 13 March 1975.

Unpublished materials

1. Charles Phillips Diary: 1877–1906, University of Ibadan Library.
2. Canon M.C. Adeyẹmi's Manuscript on Ondo Customs (1937), Ọbafẹmi Awolọwọ University Library.
3. Papers from the Ondo State Chieftaincy Declaration Tribunal, Dr. A. Anjọrin's Library, Department of History, Ọbafẹmi Awolọwọ University.

Bibliography

Abimbọla, Wande, *Ifa: An Exposition of Ifa Literary Corpus*, Ibadan: Oxford University Press, 1976.
— *Sixteen Great Poems of Ifa*, Paris, UNESCO, 1975.
— "Yoruba Traditional Religion." *Contemplation and Action in World Religions*, eds. Yusuf Ibish and Ileana Marculesau. Seattle: University of Washington Press, 1978.
— "Yoruba Religion in Brazil". *Acte du XLVIᵉ Congrès Société des Americanistes*, Vol. 6, Paris, 1979: 99–108.
Adegbamigbe, A.A., *History, Laws and Customs of the Ile-Oluji*, Ibadan: E.P. Works, 1962.
Adeyẹmi, M.C., *Ondo History and Customs*, M.S., 1934.
Ajayi, J.F. Ade and Ayandele, E.A., "Emerging Themes in Nigerian and West African Religious History." *Journal of African Studies*, Vol. 1 (Spring 1974): 1–39.
Akinjọgbin, I.A. and Ekemode, G.O., eds., *Proceedings of the Conference on Yoruba Civilization*, University of Ifẹ, Nigeria, 26–31 July, 1976.
Akintoye, S.A., "The Ondo Road Eastwards of Lagos C. 1870–1975". *Journal of African History*, 10 (1969): 581–598.
Alatas, S.H., *Reflections on Theories of Religion*, The Hague: Mouton Publishers, 1963.
Allen, Douglas, *Structure and Creativity in Religion: Hermeneutics in Mircea Eliade's Phenomenology and New Directions*, The Hague: Mouton Press, 1978.
Akinrilọla, F., "Ogun Festival," *Nigerian Magazine*, No. 85 (June 1965).
Arapura, J.G., *Religion as Anxiety and Tranquility: An Essay in Comparative Phenomenology of the Spirit*, The Hague: Mouton Publishers, 1972.
Armstrong, Robert, "The Dynamics and Symbolism of Idoma Kingship." *West African Culture Dynamics*, eds. B.K. Swartz Jr. and Raymond E. Dumell, The Hague: Mouton Press, 1980.
Atanda, J.A., *An Introduction to Yoruba History*, Ibadan University Press, 1980.
Awolalu, J.O., *Sacrifice in Yoruba Religion*, London: Longmans, 1979.
Ayandele, E.A., *The Missionary Impact on Modern Nigeria (1842-1914)*, London: Longmans, 1966.
Audrey, I. Richards, *Chisungu: A Girl's Initiation Ceremony Among the Bemba of Northern Rhodesia*, London: Faber and Faber Ltd., 1956.
Babalọla, Aaeboye, *The Contest and Form of Yoruba Ijala*, London: Oxford University Press, 1966.
Babalọla Adeboye, *Ijala*, Lagos: Federal Ministry of Information, 1968.
— "The Delight of Ijala", *Yoruba Oral Tradition*, Abimbọla Wande ed., Ilẹ-Ifẹ, University of Ifẹ Press, 1971: 631–676.
Babcock, Barbara, *The Reversible World: Symbolic Inversion in Art and Society*, Ithaca, New York: Cornell University Press, 1978.

Baird, R.D., *Category Formation and the History of Religions*, The Hague: Mouton Publishers, 1978.

Bankọle, Ayọ, Bush, Judith, Samagn, Sadet H., "The Yoruba Master Drummer." *African Arts* 8 (Winter 1975): 48–55.

Barnes, Sandra, *Ogun: An Old God for a New Age*, Philadelphia: Institute for the Study of Human Issues, 1980.

Bascom, William, *Shango in the New World*, Occasional Publications of African and Afro-American Research Institute, Austin: University of Texas Press, 1972.

— *Sixteen Cowries: Yoruba Divination from Africa to the New World*, Bloomington: Indiana University Press, 1980.

Beane, Wendell Charles, *Myth, Cult and Symbols in Shakti Hinduism: A Study of the Indian Mother Goddess*, Leiden: E.J. Brill, 1971.

Beier, Ulli, Gbadamosi, Bakare, *Yoruba Poetry: Traditional Yoruba Poems*, Ibandan: Ibadan University Press, 1961.

Belasco, Bernard I. *The Entrepreneur as Cultural Hero*. New York: Praeger, 1980.

Bellah, Robert, *Beyond Belief: Essays on Religion in a Post-Tradition World*, New York: Harper and Row, 1970.

Bender, Donald, "Agnatic or Cognatic: A Re-evaluation of Ondo Descent." *Man* (N.S.) 5 (1970): 71–87.

— "De Facto Families and De Jure Household in Ondo." *American Anthropologists* 73 (1972): 223–241.

Berger, Peter, *The Sacred Canopy: Elements of a Sociological Theory of Religion*, New York: Doubleday, 1969.

Berglund, Axel-Ivar, *Zulu Thought Patterns and Symbolism*, Uppsala: Swedish Institute of Missionary Research, 1976.

Berry, Sara, "Christianity and the Rise of Cocoa Growing in Ibadan and Ondo." *Jounal of the Historical Society of Nigeria* IV (December 1968): 439–451.

Bianchi, Ugo, *The History of Religions*, Leiden: E.J. Brill, 1975.

Bianchi, U., Bleeker, C.J., and Bausani, A. eds., *Problems and Methods of the History of Religion*, Leiden: E.J. Brill, 1972.

Biobaku, S.O. ed., *Sources of Yoruba History*, Oxford: Clarendon, 1973.

Blasi, Anthony, "Definition of Religion and Phenomenological Approach: Towards a Problematic." *Les Cahiers du CRSR* 3 (1980): 55–70.

Bleeker, C.J., *Egyptian Festivals*, Leiden: E.J. Brill, 1967.

— *The Sacred Bridge: Researches into the Nature and Structure of Religion*, Leiden: E.J. Brill, 1963.

— ed., *Initiation: Studies in the History of Religions*, Leiden: E.J. Brill, 1965.

Bodde, Derk, *Festivals in Classical China*, Princeton, NJ: Princeton University Press, 1975.

Bogdan, Robert & Steven, J. Taylor, *Introduction to Qualitative Research Methods: Phenomenological Approach to the Social Sciences*, New York: John Wiley and Sons, Inc., 1975.

Brenneman, Walter Jr., Yarian, Stanley O., and Olson, Alan M., *The Seeing Eye: Hermeneutical Phenomenology in the Study of Religion*, University Park and London: The Pennsylvania State University Press, 1982.

Brown, Judith K., "A Cross-Cultural Study of Female Initiation Rites." *American Anthropologists* 65 (1963): 837–852.

Brown, Susan Brucker, *Ritual Aspects of the Mamprusi Kingship*, African Social Rescarch Documents, Vol. 8, Leiden: African Studicentrum and Cambridge: African Studies Center, 1975.

Burton, John, *God's Ant: A Study of Atout Religion*, Studii Institute: Anthropos, Vol. 37, St. Augustine: Anthropos Institute, 1981.

Callois, Roger, *Man and the Sacred*, New York: Free Press, 1959.

Claesson, Henri, J.M. & Peter Shelnik, eds., *The Study of the State*, The Hague: Mouton Publishers, 1981.

Cohen, Ronald, "The Political Analysis." *A Handbook of Method in Cultural Anthropology*, eds. Radul Haroll and Ronda Cohen, New York: Colombia University Press, 1977.

Cohen, Yehudi A., *The Transition from Childhood to Adolescence: Cross-Cultural Studies of Initiation Ceremonies, Legal Systems and Incest Taboos*, Chicago: Aldine, 1964.

Courlander, Harold, *The Drum and the Hoe: Life and Lore of Haitian People*, Berkeley: University of California Press, 1960.

Crumsine, N. Ross, "Mediating Roles in Ritual and Symbolism: Northwest Mexico and the Pacific Northwest, *Anthropologica*, N.S. XVIII (1976) 2:142–143.

Donabari, Mara E., "Kingship Theory in the Patriarchal Narrative (Genesis 11:27, 35:29)." *American Academy of Religion, Abstract of Proceedings*, Chico: Chico Press, 1976.

Douglas, Mary, *Purity and Danger: An Analysis of the Concepts of Pollution and Taboo*, New York: Praeger, 1966.

Drewal Henry John and Drewal, Margaret Thompson, *Gelede: Art and Female Power Among the Yoruba*, Bloomington, Indiana: Indiana University Press, 1983.

Driver, Harold, "Girls' Puberty Rites in Western North America." *University of California Publications in Anthropological Records* 6 (1941): 21–90.

Droogers, Andre, *The Dangerous Journey: Symbolic Aspects of Boys' Initiation Among the Wageni of Kinangani*, The Hague: Mouton Publishers, 1980.

Dupre, Wilhelm, *Religion and Primitive Cultures: A Study in Ethno-Philosophy*, The Hague: Mouton Publishers, 1974.

Durkheim, Emile, *Elementary Forms of the Religious Life*, New York: Free Press, 1965.

Eades, J.S., *The Yoruba Today*, Cambridge: Cambridge University Press, 1980.

Egharevba, Jacob, *A Short History of Benin*, 3rd Ed., Ibadan: Ibadan University Press, 1960.

Eliade, Mircea, *Cosmos and History*, Princeton: Princeton University Press, 1974.

— *The Sacred and the Profane*, New York: Harper & Row, 1961.

— *Myths and Reality*, translated by W.R. Trask, New York: Harper & Row, 1964.

— *Rites and Symbols of Initiation*, New York: Harper & Row, 1965.

— *Patterns in Comparative Religion*, translated by Rosemary Sheed, New York: Word Publishing 6, 1963.

— *Images and Symbols, Studies in Cosmology*, translated by P. Mairet, New York: Sheed & Ward, 1969.

Eliade, M. and Kitagawa, J.M., *The History of Religion: Essays in Methodology*, Chicago: University of Chicago Press, 1959.

Ellwood, Robert, *The Feasts of Kingship: Ascension Ceremonies in Ancient Japan*, Tokyo: Sophia University Press, 1970.

Engnell, Ivan, *Studies in Divine Kingship in the Ancient Near East*, Uppsala, (1943) 1967.

Evans-Pritchard, E.E., *Theories of Primitive Religion*, London: Oxford University Press, 1965.

Fabunmi, M.A., *Ifẹ Shrines,* Ile-Ifẹ: University of Ifẹ Press, 1969.

— *Ẹsin Kristi ni Ile-Ifẹ ati Agbegbe* (Christianity in Ile-Ifẹ and District), Ile-Ifẹ: Kosalabaro Press, 1970.

Fadipe, N.A., *The Sociology of the Yoruba*, eds. Francis Olu Okediji and Oladejo Okediji, Ibadan: University of Ibadan Press, 1970.

Fallers, L.A., *Bantu Bureaucracy*, Chicago: Chicago University Press, 1965.

Fisher, H., "Conversion Reconsidered: Some Historical Aspects of Conversion in Black Africa." *Africa* 43 (January 1973): 27–40.

Frankfort, Henri, *Kingship and the Gods: A Study of Ancient Near Eastern Religion as the Integration of Society and Nature*, Chicago: Chicago University Press, 1948.

Freud, Julian, *Sociology of Max Weber*, translated by Mary Ilford, New York: Pantheon Books, 1968.

Frisbie, Charlotte Johnson, *Kinnalda: A Study of Navaho Girls' Puberty Ceremony*, Middletown: Wesleyan University Press, 1967.

Gadd, C.J., *Ideas of Divine Rule in the Ancient Near East*, London: Oxford University Press, 1948.

Gbadamọsi, Gbadebo O., *The Growth of Islam Among the Yoruba, 1841–1908*, London: Longman, 1978.

Geertz, Clifford, *The Interpretation of Cultures*, New York: Basic Book Inc. Publishers, 1973.

— *Islam Observed: Religious Development in Morocco and Indonesia*, New Haven: Yale University Press, 1968.

Gill, Sam., "Seeing with the Native Eyes." *Contributions to the Study of Nature of American Religion*, ed. Walter H. Capps, New York: Harper & Row, 1976.

Gleason, Judith, *Orisha: The Gods of Yorubaland*, New York: Atheneum, 1971.

— *Ọya: In Praise of the Goddess*, Boston: Shambhala Press, 1987.

Gluckman, Max, *Custom and Conflict in Africa*, Oxford: Blackwell, 1965.

— ed., *Essays in the Ritual of Social Relations*, Manchester: Manchester University Press, 1962.

Goody, Jack, *Succession in High Office*, Cambridge: Cambridge University Press, 1966.

Gonda, Jan, *Ancient Indian Kingship from the Religious Point of View*, History of Religion Series, Leiden: E.J. Brill, 1969.

Grunebaum, G.E., *Mohammedan Festivals: Typical Elements of Islamic Ritual Prayer*, London: Curzon Press, 1976.

Hall, T. William, ed., *Introduction to the Study of Religion*, New York: Harper and Row, 1978.

Hallen, Barry, "Phenomenology and the Exposition of African Traditional Thought." *African Philosophy*, ed. Clause Summer. Proceedings of the Seminar on African Philosophy, Addis Ababa, 1980: 57–70.

Hamnet, Ian, "Ambiguity, Classifications and Change: The Function of Riddles." *Man* 2 (September 1967): 379–392.

Herskovits, Melville Dahomey, *An Ancient West African Kingdom*, Vol. I, New York: J.J. Augustini, 1939.

Hidding, K.A.H., "The High God and the King." *The Sacral Kingship/La Regalita Sacra Studies in the History of Religion*, Leiden: E.J. Brill, 1959.

Hocart, M.M., *Kingship*, London: Oxford University Press, 1927.

Holtom, D.C., *The Japanese Enthronement Ceremonies*, 2nd Ed., Tokyo: Sophia University Press, 1972.

Hooke, S.H., ed., *Myth, Ritual and Kingship: Essays on the Theory and Practice of Kingship in the Ancient Near East and in Israel*, Oxford: Clarendon Press, 1958.

Honko, Lauri, ed., *Science of Religion, Studies in Methodology*, The Hague: Mouton Publishers, 1979.

Horton, Robin, "African Conversion." *Africa* 41 (April 1971): 85–108.

Houlberg, Marylin Hammesley, "Social Hair: Yoruba Hairstyles in Southwestern Nigeria." *The Fabrics of Culture*, eds. Justice M. Cordwell and Ronald Aswarz, The Hauge: Mouton Press, 1979.

Hudson, Alfred E., *Kazan Social Structure*, Human Relations Area Files Press, 1964.

Hultkrantz, Åke, "The Phenomenology of Religion; Aims and Methods." *Temenos* 6 (1970): 68–88.

Hunt, Cult M., *Oyotunji Village: The Yoruba Movement in America*, Washington: University Press of America, 1979.

Idowu, Bolaji, *Olodumare: God in Yoruba Belief*, London: Longman, 1962.

Ifeka-Moller, Caroline, "White Power: Social-Structural Factors in Conversion to Christianity, Eastern Nigeria, 1921–1966." *Canadian Journal of African Studies* 8 (1974): 55–72.

Issaka, Prosper Lalaye, *La Conception de la Personne dans la Pensée traditionnelle Yoruba: Approach Phénoménologue*, Berne: Herbert Land & Cie sa, (Publications Universitaires Europeennes server xx Vol. 3).

James, E.O., *Creation and Cosmology*, London: E.J. Brill, 1964.

Johnson, Samuel, *The History of the Yorubas: From the Earliest Times to the Beginning of the British Protectorate*, West Port: Negro University Press, 1921. Reproduced 1970.

Jules-Rosette, Benetta, ed., "Women as Ceremonial Leaders in an African Church: The Apostle of John Maranke." *The New Religions of Africa*, Norwood, NJ: Ablex, 1979.

— "Changing Aspects of Women's Initiations in Southern Africa: An Exploratory Study." *Revue Canadienne de Études Africanes/Canadian Journal of African Studies* 13 (1980).

Kitagawa Joseph M., Eliade, M., and Long, Charles, *The History of Religions: Essays on the Problems of Understanding*, Chicago: University of Chicago Press, 1967.

Kloos, Peter, "Female Initiation Among the Maroni River Caribs." *American Anthropologists* 71 (October 1969): 890–897.

Kristensen, W.B., *The Meaning of Religion*, The Hauge: Mouton Publishers, 1960.

La Fontaine, J.S., "Ritualization of Women's Life Crisis in Bugisu." *The Interpretation of Ritual*. Essays in Honor of A.I. Richards, London: Tavistock Publications, 1972.

Laitin, David, "Conversion and Political Change: A Study of (Anglican) Christianity and Islam Among the Yoruba in Ile-Ife," Seminar Paper, 26 pp.

— *Hegemony and Culture*. Chicago: University of Chicago Press, 1986.

Lamb, Venice and Holmes, Judy, *Nigerian Weaving*, Lagos, 1980.

Law, Robin, *The Oyo Empire C. 1600–C. 1836*, Oxford: Oxford University, 1977.

Lawuyi, Olatunde and Olupona, Jacob K., "Making Sense of the Aje Festival: Wealth, Politics and Status of Women Among the Ondo of South-Western Nigeria." *Journal of Ritual Studies* 1, 2 (Summer 1989): 97–109.

Leach, Edmund R., *The Structural Study of Myth and Totemism*, London: Tavistock Publications, 1967.
— *Dialectic in Practical Religion*, Cambridge: Cambridge University Press, 1968.
Leigh, J.A., *The History of Ondo*, Ondo, 1917.
Lessa, William A. and Vogt, Even Z. eds., *Reader in Comparative Religion: An Anthropological Approach*, New York: Harper and Row, 1965.
Levine, Daniel H., *Religion and Politics in Latin America: The Catholic Church in Venezuela and Columbia*, Princeton: Princeton University Press, 1981.
Levtzion, Nehemia, ed., "Towards a Comparative Study of Islamization." *Conversion to Islam*, New York: Holmes and Meier Inc., 1968.
Lincoln, Bruce, *Emerging from the Chrysalis: Studies in Rituals of Women Initiation*, Cambridge: Harvard University Press, 1981.
Lloyd, Peter C., "The Yoruba Lineage." *Africa* 25 (1955): 235–251.
— *Yoruba Land Law*, Oxford: Oxford University Press, 1962.
— "Agnatic and Cognatic Descent Among the Yoruba." *Man* (New Series) 1, 1966: 484–500.
— "Ondo Descent" *Man* (New Series) 5, 1970: 310, 312.
Mabogunjẹ, A.L. and Awẹ, B., eds., *The City of Ibadan*, Cambridge: Cambridge University Press, 1967.
Logboṣẹrẹ, Dudu, *Orukọ Awọn Ọba ati Adugbo ni Ondo* (Ondo King List and Names of Streets), Ondo: Regina Press, 1976.
Long, Charles, "Prolegomenon to a Religion Hermeneutic." *History of Religion* 6: 3 (February 1967): 254–264.
Lucas, J.O., *The Religion of the Yorubas*, Lagos, 1948.
Lukes, Stephen, *Emile Durkheim, His Life and Work: A Historical and Critical Study*, New York: Harper & Row, 1972.
McKenzie, R.R., "Yoruba Oriṣa Cults: Some Marginal Notes Concerning the Cosmology and Concepts of Deity." *Journal of Religion in Africa* 8 (1976):
Meyerowitz, Eva L.R., *The Divine Kingship: Ghana and Ancient Egypt*, London: Faber and Faber Ltd., 1966.
Middleton, John, "Some Categories of Dual Classification Among the Lugbira of Uganda." *Right and Left: Essays in Dual Symbolic Classification*, ed. Rodney Needham, Chigaco: University of Chicago Press, 1973.
— ed., *Myth and Cosmos*, New York: The Natural History Press, 1967.
Morton-Williams, P., "An Outline of the Cosmology of the Cult Organization of the Ọyọ Yoruba." *Africa* 34 (1964): 243–260.
Murphy, Joseph M., *Santeria: An African Religion in America*, Boston: Beacon Press, 1987.
Nadel, S.F., *Nupe Religion: Traditional Beliefs and the Influence of Islam in a West African Chiefdom*, London: Rutledge Kegan Paul, 1954. Reproduced 1970.
Needleman, Jacob and Bake, George, eds., *Understanding the New Religions*, New York: The Seabuary Press, 1978.
O'Flaherty, Wendy, *The Origins of Evil in Hindu Mythology*, London: University of California Press, 1976.
Ogunṣakin, Patrick, *Ondo: The People, Their Customs and Traditions*, Lagos: Inway, 1976.
Ojo, G.J.A., *Yoruba Culture: A Geographical Analysis*, London: University of Ifẹ and University of London Press, 1966.

Ojo, Jerome O., "Yoruba Customs from Ondo," *Acta Ethnologica et Linguistica* No. 3, Series Africana 10, Wien, 1976.

Ojo, Lucretia, *Odun Oba ni Ilu Ondo* (The King's Festival in Ondo), N.C.E. Long Essay, College of Education, Ikere, Nigeria, June, 1980.

Ojo, S. (Bada of Saki), *Iwe Itan Ondo*, N.P. 1940, 4th Pub. Ondo, 1962, *Ondo State of Nigeria*.

Olupona, Jacob K., "Some Notes on the Religion of the Ondo People: A Phenomenological/Anthropological Study. *Bulletin of the International Committee on Urgent Anthropological and Ethnological Research*, No. 27, 1987: 45–58.

Ondo State of Nigeria, N.P. *Report of the Morgan Chieftaincy Review Commission*, Vols. I–IV.

Otto, R., *The Idea of the Holy*, translated by John W. Harvey, New York: Oxford University Press, 1936; [1917].

Parrinder, E. Geoffrey, *Religion in African City*, London: Oxford University Press, 1958.

Peel, J.D.Y., "Religious Change in Yorubaland." *Africa* 37 (1967): 292–306.

— *Aladura: A Religious Movement Among the Yoruba*, London: Oxford University Press, 1968.

— "Conversion and Tradition in Two African Societies." *Past and Present* 77 (1977): 108–141.

Pemberton, John III, "A Cluster of Sacred Symbols: Orisa Worship Among the Igbomina Yoruba of Ila-Orangun." *History of Religions* 17 (August 1977): 1–28.

— "Sacred Kingship and the Violent God: The Worship of Ogun Among the Yoruba, *Berchire Review*, Vol. 14, 1979: 85–106.

Penner, Hans "Is Phenomenology a Method for the Study of Religion?" *Bucknell Review* XVIII (Winter 1970): 29–51.

Pentikäinen, Juha, "The Symbolism of Liminality." *Religious Symbols and Function*, ed. Haralds Biezais, Stockholm: Almqvist and Wiksell International, 1969.

Pettersson, Olof, *Chiefs and Gods: Religious and Social Elements in the South Eastern Bantu Kingship*, Lund, 1953.

Pettersson, Olof and Åkerberg, Hans, *Interpreting Religious Phenomena: Studies with Reference to the Phenomenology of Religion*, Stockholm: Almqvist and Wiksell International, 1981.

Pilgrim, Richard B., "Ritual." *Introduction to the Study of Religion*, pp. 64–68, ed. William Hall, New York: Harper & Row, 1978.

Platvoet, J.G., *Comparing Religions: A Limitative Approach: An Analysis of Akan Para-Creole, and Ifo Sananda Rites and Prayers*, The Hauge: Mouton Press, 1982.

Price, Theodural Hadzistelon, *Kourothropos: Cults and Representation of the Greek Nursing Deities*, Leiden: E.J. Brill, 1970.

Pye, M. and Morgan, eds., *The Cardinal Meaning: Essays in Comparative Hermeneutics: Buddhism and Christianity*, The Hague: Mouton Publishers, 1973.

Radin, Paul, "Religion of the North American Indians." *Anthropology in North America*, American Academy of Religion Papers, New York: Kraus Reprint Co., 1972.

Ray, Benjamin, *African Religions: Symbol, Ritual and Community*, Englewood Cliffs N.J.: Prentice-Hall Inc., 1976.

Reefe, Thomas A., *The Rainbow and the King*, Berkeley: University of California Press, 1981.

Reichard, Gladys A., *Prayer: The Compulsive World*, Washington: University of Washington Press, 1944.
— *Navaho Religion: A Study of Symbolism*, New York: Pantheon Books, Bollingen Series XVIII, 1963.
Ryder, A.F.C., "An Early Portuguese Voyage to the Forcados River." *Journal of the Historical Society of Nigeria* 1, 49, 1959.
Richards, Audrey, *Chisungu: A Girl's Initiation Ceremony Among the Bemba of Northern Rhodesia*, London: Faber and Faber Ltd., 1956.
Ryan, Patrick J., *Imalẹ: Yoruba Participation in the Muslim Tradition*, Montana: Scholar Press, 1975.
Sharpe, Eric., *Comparative Religion: A History*, New York: Schribners, 1975.
Shaughnessy, Jane M., ed., *Roots of Rituals*, Grand Rapids, MI: Grand Rapids Press, 1973.
Shippee, Arthur, *Mircea Eliade's Concept of Myth: A Study of Its Possible Relevance to an Understanding of Islam*, Ph.D. Dissertation, Hartford Seminary Foundation, 1974.
Silverstein, Stella Bobbie, "Structural Analysis of Ifa Divination of the Yoruba People of Nigeria." Unpublished Paper, 67 pp.
Smith, Bardwell, L., *Religion and Legitimization in South Asia*, International Studies in Sociology and Social Anthropology, Leiden: E.J. Brill, 1978.
Smart, Ninian, *Worldviews*, New York: Schribners, 1983.
— *Religion and the Western Mind*, New York: State University Press, 1987.
Smith, W. Cantwell, *The Meaning and End of Religion*, London: SPCK, 1978 [1962].
Ṣoyinka, Wọle, *Myth, Literature and the African World*, Cambridge: Cambridge University Press, 1976.
Sudarkasa, Niara, *Where Women Work: A Study of Yoruba Women in the Market Place and in the Home*, Ann Arbor: The University of Michigan Press, 1973.
Tambiah, Stanley Jeyaraja, *Culture, Thought and Action*, Cambridge, Ma.: Harvard University Press, 1985.
Thornton, Robert J., *Space, Time and Culture Among the Iraqwa of Tarzania*, Studies in Anthropology, New York: Academic Press, 1980.
— *A History of Islam in West Africa*, London: Oxford University Press, 1962.
Turner, Harold, *Religious Innovation in Africa: Collected Essays On New Religious Movements*, Boston: C.K. Hall & Co., 1979.
Turner, Victor, *Forests of Symbols*, Ithaca: Cornell University Press, 1967.
— *The Ritual Process*, Chicago: Aldine Publishing Co., 1969.
— *Drama Fields and Metaphors*, Ithaca: Cornell University Press, 1971.
— *Process, Performance and Pilgrimage: A Study in Comparative Symbology*, Ranchi Anthropological Series No. 1, New Delhi: Concept Publishing Company, 1979.
Turner, Victor and Turner, Edith, *Image and Pilgrimage in Christian Culture: Anthropological Perspectives*, New York: Columbia University Press, 1978.
Vaughan, Robert, "A Reconsideration of Divine Kingship." *Exploration in African System of Thought*, eds. Ivan Karp and Charles S. Bird, Bloomington: Indiana University Press, 1980.
Van Baaren, Th. P. and Drijvers, A.J.W., eds., *Religion, Culture and Methodology*, The Hague: Mouton Publishers, 1973.
Van der Leeuw, G., *Religion in Essence and Manifestation: A Study in Phenomenology*, 2 Vols. Trans. J.E. Turner, New York: Harper & Row, 1963.
Van Gennep, Arnold, *Rites of Passage*, Chicago: University of Chicago Press, 1961.

Verger, Pierre, *Awọn Ewe Ọsanyin*, (Yoruba Medicinal Leaves), Ile-Ifẹ: African Studies Institute, 1967.

— *Notes sur les culte des Orisa et Vodun a Bahia, la Baie de tous les Saints, au Brasis et L'ancienne Côte des Esclaves en Afrique*, Memoires de L'IFAN, No. 51, Dakar, IFAN, 1957.

Vizedom, Monika, *Rites and Relationships: Rites of Passage and Contemporary Anthropology*. California: Beverly Hills, Sage, 1976.

Voegelin, Eric, *Order and History*, Vol. II, Louisiana: State University Press, 1956.

Vogt, Evon Z., "On the Symbolic Meaning of Percussion in Zinacanteco Ritual." *Journal of Anthropological Research* 33 (1977): 231–244.

Waardenburg, J., *Classical Approaches to the Study of Religion*, 2 Vols. The Hague: Mouton Publishers, 1974.

Ward, Edward, *Marriage Among the Yoruba*, Washington D.C.: Catholic University of America, 1938.

— *The Yoruba Husband-Wife Code*, Washington D.C.: Catholic University of America, 1936.

Weber, M., *The Sociology of Religion*, translated by E.F. Shoff, Boston: Beacon Press, 1963.

— *The Theory of Social and Economic Organization*, translated by Talcott Parsons, New York: The Free Press, 1947.

Whythe, R.W., "On the Rationality of the Devout Opposition." *Journal of Religion in Africa* XI (1980):

Williams, Daniel, *Icon and Image: A Study of the Sacred and Secular Forms of African Classical Art*, New York: New York Univ. Press, 1974.

Willis, R.G., "Traditional History and Social Structure in Ufipa." *Africa* XXIV, 4, 1964.

Wilson, John P., *Public Religion in American Culture*, Philadephia: Temple University Press, 1979.

Wilson, Monica, *Divine Kingship and the Breath of Men*. The Frazer Lecture, Cambridge: Cambridge University Press, 1959.

Young, Frank W., *Initiation Ceremonies: A Cross-Cultural Study of Status Dramatization*, New York: Bobbs Merill, 1965.

Young, M.W., "The Divine Kingship of the Shilluk." *Africa* 36 (1966):

Zahan, Dominique, *The Religion, Spirituality and Thought of Traditional Africa*. Translated by Katezva Martin and Lawrence M. Martin. Chicago: University of Chicago Press, 1979.

Zeusse, M. Evan, *Ritual Cosmos: The Sanctification of Life in African Religions*, Athens: Ohio University Press, 1979.

Index